Jesus

Our
Salvation

Author Acknowledgments

Many people deserve thanks and praise for their assistance in seeing this project to its completion. First of all, Leslie Ortiz at Saint Mary's Press has shepherded this endeavor for over a year, and her expertise has enhanced every aspect of the book. The team of copy editors and readers have thoroughly critiqued and reshaped the final product and improved it immensely. My wife, Debra Faszer-McMahon, has corrected and revised several drafts of the manuscript with her pedagogical insights, her evangelical sensibilities, and her brutally honest editorial suggestions. Last, I would like to thank William Loewe and the faculty at Catholic University for their "patient endurance" in teaching me how to think and believe at the same time. As always, the invaluable assistance of those mentioned above does not diminish my responsibility for the book, and any shortcomings or errors are my own.

Publisher Acknowledgments

Thank you to the following individuals who advised the publishing team or reviewed this work in progress:

Terrence W. Tilley, PhD, Fordham University, New York
Sr. Shannon Schrein, OSF, PhD, Lourdes College, Ohio
Ralph Del Colle, PhD, Marquette University, Wisconsin
Sr. Mary Ann Baran, SND, Notre Dame College, Ohio

An Introduction to Christology

CHRISTOPHER MCMAHON

Saint Mary's Press®

The publishing team included Leslie M. Ortiz, general editor; John B. McHugh, director of college publishing; prepress and manufacturing coordinated by the production departments of Saint Mary's Press.

Cover image royalty-free from Shutterstock. Interior photo images royalty-free from iStock.

Printed in the United States of America

ISBN 978-0-88489-958-7

7003

Library of Congress Cataloging-in-Publication Data

McMahon, Christopher
  Jesus our salvation : an introduction to Christology / McMahon
      p. cm.
   ISBN 978-0-88489-958-7 (pbk.)
   1. Jesus Christ—Person and offices. I. Title.

   BT203.M38 2007
   232—dc22
                                    2007025888

Contents

List of Charts and Sidebars

Chapter 5

Chapter 6

Chapter 7

Chapter 8

A Note to Instructors

Allow me to begin by thanking you for choosing *Jesus Our Salvation* for your course. On behalf of the Saint Mary's Press college publishing division, it is my hope that you find the text to be an engaging and helpful resource for your class, one that is both approachable and challenging. I have tried my best to provide students with a serviceable account of the contours and challenges the history of Christology poses for the contemporary discipline. Although the presentation is centered in the Roman Catholic tradition, such centering also acknowledges that this tradition has become increasingly open to and conversant with Protestant theologies and the religious outlooks of other traditions. The merits of this cross-fertilization of contemporary Christology will be evident to all readers.

Organization

The text unfolds in three parts: the quest for the historical Jesus, the emergence of the christological tradition, and contemporary christological issues. Part one charts a well-traveled path through historical Jesus research and privileges the work of John Meier and N. T. Wright. Meier and Wright, for better or for worse (I think for better), have provided accounts of the historical Jesus and of historical Jesus research that are most in keeping with the christological tradition, though William Loewe's assessment of the limits of historical Jesus research sounds an appropriate caution about the relevance of such research for contemporary Christian thought.

Part two begins by walking a tightrope in the discussion of the Resurrection of Jesus, and the position taken in the text is open to the scrutiny of readers, teachers, and students (whether they are readers or not). I have regularly found the chapter on the Resurrection to be some of the most difficult and troubling material for students to engage, and it is my hope that the presentation here will open up a rich and fruitful classroom conversation. From there the Christology of the early church is traced out using a Lonerganian approach, which recognizes innovation as the hallmark of orthodoxy as well as the importance of various realms of meaning in doctrinal formulation. This approach, I believe, will be of some benefit to students who may otherwise have difficulty finding their bearings in such a discussion. Additionally, a Lonerganian approach provides a general account of the immense value of doctrines as well as their limitations. The chapter on the soteriological tradition offers a balanced presentation of biblical, patristic, medieval, and Reformation approaches.

The final part of the book is devoted to issues in contemporary Christology—an area so expansive that a survey such as this cannot hope to provide anything more than a snapshot. Such a snapshot inevitably is limited by the narrow focus of the camera's lens, and so it is with the third and final section of the text. Building on the previous chapter on the soteriological tradition, part three begins by mapping a new approach to soteriology articulated in the work of William Loewe—it is a soteriology that emphasizes the concrete difference Christian faith makes in a world marred by violence and evil. Such an approach draws attention to the theologies of J. Moltmann and E. Johnson as well as the emergence of postcolonial theology in Asia, and provides a segue into perhaps the most important christological question of the twenty-first century: the relationship between Christian convictions about Jesus and the prevalence of other traditions that do not accept or recognize those convictions. Within this context, at the end of the paradigm shift to a low-ascending Christology, the text moves to a presentation on the theology of Hans Urs von Balthasar, who questioned the import or appropriateness of such a shift, leaving us with a renewal of the high-descending approach.

Text Features

I have tried to include enough quotations and enough references to make the book a helpful starting point for some basic undergraduate research, but no attempt has been made to be exhaustive. Additionally, I have included a number of charts and peripheral discussions of important topics and personalities throughout the text. These features are meant to engage students in interesting (even if occasionally digressive) conversations and provide background knowledge on material presented in the chapter.

Each chapter concludes with a series of questions. The "Questions for Understanding" ask students to recall basic facts from the chapter; they can be used to hold students accountable for reading a significant part of each chapter. The "Questions for Reflection" ask students to go beyond recalling information presented in each chapter to deal with the implications of that information. Instructors may find it useful to assign "Questions for Understanding" for students to complete individually and use the "Questions for Reflection" for small-group discussion or as a springboard for additional research.

Instructional Design and Latitude

The book certainly is not *the definitive guide* to contemporary Christology, yet it is my sincere hope that what this work lacks in comprehensiveness, it makes up for as a learning guide that will help students connect with the tradition so that they may evaluate and participate in christological debates.

I have made an effort to include a variety of voices within the tradition in such a way that instructors with various perspectives may find the text engaging, but some teachers will be concerned that important contemporary voices such as those of eco-feminist, womanist, or *mujerista* theologians, among others, are not featured here. While I accept that critique, I urge instructors to use the text to set up supplemental presentations of alternative Christologies. Additionally, teachers of more advanced students may find the text helpful as a springboard from which to approach and engage primary sources in the history of Christology.

As a guide for beginning undergraduates, *Jesus Our Salvation* provides students with an integration of a relatively detailed presentation of the christological tradition and a survey of contemporary approaches to Christology. This integration always acknowledges the presence of the tradition—an historic, not just a contemporary, community of thinkers and believers.

Introduction

An Invitation and Some "Ground Clearing"

Imagine that tomorrow morning, just as the sun peaks over the horizon, your alarm clock goes off as usual and you make three or four sleepy half-blind swipes at the "snooze" button. Halfway through your morning coffee, you find yourself reasonably awake and in pretty good spirits. But as you begin to move around your room, the crucifix on your wall catches your eye—the one you received as a confirmation gift from your godparents—and you realize at that moment that your faith in Jesus Christ is gone.

Generally people do not actually "lose" their faith overnight—coming to faith and abandoning it are both complex experiences—but imagine that it did happen as instantaneously as described. From this point forward, how would your day be any different than any other day? How would your life change?

For a non-Christian the hypothetical scenario has no point—of course one's life would not change. But for many Christians in the early twenty-first century, a meaningful answer to this question is often elusive. Some might say, after pondering the question for a moment, that they would stop praying, quit going to church, or that they would no longer believe that there is a God. Others might say that they would no longer feel obligated to treat their neighbors with love and respect. Of course, not believing in Jesus Christ is different from not believing in God; after all, billions of people believe in God but do not believe in Jesus. These same people also treat their neighbors with care and concern. And if your response to the question revolves around what prayers you might say or what church you might attend, many people feel so connected to the people in their communities of worship that despite losing faith in Jesus Christ, they might just keep on going to their church and maintain their involvement in a variety of activities.

The hesitancy and uncertainty that many Christians experience when wrestling with the practical implications of their faith in Jesus may help function as a barometer for measuring two realities. First, such hesitancy may reflect the relative strength of our beliefs about Jesus. Do we have real convictions about Jesus and the God he reveals to us, or are these so-called convictions merely a set of general assumptions Christians share but don't take too seriously? Is Jesus simply an empty concept into which we may pour our own agendas, or project our hopes and fears? What is the relationship between the act of faith or trust in God, and our beliefs, the content of that faith? Second, the hesitancy of our response may be a barometer for assessing how our convictions or beliefs about Jesus do or do not structure a distinctive way of living.

Increasingly, Christians find themselves in a **post-Christian** culture, struggling to integrate their faith life with daily economic and political concerns. Christians' strongest convictions about the world are all too often determined by the values of the dominant culture, so that one cannot easily distinguish between the values one holds as a follower of Christ and the values one holds as a twenty-first-century consumer. As we stand twenty centuries removed from the life of Jesus of Nazareth, the relevance of his life and the relevance of doctrinal statements about him often escape us, even if today we find comfort and fellowship in church communities formed in his name. In these churches we often avoid wrestling with Jesus—he is too historically specific, too particular, and church doctrines about him are too elusive. Instead, we prefer to concentrate on our own lives—we interpret our lives in an attempt to find religious meaning, while the stories of Jesus supply the superstructure, the set of images, that provide us with a point of reference for this reflection. Or we bring Jesus to life as our invisible friend, walking beside us or "carrying us" through the tough times as in the famous devotional work "Footprints." Such activity is understandable and has its place in the faith life of Christians, but our devotional life, our liturgical life, and our life as Christians in a world threatened by sin and violence need to reflect the deep and rich mystery of our faith in Jesus.

The history of theology is in some ways a history of forgetting. This is especially true of the discipline known as Christology, critical reflection on the religious significance of Jesus. The christological tradition is regarded by many Christians as largely irrelevant for contemporary faith, and many choose to ignore it or just forget about it. Such sentiment has been expressed widely, even among those theologians who, in the nineteenth and twentieth centuries, attempted to drive out what they regarded as the demons of medieval and ancient Christology and its creeds.

Dissatisfaction with what might be called creedal Christianity has driven many contemporary Christians to emphasize the Bible in the hope that an unambiguous affirmation of a collection of texts might provide simple assurance and affirmation of basic Christian faith. Yet even the biblical accounts of Jesus have suffered attack. Increasingly, skeptics have tried to get behind the Gospels to find the Jesus whom they claim has been hidden and distorted by the early Christian church. Such sentiment was behind the widely popular book and film *The DaVinci Code* as well as the spate of popular books on the so-called historical Jesus in the 1980s and 1990s.

Given the apparent demise of christological doctrines within modern culture and the pathological suspicion of Scripture that culture engenders, it is understandable that individualism has come to reign within the devotional lives of so many Christians. Insulation can be comforting. As long as one remains within the devotional life of the individual or small group, the personal relationship with Jesus can remain largely unassailable. I certainly do not wish to assail a personal relationship with Jesus— the language of a personal relationship has long served to designate the powerful transformative presence of Christ in those who have come to believe, not merely participate in religious observances. Nevertheless, one must recognize that confession of faith in Jesus is always mediated, made available, through a believing community. Those who self-identify as Christians do so because the faith has been witnessed to them, and the resources supplied by the tradition (the Bible, worship, prayer) have summoned them to deeper faith. There is a famous saying from the early church: "One Christian is no Christian." This book invites those tempted to marginalize the religious significance of Jesus, either through a rampant skepticism or through a retreat into personal piety, to discover or, rather, to remember the joy and the beauty of the tradition, the questions it poses, and the resources it offers for renewing an understanding of the religious meaning of Jesus, our salvation.

Shifting Terrain

For a time Christology was a rather straightforward discipline. In Roman Catholic circles, a course on Christology had a mathematical precision to it. One simply investigated how God became human in Christ, what powers Christ had, and how the death and resurrection of Christ saved us. As you have probably guessed, the account of Christology offered in these pages will not progress in such a straightforward manner. Times and people have changed. It is now expected that an introductory Christology text should begin by discussing how modern times have shifted the terrain of all theology, Christology included.

There has been a paradigm shift in the way Christology is done and taught. Karl Rahner, one of the giants of twentieth-century theology, was perhaps the greatest and most vocal advocate for this shift. Rahner was critical of the christological mentality that prevailed within the church in the middle of the last century.[1] He was particularly concerned with how the modern church had all but forgotten its own christological teaching regarding the full humanity and full divinity of Jesus. This doctrine had been established at the Council of **Chalcedon** in 451, but in the common language and practice of the church, this teaching was only verbally acknowledged, while in the practice of theology and in the lives of the laity it was nonoperative—that is, it was irrelevant to how people believed and lived. Rahner believed that the teaching of Chalcedon, and indeed all church teaching on Christ, represented both an obstacle and an opportunity for the renewal of Christology.

Chalcedon enshrined what many have called a **high-descending** approach to Christology. The prologue to John's Gospel is the best example of a high-descending approach to Christ. In that text the Word of God descends from heaven and becomes flesh, is glorified in death, and returns to the Father in heaven. In Christian art we often see images of the Annunciation represented with a tiny person (often carrying a cross, as in Robert Campin's *Annunciation Triptych*) who flies down from heaven and occupies the womb of the Blessed Mother. Such an approach to Christology makes perfect sense in the worldview of ancient peoples, but, as Rahner argued, it has become perilously out of date and theologically dangerous within our present context.

A high-descending approach has burdened many Christians with a warped and unorthodox Christology that Rahner termed *crypto-mono-physitism*. This phrase—a real mouthful—is comprised of both Latin and Greek terms: Greek *crypto* ("hidden"), Latin *mono* ("one"), and Greek *physis* ("nature"). Rahner's point is that modern Christians, while verbally affirming the full humanity and full divinity of Christ, actually have an unacknowledged tendency to ignore the human nature of Christ and emphasize only his divine nature. The neglect of Jesus' humanity is entirely understandable given the high-descending approach that dominated christological discourse and popular piety for centuries. But this approach has also produced a mythical understanding of Jesus that disconnects him from our experience as human beings and disconnects him from history. This disconnect represents an attack on the authentic teaching of the church, for Chalcedon affirmed the full and complete humanity of Jesus along with his divinity.

Rahner argued for a shift in christological thinking away from the high-descending approach to an emphasis on the humanity of Christ as the appropriate path to a recovery of the church's teaching. Such a shift, he argued, would act as a counterbalance to the longstanding crypto-monophysitism that dominated the church. Some theologians, however, objected to this move, arguing that a low-ascending approach would diminish the divinity of Christ. But Rahner rightly anticipated such concerns when he wrote, "Anyone who takes seriously the historicity of human truth (in which God's truth too has become incarnate in Revelation) must see that neither the abandonment of a [theological] formula nor its preservation in a petrified form does justice to human understanding."[2] Just because you say it does not mean that you really believe it, for you might not act in accordance with it. For example, if I say, "I love you," but I regularly act impatiently, react with anger, and am constantly preoccupied with myself, have I really understood and affirmed the truth of my statement? Similarly, the mere repetition of christological doctrines and formulas does not mean that they have been properly understood or adequately appropriated. When talking about God, something more is always possible. Therefore, the shift to a low-ascending Christology is not really a challenge to traditional Christology; rather, it is the means by which contemporary Christians do homage to the tradition and renew it.

As such, this book will follow a low-ascending approach, though with the recognition that such an approach will inevitably raise issues that can also prove both helpful and problematic for articulating a contemporary Christology that is faithful to the tradition.

A Road Map for What Follows

There is always something more to say about a given subject—especially when that subject is Jesus. This book represents one attempt to frame contemporary debates on the religious meaning of Jesus. Although many issues and personalities have been omitted in this text, the material included here reflects a twofold concern: to provide students who have little or no background in theology with a reasonably complete and accessible overview of important developments in the history of Christology, and to introduce students to the major questions that constitute the contemporary conversation in Christology. Because the contemporary conversation includes an assessment and appropriation of the history of Christology and its language, one cannot easily separate these concerns.

The threefold division of the text follows the logic of a low-ascending approach to Christology mentioned above. That approach begins with the human being Jesus and proceeds to ask, "What was it about this human being from the distant past that claimed the attention and devotion of so many people—both those who knew him and those who did not?" The first two chapters address the question of the human being Jesus from the perspective of history. Chapter 1 surveys the debate concerning the relevance, possibilities, and limitations of historical Jesus research. The chapter concludes with a warning that historical Jesus research cannot be the sole norm for theological reflection on Jesus. Chapter 2 outlines what one might call the middle ground in historical Jesus research. Using the work of John Meier and N. T. Wright, the chapter establishes the religious character of Jesus' life and ministry, and raises questions about how Jesus understood himself, his ministry, and his death. As one wrestles with the historical portrait of Jesus, one begins to recognize the difficulties and ambiguities inherent in the older forms of Christology. In the end, one has to deal with the human reality of Jesus of Nazareth and not simply retreat into the doctrinal claims of traditional Christology.

Part two steers the reader through the complex history and developments of christological doctrine. The resurrection of Christ stands at the origins of the Christian tradition, and for all the diversity of early Christianity, N. T. Wright correctly insists that there was no form of Christianity that did not proclaim the resurrection of Jesus. Chapter 3 addresses the experience of Jesus' resurrection as the catalyst for the earliest christological affirmations. Chapter 4 addresses the complex question of how the resurrection of Jesus, as well as the context of his life and ministry, created a new situation for the early followers of Jesus. Within the context of Jewish belief in one God, early believers affirmed that God was present in Jesus, bringing about a dramatic fulfillment to the story of Israel and hope amid the world's despair. The New Testament affirmations, however, were manifold; they did not provide a single encompassing vision of Christ and his relationship to God. In chapter 5 the long road to doctrinal orthodoxy (correct belief or teaching) passes through the first five centuries of the Christian era and beyond. The tension between fidelity to the biblical narratives and the need to articulate the Christian experience of salvation in Christ echoes the need for theological innovation already evident in the pages of the New Testament. In the creation of a new language about God, christological orthodoxy begins to emerge, though not without the tragedy and scandal of imperial politics and divisions within the church. Part two concludes with the exploration of Christ's saving work, or soteriology, in chapter 6. Biblical, patristic, and medieval doctrines create a rich theological tapestry, though at the expense of doctrinal clarity. The Western tradition is left with a maze of approaches, but seems to place violent imagery at the center of Christ's saving work.

Part three begins with an acknowledgement of a crisis regarding the credibility of Christian faith in the contemporary world. As traditional doctrines are increasingly subject to the scrutiny of a contemporary world defined by science and the norms of reason and secular values, the theological response to the contemporary situation shifts to a concern for the social effectiveness of Christian convictions, asking the question, "What difference does Christian faith make?" Chapter 7 begins with William Loewe's recasting of the soteriological question in terms of conversion and offers an account of how Christ saves us by making human transformation possible through the reversal of sin. The chapter then moves on to treat the revolutionary Christologies of Jürgen Moltmann and Elizabeth Johnson. Both Moltmann and Johnson suggest that modern Christology must undergo a revolution to become a catalyst for people oppressed by violence and dominated by suffering, and both also challenge the traditional boundaries or limits of christological reflection. The chapter concludes with reflections on the suffering caused by colonialism and the way theologians, especially in Asia, have come to articulate their own experience of suffering by formulating distinctly Asian postcolonial Christologies. Chapter 8 brings the discussion of contemporary Christology to a close by asking, "How can Christians affirm their faith in Christ while living in a world of non-Christians?" The approaches of numerous theologians are addressed, with particular emphasis on the ideas of Roger Haight and Jacques Dupuis. The chapter concludes with a brief presentation of the great Swiss theologian Hans Urs von Balthasar and his aesthetic and dramatic Christology. Though it may seem odd to include his theology within a chapter dedicated to religious pluralism, some theologians regard his approach to Christology (and to theology as a whole) as a way to move forward from the critical Christologies that seem to threaten the integrity of the tradition, especially the centrality of Christ. While von Balthasar's Christology represents a return to the high-descending approach, his theology avoids the mythological worldview of older Christologies and offers a thoroughly post-modern engagement with the tradition.

Endnotes

1 Karl Rahner, "Current Problems in Christology," in *Theological Investigations* (Baltimore: Helicon, 1961), 1:149–200.

2 Ibid., 150.

The Story of the Quest(s)

The shift to a low-ascending approach to Christology mentioned in the introduction (i.e., the approach that begins by looking at the first-century human being Jesus) has been responsible, in part, for the wave of books, films, and documentaries on Jesus we have seen over the past two decades. These media have often presented pictures of Jesus that many Christians have found disconcerting: Jesus as a violent revolutionary, a confused and naïve religious reformer, a magician, and a philosopher. The diverse depictions of Jesus have one important feature in common: they all purport to offer a view of the person behind the Gospels, the historical human being rather than the religious figure proclaimed by the Christian church. Scholars generally designate any sketch of this historical human being "the historical Jesus." In the face of all these images of Christ, one might fairly ask questions like, why not stick with what the Bible says—isn't the Bible enough? or, how do we know who this Jesus behind the Gospels was? These are excellent questions, and perhaps the best way to begin addressing them is to explain how and why this quest for the Jesus "behind the Gospels" developed. The brief account offered here will address the important insights as well as the problems inherent in any talk about the historical Jesus in contemporary Christology.

The Old Quest: The Challenge of the Enlightenment

The Enlightenment provides the basic backdrop against which the so-called old or original quest for the historical Jesus is best understood. The historical parameters for the Enlightenment are often disputed and, as with all large movements, the identification of a specific inaugurating event proves elusive. One development, however, may help us understand both its historical context and its general philosophical and political concerns, namely the "wars of religion" sparked by the **Reformation** and the **Counter-Reformation** and extending to the Peace of Westphalia (1648). Europe witnessed decades of wars between allegedly Christian (Catholic and Protestant) rulers who, with perverse irony, were busy killing one another in the name of Jesus. These wars helped to discredit religious authority in Europe: if Christian authorities on either side of the conflicts could cite divine sanction for their violent crusades, logically their respective accounts of that authority must be highly selective and self-serving, to say the least.

The discrediting of religious authority prompted many thinkers to look outside religion for answers to questions of reason, truth, and morality. As one of its main principles, the Enlightenment cultivated a pervasive suspicion of religious authority—those people, documents, and institutions that appealed to God for their exercise of power were not to be trusted. Instead, the Enlightenment celebrated the work of the individual mind that was free from authoritarian constraints, including religious authority. In part, the Enlightenment set the stage for the **old quest** for the historical

Important Movements and Eras

All movements and eras, all periods in history, are constructed. That is, they are devices used by scholars to understand how history has unfolded and to differentiate one set of developments from another. Below is a chart representing some of the movements or eras discussed in chapter 1.

Reformation	Enlightenment	Romanticism	Modernism and Post-Modernism
The Reformation established the primacy of the literal sense of Scripture (as opposed to allegory) and the autonomy of the individual believer in the interpretation of Scripture. The Reformation was a political and social movement as well as a religious one. It was inaugurated by Martin Luther in 1517, though there were many less successful reformers before him.	The Reformation and the Counter-Reformation spawned considerable violence in Europe: the "wars of religion." As this violence came to an end in the 1600s, European thinkers began to look to human reason rather than religious authority as their guiding principle. At this time the natural sciences began to emerge as true sciences, whereas religious assertions were increasingly viewed with suspicion. The political repercussions of the Enlightenment include the French and American revolutions, which replaced the authority of kings with "government by the people." In France this resulted in the tyranny of Robespierre and Napoleon, while in the U.S. it resulted in the Constitution and the founding of the Republic.	Romanticism was concerned less with science than with humanity, art, and a sense of transcendence. The Romantic movement was a reaction to the excesses of the Enlightenment. As a movement, the Enlightenment and its effects were still felt throughout the nineteenth and twentieth centuries, but Romanticism tempered that influence in the nineteenth century through its appeal to narrative, image, the past, and the individual.	Modernism, or "modernity," emerged in the nineteenth century as a response to traditional forms of philosophy, art, and politics. Modernity sought to overcome every aspect of tradition that held back "progress." Post-modernism was a reaction against the emphasis on progress. In the middle and later part of the twentieth century, notions of progress and disdain for tradition came under scrutiny. Many claims of progress and objective science were unmasked as destructive ideologies.

| 1500 | 1600 | 1700 | 1800 | 1900 |

Wars of Religion (1618–1648)
American Revolution (1776–1781)
French Revolution (1789)

WWI (1914–1919)
WWII (1939–1945)

Jesus that emerged in the nineteenth century by discrediting traditional Christianity and its source of authority: Scripture.

But the Enlightenment's hostility to organized religion provides only one piece of the background necessary for understanding the old quest. The other piece involves the Enlightenment's successor, Romanticism. Whereas the Enlightenment had emphasized the cool logic of scientific reason as the sole criterion of truth and value, Romanticism emphasized the emotional, mystical, and more natural aspects of human existence. Like the Enlightenment, Romanticism prized individual experience and remained suspicious of organized religion and religious authority. However, Romanticism was much more comfortable creatively engaging traditional Christianity than was the Enlightenment, albeit in a subversive way. Together Romanticism and the Enlightenment, to varying degrees, fueled the major efforts of the old quest.

The Old Quest: Looking for Jesus amid Social and Cultural Revolution

The French Revolution (1789) was a watershed event in the political, social, and religious life of Europe. The insights and challenges posed by Enlightenment thinkers came to fruition in what amounted to a wholesale rejection of the old order of Europe in which the Christian church had held a position of considerable cultural and political influence. At this time the father of historical Jesus research, Hermann Samuel Reimarus (1694–1768), inaugurated what has come to be known as the old quest for the historical Jesus. The general indictment of the church that accompanied the French Revolution seems to have played a role in his description of the origins of Christianity and the place of Jesus therein. Reimarus suggested that Jesus' proclamation of the kingdom of God stood in contrast to the disciples' emphasis on Jesus and the church. Jesus' ministry was primarily a nationalist religious and political reform movement (much like the French Revolution), while Jesus' disciples, through their preaching and writing, misrepresented the message of Jesus for their own purposes. Reimarus concluded that traditional Christianity was, simply stated, a fraud, a deception that an investigation into the life of Jesus behind the Gospels helps to unmask. Such an account of Jesus and the origins of the church further eroded the power of the church while giving solace to those who sought political and social reform.

The attack on the Christian church as a fraud certainly resonated within many quarters in nineteenth-century Europe, but the profound religious and philosophical sensibilities of the culture also admitted a more nuanced revision of the origins of Christianity, such as that offered by David Friedrich Strauss (1808–1874). His major work, *The Life of Jesus Critically Examined* (1836), went through several editions during Strauss's own lifetime. An admirer of the German philosopher G. F. Hegel, Strauss argued that the Gospels were **myth** and attempted to communicate a reality that Hegel designated the ideal of "God-manhood." This ideal is somewhat complicated, but in broad terms it describes human life lived

Person of Interest

Bruno Bauer

Bruno Bauer (1809–1882) was a philosopher, historian, and theologian. Bauer was a student of the great German philosopher G. F. Hegel and the teacher of Karl Marx. Bauer's thought stressed rational autonomy of the human person as well as the notion of historical progress. His research on the origins of Christianity may be the best-known aspect of his work. He contextualized its origins in the experience of alienation and disaffection with terrestrial existence. Such alienation spurred the human mind to project the notion of irrational transcendent powers—i.e., "God"—over the individual. This projection sanctioned the specific interests, both material and ideological, of the Christian sect. Furthermore, Bauer located the origins of Christianity in the second century CE rather than the first century and argued that the Gospels were written much later than people had supposed. In reconstructing the genealogy of basic Christian beliefs, Bauer argued that Christianity had only a vague connection with Judaism; rather, its most distinctive beliefs were derived from Greek thought and religion. But Bauer also believed that Christianity emerged as a revolutionary force in the Roman Empire—it promoted liberation for the economically and politically marginalized. As such, Christianity stood as an important moment of progress in Roman history. Bauer's account of the historical origins of Christianity were positive from a social point of view (though heretical from a Christian point of view), but his account of nineteenth-century Christianity was far less optimistic. Bauer saw the growing emphasis on religious feeling rather than reason as a sign of Christianity's impending demise.

toward the goal of actualizing the great spiritual orientation of our existence: a union with God. Jesus therefore is not the incarnation of God, but a sign, or example, of what human beings might become if they are awakened to the spiritual foundations of their existence. Strauss's understanding of myth has proven influential over the years.

For Strauss, the disciples' desire to communicate the dynamics of a personal encounter with Jesus could only be effective if that communication were evocative—it had to invite people to respond or react in a certain way, rather than merely describe or report the events of Jesus' life. Myth was the means by which the literary and religious conventions of the first century were unconsciously used by early Christian writers to bring the encounter with Jesus alive and thus make the realization of God-manhood possible in a way that mere description could not. For Strauss, Christianity was not a fraud but a mistake or a misunderstanding of this basic dynamic, a mistake that could be corrected. This correction, however, necessitated the demise of traditional Christianity, but at the same time would create a new, more authentic, and non-dogmatic religion.

Around the time of Strauss, a movement emerged within theological circles that sought to find middle ground between the principles of the Enlightenment and traditional Christianity. This position came to be known as **liberal theology**, and one of its most popular exponents at the turn of the twentieth century was the great historian Adolf von Harnack (1851–1930). Liberal theology, evolving from the work of a group of theologians known as rationalists in the eighteenth and early nineteenth centuries, sought to accommodate the principles of the Enlightenment and Christianity—usually by adopting a thoroughly modern outlook, retaining aspects of traditional Christianity that fit, and abandoning elements that did not. For example, the **miracle** stories were given naturalistic and moral interpretations. Jesus' healings had natural explanations, and so-called nature miracles like the feeding of the multitude had moral significance (when we share, we find that there is more than enough to go around). In his famous book *What Is Christianity?* (1900), Harnack depicted Jesus as an eminently reasonable human being and did away with any hint of the supernatural. The resultant portrait of Jesus and his mission revolved around three central ideas: (1) the kingdom of God as a present interior reality, (2) the infinite value of the human soul, and (3) the law of love as the supreme religious and moral value. For Harnack, Jesus did not point to himself; rather, he directed all people to God as a loving Father. Harnack, like Strauss, rejected the doctrines of traditional Christianity, but he did so not because they are a misunderstanding of Jesus. Rather, Christian doctrines, even those in Scripture, are historically and culturally determined—the product of Greek and other influences—and only of passing value.

Harnack was an important and serious church historian, and he was closely connected to many of the Romantic and "liberal" approaches to the historical Jesus that emerged in the middle and latter part of the nineteenth century. These approaches imaginatively narrated the life and ministry of Jesus so that the worldview of Jesus was made to fit with that of modern European intellectuals. Around the turn of the nineteenth century, many began to wonder whether the quest for the historical Jesus was sufficiently self-critical.

The End of the Old Quest: The Limitations of Historical Investigations

The old quest was brought to a close through important developments in two areas of New Testament study: the development of a better understanding of the formation and purpose of the Gospels, and a better (though still imperfect) understanding of first-century Palestinian Judaism and its theology. First, it had been argued for the better part of Christian history that the Gospels represented eyewitness accounts of the life and death of Jesus (particularly the Gospel of Matthew, the "first Gospel"). The Markan hypothesis challenged this assumption and thereby revolutionized how most scholars read the canonical Gospels. Beginning in the middle of the nineteenth century, Mark came to be regarded as the first Gospel, a kind of bare-bones account of Jesus' life and ministry with few theological accretions. In some circles Mark was confidently regarded as a basic historically reliable account of Jesus' life, whereas the other Gospels were thought to have comparatively little historical value.

At the close of the nineteenth century, the historicity of Mark came under fire in the work of William Wrede (1859–1906), who suggested that even Mark's Gospel was suffused with the theology of the early church.

He claimed that one example of this was the so-called **messianic secret** material in Mark. The messianic secret refers to passages in Mark where those who have witnessed Jesus' divine power (e.g., in a healing or exorcism) are instructed not to tell others of Jesus' identity as the divine agent, but to be silent about what they have seen (Mark 1:40–45; 5:21–24, 35–43; 7:31–37; 8:22–26). Wrede saw this feature of Mark as an apologetic tool—a means to defend the truthfulness of Christian faith—and attributed it to the *Sitz im Leben* (life-setting) of Mark's audience rather than to Jesus' own ministry. In other words, Wrede claimed that primitive Christians had understood that Jesus became the Messiah after his death (we will discuss the development of New Testament Christology in a later chapter). As Christology developed, Jesus' identity as Messiah was read back into the stories about his ministry, but this created a tension—was Jesus the Messiah before or only after his death? Wrede believed that Mark's community resolved this tension by creating the messianic secret: Jesus was the Messiah during his life, but he hid his identity and revealed it only after his Resurrection.

This feature of Mark's Gospel was but one example of how later concerns and developments within early Christianity came to dominate the proclamation of the gospel. For Wrede, the Gospels were excellent sources for the study of earliest Christianity but poor, or even inadequate, sources for the reconstruction of the historical Jesus.

The critical account of the historicity of the Gospels was also fueled by the emergence of a more complex account of first-century Judaism and its theology. Johannes Weiss (1863–1914) put another nail in the coffin of the uncritical assumptions of the old quest with his book *Jesus' Proclamation of the Kingdom of God* (1892). Weiss argued that one may indeed gain some knowledge of the historical Jesus by reading the Gospels, but the picture that emerges makes Jesus irrelevant to modern human beings because his message and his actions all revolve around an ancient understanding of the world and God.

Weiss claimed that Jesus' preaching and ministry was informed by first-century Jewish apocalypticism, or more precisely, **apocalyptic eschatology**. The expression comes from two Greek words: *apocalypsis,* "revelation," and *eschatos,* "last" or "end." We will discuss apocalyptic eschatology in more detail in another chapter, but some initial background may be helpful at this point. Apocalyptic eschatology is a term developed by scholars to get a handle on the unique features of a particularly Jewish and Christian perspective that flourished from the second century BCE to the second century CE. The term refers to a theological genre of literature as well as a theological movement that prevailed in many sectors of Palestinian Jewish society in the years before and after the time of Jesus. This eschatology was blended with ideas from Persia and Greece and began to focus on the idea that God would shortly intervene in history, raise the dead, give both the wicked and righteous their just rewards, and reestablish Israel as an independent kingdom ruled by God. Apocalyptic eschatology usually involved the communication of this message or revelation of hope to a persecuted community through the work of an intermediary—sometimes an angel, other times a famous figure from the history of Israel. Needless to say, if Weiss was correct about the basic content and meaning of Jesus' ministry and self-understanding, then the entire project of liberal theology would be undercut. In fact, the entire historical Jesus quest would be vain because it could not supply a picture of Jesus that would be useful for modern people.

Albert Schweitzer, notable composer, physician, medical doctor, winner of the Nobel Peace Prize, and theologian, brought the old quest for the historical Jesus to a halt in 1906 with the publication of *The Quest of the Historical Jesus: A Critical Study of its Progress from Reimarus to Wrede.* In this book Schweitzer traced the progress and aberrations of the various attempts to discover the historical Jesus in the nineteenth century. Schweitzer made use of George Tyrell's famous image of historical Jesus research at the time: such research is like looking down a dark well—what one sees is simply one's own reflection. In other words, the political philosopher and revolutionary see Jesus as a revolutionary, the Hegelian philosopher sees Jesus as a Hegelian philosopher, and the humanist sees Jesus as a humanist. Schweitzer's own position was similar to that of Johannes Weiss and his thoroughgoing eschatology. Schweitzer contended that the Jesus of history was so thoroughly immersed in the situation of first-century Palestine and its concern with eschatology that any attempt to bring him into the modern period does so only through violence and distortion. The historical Jesus is alien to modern ways of thinking.

Person of Interest

Albert Schweitzer

Albert Schweitzer (1875–1965) was one of the most important figures within twentieth-century Western culture. His family was deeply religious as well as musically and academically inclined, and this helped to chart Albert's future. His greatness first manifested itself in Albert's musical abilities: he was nine when he first performed at his father's church is Strasbourg. Schweitzer's musical interest continued unabated to the end of his life—he was internationally renowned. His performances and musical publications earned him substantial financial resources with which to continue many endeavors over the years, but as a young man, he used these resources to further his education. Initially Schweitzer entered into theological studies at the University of Strasbourg, where he completed his doctorate in philosophy (1899). He also received a licentiate in theology a year later. Afterward he took up posts as a pastor and professor over the next decade, during which he wrote several important books, including his celebrated account of the old quest for the historical Jesus (*The Quest of the Historical Jesus*, 1906). Around the same time, Schweitzer decided to go to Africa as a medical missionary and proceeded to earn a medical degree in 1913. He founded a hospital at Lambaréné in French Equatorial Africa, which he operated until his death in 1965. The hospital could serve as many as five hundred patients at its height, and Schweitzer had multiple roles there: physician, surgeon, pastor, administrator, and janitor. He was awarded the Nobel Peace Prize in 1952.

In his account of the progress of the old quest for the historical Jesus, William Loewe identified four major positions at the end of the nineteenth century:[1] (1) the historical Jesus is the Jesus of the Gospels (the position of fundamentalists or reactionaries), (2) the historical Jesus is the Jesus of philosophers and humanists (liberal theologians), (3) the historical Jesus cannot be reconstructed from the Gospels (Wrede), and (4) the historical Jesus is freakish and irrelevant to our time (Weiss and Schweitzer). Within academic circles in Europe, positions three and four carry the day, but positions one and two enjoy significant popularity. The result of this division between academics and the broader culture was the general acceptance of the position outlined in Martin Kähler's book *The So-Called Historical Jesus and the Historic Biblical Christ* (actually published before Schweitzer's book). For Kähler, the "historical" (*geschich-tlich* in German) Jesus cannot be identified as the object of faith; rather, it is the Christ proclaimed at Easter that is the object of proclamation and belief, and it is this "historic" (*historisch* in German) Jesus that makes a difference in history. Kähler's distinction between the historical person and the Christ of the faith community would be influential over the next several decades.

Beyond the Question of the Historical Jesus

Few figures have dominated theological debates as did Rudolf Bultmann (1884–1976) in the middle decades of the twentieth century. Bultmann, a Lutheran, helped to move theology away from the seemingly intractable

The Historical Jesus at the Turn of the Nineteenth Century

At the close of the nineteenth century, the quest for the historical Jesus had all but come to an end in one of four major positions.

The historical Jesus is the Jesus of the Gospels. For many Christians the rise of biblical criticism in the wake of the Enlightenment seemed obviously contrary to the spirit of Christianity; they responded by rejecting any separation between Jesus in the Gospels and accounts of the historical Jesus. Many Christians today continue to find such distinctions troubling since they seem to cast doubt on the truthfulness of the Gospels.

The historical Jesus is the Jesus of philosophers and humanists. Not all Christians viewed the contributions of the Enlightenment, and the modern world in general, as destructive. Liberal theology was a widely popular movement that saw the Enlightenment as an opportunity to formulate a new understanding of Christianity. Liberal theology worked tirelessly to construct a positive account of Jesus as the ultimate humanist and philosopher. Such

an account was to replace traditional dogmas that identify Jesus as the incarnate **Son of God**.

The historical Jesus cannot be reconstructed from the Gospels. William Wrede determined that Christian confidence in the Gospels as a source for uncovering the life and ministry of Jesus was misplaced. Wrede saw the Gospels as good resources for understanding the early church, which created the Gospels to help them deal with their own particular situation. Christians, therefore, are left without any sure historical resource for their faith.

The historical Jesus is freakish and irrelevant. Weiss and Schweitzer both attacked the supposition of liberal theology that Jesus could best be understood through an appeal to modern ideas. Rather, they insisted, Jesus was a unique individual who was a product of a first-century Jewish worldview: he thought that the world was coming to an end in the fiery and dramatic advent of God. His Crucifixion was, therefore, a failure, a last desperate attempt to force God to act.

situation created by the demise of liberal theology and the old quest to locate an authentic religious expression of Christianity within a modern context. The movement became known as dialectical theology. Dialectical theology did not share with liberal theology its optimism regarding human history and progress; rather, God was understood as entirely "other"—apart from the world—and such a position carries some important implications for the study of the historical Jesus.

Bultmann denied the theological significance of the historical Jesus beyond the mere fact of his existence. The fact of Jesus' existence (*das Dass*) was simply the precondition for the proclamation of the early church. Bultmann was concerned instead with historical issues surrounding the formation of the Gospels within the early church. He and other form critics (especially Martin Debelius) sought to deconstruct the Gospels into individual units to determine the original life setting of the early church that gave rise to these units. By doing this Bultmann hoped to gain an understanding of the manner in which the early church came to understand and communicate its faith in Christ. Armed with this knowledge, the contingencies that formed much of the New Testament could be relativized or dismissed in a project of **demythologizing**. For Bultmann, as for Kähler, the proclamation, or **kērygma** of the risen Jesus has import for believers, not a historically reconstructed figure of the past. The main features of Bultmann's theology and his approach to historical Jesus research are outlined in his famous essay on demythologizing the New Testament.[2]

For Bultmann, the New Testament presents a mythical worldview and a corresponding mythical view of salvation. The world of the New Testament is a three-story structure (heaven is "up there," earth is "here," and hell is "down there"); the course of human history is governed by spiritual powers; salvation occurs as a result of the God-man's atoning sacrifice and the victory this gives him over the powers of evil; anyone who belongs to the Christian community is guaranteed resurrection. For Bultmann, one cannot recover this worldview—one cannot go back to olden times and adopt a "flat-earth worldview"; rather, the worldview of the New Testament must be deconstructed. The mythical worldview of the New Testament has its roots in the mythology of either first-century Judaism or that of the Greco-Roman world. Christians cannot accept

The Reformation and Contemporary Christianity

Although the history of Christianity from earliest times bears witness to its great diversity, both practical and theological (note the churches of Greece, Russia, Egypt, Armenia, and Lebanon), the Reformation gave rise to numerous expressions of Christianity in the West and dramatically changed the landscape of the faith. The sixteenth-century reformers and the movements they founded all took exception to the Church of Rome (the Roman Catholic Church) to which virtually all people living in Western Europe belonged until that time (note that *catholic* means "universal"). Two important theological principles unite virtually all Reformation or Protestant Churches: (1) Scripture is the sole authority for governing Christian thought and practice, and (2) justification ("being made right with God") is given to human beings by God as a gift (i.e., grace) through faith and not through any good works on our part. In the chart below, the four major trajectories of the Reformation are presented along with the general aspects of the tradition, the contemporary churches in those traditions, and the characteristic elements within these traditions. The chart paints Protestant Christianity with a broad brush, and is meant to give readers a reference point and not a full-scale account of any denomination or the history of the Reformation. Many important Protestant churches are not represented here because they emerged more recently (e.g., pentecostal churches).

	Lutheran Churches (R. Bultmann)	Reformed / Presbyterian Churches (K. Barth)	Anabaptist and Baptist Churches	Anglican / Episcopalian and Methodist Churches
Leaders	Martin Luther (1483–1546) Philip Melancthon (1497–1560)	John Calvin (1509–1564) John Knox (1505–1572)	Ulrich Zwingli (1484–1531) Menno Simons (1496–1561)	Ulrich Zwingli (1484–1531) Menno Simons (1496–1561)
General Tradition	Lutheran churches are the direct descendants of Luther's movement. Lutheran churches generally emphasize the importance of Scripture, of preaching, and of salvation by grace through faith, but also celebrate Communion on a regular basis and maintain a hierarchy (i.e., bishops).	The Reformed movement was distinct from that of Luther in emphasizing the irresistibility of grace (i.e., God gives grace to human beings and they cannot reject or lose that grace), and predestination (God chose those human beings who would be given God's grace before they were created). Administrative authority rests in a body of elders (or "presbyters") in each congregation.	This "radical" branch of the Reformation has less coherence than other branches. While Zwingli opposed the ideas of the Anabaptists like Menno Simons, they both agreed on the importance of congregational authority rather than on bishops or elders (hence the term *free churches*). Of the Protestant churches, these tend to be the most conservative in their handling of the Bible, but the most	The Church of England became a separate entity not on theological grounds but jurisdictional: it rejected the authority of the Pope. The Anglican tradition does not usually consider itself "Protestant," for while it (cautiously) adopted many of the practices and much of the theology of the Reformers, it also retained much of the catholic heritage, such as the authority of bishops (*Episcopal* comes from

The Reformation and Contemporary Christianity *(continued)*

	Lutheran Churches (R. Bultmann)	Reformed / Presbyterian Churches (K. Barth)	Anabaptist and Baptist Churches	Anglican / Episcopalian and Methodist Churches
General Tradition			critical of church tradition, including traditional doctrines and the creeds.	*episcopos*, "bishop"). Wesley, an Anglican priest, began a revival movement that grew into a denomination (the Methodists) in its own right. Today, Episcopal and Methodist churches are among the most theologically progressive communities.
Some Contemporary Denominations	ELCA, Missouri and Wisconsin Synod Lutheran Churches (LCMS and LCWS), The Worldwide Lutheran Federation (to which ELCA belongs)	Reformed Churches (Dutch, Swiss, etc.), Presbyterian Churches (PCUSA, PCA, etc.)	Anabaptists (Mennonites, Amish). Modern Baptists are related to this movement but stand between the Reformed, Anabaptist, and even Anglican / Episcopalian traditions. Most non-denominational Evangelical churches stand in this tradition as well.	The Church of England and its sister churches forming the worldwide Anglican communion (Episcopal Church in America, Church of Canada, Australia, etc.). United Methodist and other Wesleyan Churches sprang from this tradition.
Some Distinguishing Characteristics	Luther's reverence for the celebration of the Eucharist (Communion) and emphasis on the proclamation of Scripture in the assembly make Lutheran worship similar to contemporary Roman Catholic (i.e., post–Vatican II) worship and general practice.	In this tradition the holiness and sovereignty of God are emphasized, especially in the doctrine of predestination and the denial of free will, though these last two are still debated among many Reformed Christians, with many churches taking a less Calvinist position.	These churches reject infant baptism in favor of believer's (adult) baptism. They emphasize the relationship between God and the individual, and tend to be suspicious of the state.	Episcopal churches grew out of the Church of England and are therefore "national churches." They stand between the Reformed and Catholic traditions in many ways. Methodist churches emphasize the spiritual and emotional experience of God's love.

The Reformation and Contemporary Christianity *(continued)*

Many Christians today belong to non-denominational churches, which often purport to be free from denominational concerns. Although these churches provide new and exciting visions of doing church, they also emphasize a basic form of Evangelical Christianity that is more often than not rooted in some form of traditional Protestant Christianity (usually Baptist). For example, Saddleback Church, from which comes the *Purpose-Driven Life* series of books, was affiliated with the Southern Baptist Convention. The Willow Creek Churches (WCA), though non-denominational, nonetheless espouse an Evangelical faith that finds strong support from Baptist churches. This is not a bad thing, but Christians must be conscious of their theological roots and wary of evacuating the Christian tradition of its history. Christians believe that God is made known through history—that is a complex, beautiful, frustrating, and redemptive reality!

this worldview because (1) there is nothing specifically Christian about this worldview, and (2) no one can appropriate this worldview today in light of modern culture. The revision of the New Testament worldview springs forth most obviously from the natural sciences. Geology, biology, astronomy, and the other scientific disciplines help us to construct a scientifically responsible worldview. More important for Bultmann, however, is the way our self-understanding as modern people helps to shape our worldview, and this has great implications for our understanding of salvation.

Demythologizing does not imply a cafeteria approach to Christianity—taking what fits with our modern worldview and leaving behind ideas or doctrines that do not conform to our modern sensibilities. Rather, Bultmann insists, "We can only accept the mythical world picture or completely reject it."[3] He contends that the mythic picture of the New Testament will be done away with as we uncover the real intention of the New Testament and its use of myth. For Bultmann, myth is to be understood not in cosmological terms but in anthropological terms. It gives expression to the "beyond" or the limit of human existence that lies beyond the familiar disposable world that we take for granted. In other words, myth must be understood as disclosing the mystery of human existence (what it means to be human).

This is not an altogether novel approach to the gospel; rather, Bultmann insists that the task of demythologizing is already undertaken in the New Testament itself. Earlier attempts at demythologizing the New

Testament were offered in the nineteenth century, most notably by Strauss and by some within liberal theology. These attempts, however, failed to understand the kērygma (the faith proclamation of the church). An existential interpretation of the New Testament myths is needed, an interpretation that will speak to the difficulties of human existence in the modern world.

The understanding of "being" that underlies the Christian kērygma contrasts existence (or "human being") with faith and without. The human being outside faith—one who lives "according to the flesh"—is subject to the impermanence and decay associated with the world. However, in faith, human beings live "according to the Spirit" because their lives are based on what cannot be seen and what is not disposable. For Bultmann, the eschatology usually associated with Jewish apocalypticism is now to be read as the new life of the believer, a new creation, free from the trouble of this transitory and disposable world.

Bultmann contends that this discovery is dependent on the New Testament. The revelation that takes place in Christ is the revelation of the love of God. This love frees us from ourselves and opens us up to freedom and future possibility. Christian faith recognizes the act of God in Christ as the condition for the possibility of our love and our authenticity. That is why, for Bultmann, the significance of the Christ occurrence rests not in historical questions but in discerning what God wants to say to us in the proclamation of Christ. The cross of Christ is to be understood not as an occurrence outside of ourselves and our world; rather, the meaning of the cross is found in the lives of believers who commit to the suffering that authentic freedom demands.

The project of demythologizing the New Testament preserves the paradox (apparent contradiction) of the Christian faith because the transcendent God—the God that is totally beyond us—becomes present in the concrete history and lives of people. Bultmann's project, though criticized during his lifetime, was eminently pastoral (rather than simply academic) since it tried to outline how Christians are to believe within the modern world. Bultmann's project began to be dismantled in the latter part of the twentieth century at the hands of some of his own students.

Christianity and Existentialism

Existentialism, a philosophical movement that flourished in the middle of the twentieth century, rejected classical philosophy and its insistence on abstractions like "essence." The famous existentialist philosopher Jean-Paul Sartre defined existentialism in the maxim "existence precedes essence." In other words, human beings are thrown out into the world—"thrown toward death," to use Martin Heidegger's expression—without any definition or foundation to guide them. According to existentialism, one is forced to wrestle with one's own existence and, through the exercise of will, responsibly create one's own essence. Such a project no doubt explains why human beings are so anxious, consumed by the desire to possess and control, under the illusion that the one who controls or owns the most "wins."

While some of the most famous existentialists were atheists (Sartre, de Beauvoir, Camus), the movement had its roots in the work of the Danish theologian and philosopher Søren Kierkegaard (†1855). Kierkegaard, deeply dissatisfied with the modern emphasis on science and a corresponding concern with universals in accounts of human existence, emphasized the problems of individual existence. Gabriel Marcel, a twentieth-century existentialist philosopher, frames the issue simply: the primary task of human life is not to have or control but to be or become. Such an outlook transcends the scientific emphasis of the modern world without rejecting its advances. Thus the modern world is neither vilified nor glorified.

Both of the founders of dialectical theology (Karl Barth and Rudolf Bultmann) appealed to the thought of Kierkegaard, though Bultmann was well acquainted with the thought of the German philosopher Martin Heidegger as well. For dialectical theology, existentialism helped to move Christianity away from liberal theology's problematic embrace of modernity and the dangerous idea of "progress." Existentialism helped to emphasize the precarious position of the human person and the need to abandon oneself to God in an outrageous leap of faith. As such, existentialism helped to reinforce the Reformation's emphasis on salvation as a gift that cannot be earned.

The New Quest

The dismissal of the historical Jesus from the scope of theology was a difficult position for many to accept, even among those who closely supported Bultmann's overall project. Ernst Käsemann (1906–1998), one of Bultmann's former students, launched the **new quest** for the historical Jesus when he took exception to Bultmann's position on the historical Jesus. In a paper delivered at a meeting of Bultmann's former students on October 20, 1953, Käsemann asserted (1) there was a danger of heresy in Bultmann's dehistoricizing the kērygma, (2) the Gospels were composed because the early church was in fact concerned with the earthly Jesus, and (3) the Gospels identify the risen Christ of the kērygma with the earthly Jesus. These points combine to argue that the quest for the historical Jesus, contrary to Bultmann's assertion, was not only possible but also theologically necessary.

Käsemann positively regarded the basic theological insights of Bultmann, and was sympathetic to Bultmann's dissatisfaction with liberal theology and the old quest. Though Bultmann's concern to present a thoroughly modern yet Lutheran approach to the gospel is successful in many ways, Bultmann's denial of the theological significance of historical Jesus research comes dangerously close to embracing the early heresy know as Docetism. Docestism (from the Greek verb *dokeō*, meaning "to think" or "to seem") was the heresy that denied the reality of the Incarnation, saying instead that Jesus only "seemed" or appeared to be human, but since he was divine, he could never be a real (material) human being. Käsemann argued that the denial of the theological significance of historical Jesus research in favor of the kērygma was almost the same as denying the Incarnation.

The second and third points on which Käsemann criticized Bultmann are directly related to one another. First, Bultmann fails to deal with the fact that the kērygma of the early church developed into the narratives of Jesus' life and ministry that we call the Gospels. This happened, Käsemann argued (his third point), because the earliest Christians wanted to make the explicit connection between the faith to which the kērygma calls us and the life of the human being that was the basis for the kērygma.

Among Bultmann's students, few full-length works on the life and ministry of Jesus emerged, with the notable exception of Gunther Bornkam's *Jesus of Nazareth*, which was widely read and influential for almost two decades. Among Roman Catholics, however, historical Jesus research quickly became a focal point of christological reflection. One of the most prominent and influential books released was by the Dutch Dominican Edward Schillebeeckx (1914–). Schillebeeckx's major work appeared in two volumes: *Jesus: An Experiment in Christology* and *Christ: The Experience of Jesus as Lord*. Schillebeeckx, while not sharing the same history or commitments as Bultmann's students, nonetheless offers a work that in some ways was characteristic of the new quest. Schillebeeckx offers readers an outline of what historians can reasonably assert, a critically assured minimum of information about Jesus. This initial sketch focuses on the words of Jesus and his association with the marginalized and suffering. From this point Schillebeeckx reflects on the development of Christology in the New Testament. It is the "experience" (an important concept in Schillebeeckx's theology) of the early disciples that provides the basis for their subsequent proclamations about Jesus' identity as Messiah. Because of this, Schillebeeckx has been accused of blending his historical reconstruction of Jesus with his own theology, the theology of experience. This is a common accusation raised against the entire new quest: it aims to uncover the unique personality of Jesus and thereby gain an understanding of how Christian faith emerged from the personal encounter with Jesus. In other words, there seems to be a theological agenda that controls the historical reconstruction of Jesus.

The new quest rescued historical Jesus research as an integral part of contemporary Christian faith. But the precise place of historical Jesus research within contemporary Christology is still a matter of considerable debate, a debate that has animated the so-called **third quest**.

The Third Quest: Some Distinguishing Features

The British scholar (and bishop in the Church of England) N.T. Wright coined the expression "third quest" to describe the wave of Jesus research that took place from the mid-1980s to today. Generally, this wave of Jesus research has several features that distinguish it from the earlier quests, but in any given author one can also trace some or many of their concerns to a previous generation of scholarship. For example, the Jesus Seminar, a group of scholars and other interested individuals, have produced a series of works that seem, in many ways, to continue the old quest objective of using historical Jesus research to attack traditional forms of Christianity. John P. Meier, however, argues that the third quest for the historical Jesus represents a significant departure from previous quests. He identifies seven notable gains that define the third quest:[4]

1. The third quest has an ecumenical and international character (whereas earlier quests were almost exclusively male, German, and Protestant).

2. It clarifies the question of reliable sources (the New Testament is viewed as the primary source for research, and other texts and artifacts like the apocryphal gospels or the Dead Sea Scrolls are only secondary sources).

3. It presents a more accurate picture of first-century Judaism (as opposed to the tendency in previous quests simply to contrast Jesus and first-century Judaism).

4. It employs new insights from archaeology, philology, and sociology.

5. It clarifies the application of criteria of historicity (i.e., unlike previous quests it consistently and carefully applies certain criteria for sifting the New Testament and other sources for historically reliable material).

6. It gives proper attention to the miracle tradition (as opposed to the previous quests, which relegated the miracle tradition to the status of legend or myth).

7. It takes the Jewishness of Jesus with utter seriousness (Jesus is to be portrayed as a first-century Jew).

Perhaps the two most important of these unique features of the third quest—the Jewish background of Jesus (items 3 and 7) and the use of criteria (5)—deserve further comment.

Since the end of the Second World War and coming to terms with the Holocaust, Christian churches, and Catholics in particular, have gradually acknowledged that their understanding of Judaism, especially the Judaism of the first century, has been slanted and incomplete. For example, in both the old and new quests as well as in Bultmann's theology, Judaism acted as a foil for the presentation of Jesus. First-century Judaism was petty, materialistic, and oriented toward earning salvation from God through good works. This is a caricature, a false exaggeration, of Judaism rather than a historically and theologically responsible portrait. Rooted in the work of G. F. Moore in the 1920s, the writings of E. P. Sanders in the 1970s revolutionized Christian scholarly descriptions of first-century Judaism, which subsequently became much more complex and sympathetic. Additionally, the discovery of Jewish sectarian texts (writings that are special or holy for a small group) in the wilderness of Qumran near the Dead Sea (the Dead Sea Scrolls) helps make the picture of first-century Judaism more diverse and, therefore, less authoritarian and uniform. These factors help to situate Jesus within Judaism as a faithful or perhaps prophetic critic, someone on the margins but nonetheless recognizable as a first-century Palestinian Jew.

Qumran and the Dead Sea Scrolls

In 1947, a young shepherd was wandering in the wilderness near the shores of the Dead Sea in Palestine at a place called Qumran. As he threw stones into some caves located above him, he heard a sound of breaking pottery, and so signaled one of the most sensational archeological discoveries of the twentieth century. The caves contained dozens of clay jars filled with ancient manuscripts of both biblical and non-biblical books that had remained untouched for almost two thousand years. These manuscripts were deposited in the caves at Qumran by a group or sect within early Judaism known as the **Essenes**. They copied and preserved both biblical manuscripts as well as many sectarian documents (documents that reflected the group's distinctive theology). When their monastic community came under threat from the advancing Roman legions near the end of the first century BCE, they hid their sacred texts in caves. After their community was destroyed, the documents remained hidden and undisturbed for almost two thousand years.

For Christians, the scrolls are important for at least two reasons. First, the scrolls give us some of the oldest biblical manuscripts we have. Prior to the discovery of the caves, the oldest complete text of any portion of the Old Testament in our possession was from the early Middle Ages. The commentaries, translations, and expansions of biblical books are also helpful for exegesis (biblical interpretation) and textual criticism (determining what the original manuscripts of the Bible actually said). Second, and perhaps most important, the scrolls bear witness to the theological diversity of Palestinian Judaism around the time of Jesus, particularly as it pertains to

eschatology, or discourse about the culmination of human history. Before the discovery of the scrolls at Qumran, many scholars thought that certain beliefs about eschatology held by early Christians were borrowed from the Greek world and were alien to Judaism. However, with the discovery of the scrolls it was apparent that Christian eschatology—apocalyptic eschatology—had its roots in Judaism. The sectarian documents found at Qumran envisioned a community of purified believers who awaited a final cosmic battle to bring about the defeat of their enemy and the victory of God. Central in this battle are the role of an enigmatic figure called "the Teacher of Righteousness" and the segregation of the world into two camps: "the Sons of Light" and "the Sons of Darkness." Before that battle, the Essenes were called upon to live as a holy people, set apart from the rest of the world. This separation was certainly geographical at Qumran—they were far outside Jerusalem in a desert—but it was also spiritual and ideological. Those who were to become members of the community dedicated themselves through rituals of water immersion (baptism) and communal eating that set them apart from the rest of the world.

Among the most noteworthy of the biblical texts found at Qumran are the complete leather scroll of Isaiah, parts of the book of Ezekiel, and copies of the Psalms. In addition there are important translations of books *(targummim)* in Aramaic—few people read Hebrew in first-century Palestine—as well as commentaries *(persharim)* and other creative expansions of biblical books. Among the sectarian documents at Qumran, four texts are particularly important: the

Qumran and the Dead Sea Scrolls *(continued)*

Community Rule, also called the Manual of Discipline (1QS); the Hymn of Thanksgiving (1QH); the War Scroll (1QM); and the Temple Scroll (11QTemple). Additionally, fragments were found of a strange work called the Damascus Document or Damascus Covenant (DC), already known from a medieval copy discovered in 1896 in a Cairo geniza (a repository for sacred texts no longer in use—reverence for the sacred word prohibits "throwing out" sacred books). It was published in 1910 without any sense of its importance. The discovery of fragments at Qumran confirmed that DC was indeed a Qumran document, one of the Dead Sea Scrolls found some distance from the Dead Sea!

Scholars cite the Dead Sea Scrolls following a complex system, first referencing the cave in which the document was found. For example, if a document was found in cave 1 of Qumran the citation would begin 1Q. The next part of the citation varies considerably. If it is a copy of a biblical book, the abbreviation for that book comes next. For example, the beautiful leather scroll of Isaiah from the second century BCE was found in cave 1. The citation for that document is 1QIsa. Additionally, there are copies of commentaries, translations, and expansions of biblical books. An Aramaic translation of Job, called a *targum*, was found in cave 11. That citation

is 11QtgJob (the "tg" signifying *targum*). The commentary, or *pesher*, on the prophet Habakkuk from cave 1 is cited 1QpHab. The sectarian documents, like the War Scroll found in cave 1, follow a similar pattern. It is abbreviated 1QM. The "M" stands for *milhama* ("war").

The sectarian documents in particular have caused a stir ever since their discovery. Wild speculation about their contents and their significance in relation to the New Testament has often been overstated. One urban legend holds that the Vatican has been orchestrating a cover-up and preventing the publication of many manuscripts. Such speculation sells newspapers but has little connection to the reality behind the complex process of deciphering and translating the documents. In fact, many of the scrolls were made available almost immediately: 1QIsa and 1QpHab were published in 1950 and 1QS in 1951. Many other fragments were published in a series known as *Discoveries in the Judean Desert* (published between 1955 and 1982) and then in a single volume (*The Dead Sea Scrolls in English*, ed. G. Vermes, rev. ed. [New York: Penguin, 2004]). The political situation in Palestine/Israel as well as the deliberate (i.e., slow) pace of some scholars working on the project delayed the process of publication, but no conspiracy existed, let alone one led by the Vatican!

Meier also zealously defends the use of criteria in historical Jesus research. In his voluminous treatment of the historical Jesus, *A Marginal Jew*, Meier often insists that whether we affirm or deny the historicity of a particular story from the New Testament, we must know why we do so, why we make the particular judgment. In fact, one could argue that of greatest importance for Meier is the historical autonomy of the third quest: history guides the quest, not theology. The following quote from Meier is characteristic of his concern:

It is only in the light of this rigorous application of historical standards that one comes to see what was wrong with so much of the first and second quests. All too often, the first and second quests were theological projects masquerading as historical projects. Now, there is nothing wrong with a historically informed theology or christology; indeed, they are to be welcomed and fostered. But a christology that seeks to profit from historical research into Jesus is not the same thing and must be carefully distinguished from a purely empirical, historical quest for Jesus that prescinds from or brackets what is known by faith. This is not to betray faith. . . . Let the *historical* Jesus be a truly and solely *historical* reconstruction, with all the lacunae and truncations of the total reality that a purely historical inquiry into a marginal figure of ancient history will inevitably involve. After the purely historical project is finished, there will be more than enough time to ask about correlations with Christian faith and academic Christology. ("The Present State of the 'Third Quest' for the Historical Jesus: Loss and Gain," *Biblica* 80 [1999]: 459–87, 463)

In short, Meier's concern is to defend the idea, rooted in the goals of the new quest, that historical Jesus research is primarily an academic project that can defend the reasonableness of Christian faith. Yet Meier's concerns about the historical integrity of Jesus research emanates from his frustration with the way liberation theologians (including both Latin American and feminist theologians) have understood the nature of historical inquiry and the use of historical Jesus research.

The Problem of History: Understanding the Limits and Value of History

In the mid-1980's, Elizabeth Johnson, in a debate with David Tracy, offered a good example of the liberationist position on historical Jesus research.[5] For Johnson, a critically assured minimum of knowledge about the historical Jesus can be obtained through historical research. This basic set of data can then be cast into a particular interpretive mold or framework, and can yield multiple Christologies given the particular sets of concerns or locations of the theologian. But Johnson went beyond that position by emphasizing the theological necessity of the historical Jesus as "the memory image" by which the church and the tradition have always referred to a reality that existed before the church. As such, even though the historical Jesus is the product of modern historical research (in the Middle Ages no one was asking questions about the historical Jesus), it still functions as the symbol that mediates the reality of God's saving activity. In this way, Johnson contended, a sketch of the historical Jesus can provide necessary content for Christian faith and can also be used to test competing representations of Jesus and judge which representations are valid. For example, if our historical sketch of Jesus conclusively proved that Jesus prohibited violence, then images of Christ, or Christologies, that portray Christ as a warrior could be rightly criticized on the basis that such Christologies contradict the basic data on the historical Jesus. While this use of historical Jesus research might seem completely reasonable, Johnson claimed that historical Jesus research functions as a norm or foundation for Christology. This last point has proven contentious among theologians.

In 2000 William Loewe updated the parameters of the debate concerning the theological relevance of historical Jesus research and challenged those who would argue for the **normative** value of historical research.[6] He concluded that while there has been a shift to historical Jesus studies in contemporary Christology, this shift has significant limits. Perhaps the most obvious limitation to the theological significance of historical Jesus research is its provisional character—such research is always open to revision. What historians and biblical scholars affirm about Jesus in one decade may have to be revised significantly in the next decade in light of a new archaeological find, a previously neglected piece of data, or a more precise and encompassing theory. Additionally, there seems to be less and less consensus concerning what one can affirm of the historical Jesus. For instance, while John Meier concludes that "the Twelve" (the twelve disciples) was a feature of Jesus' own ministry, John Dominic Crossan contends that it is a creation of the early church and runs counter to Jesus' practice of inclusive discipleship—Jesus treated everyone as equals and would not have privileged one group over others. This lack of consensus among scholars, therefore, challenges the naïve assumption that there is one established account of *the* historical Jesus and compromises any talk of historical Jesus research as normative.

Loewe therefore concludes that the historical Jesus cannot be the ground of either Christian faith or Christology. Rather, historical Jesus research helps Christology to move away from an ahistorical, metaphysical approach, characteristic of those who would simply leave Christology with the reading of Scripture or repeat the formulas of church councils and old catechisms. Instead, historical Jesus research enables us, in part, to focus on a historical and genetic account of the christological tradition. By enabling us to get a sense of Jesus as an historical figure, how he interacted with the world of the first century and came to challenge it, we can more fully appreciate the dynamics of his ministry. In turn, a historical sketch of Jesus' ministry may help us to understand why and how the earliest Christians came to believe that this human being, Jesus, was God's own self-expression to the world, God's agent for conquering sin and evil. In this way, historical Jesus research helps us to offer constructive statements on Christology and its contemporary significance. But this importance must not be overestimated, for historical Jesus research is not the foundation or norm of Christian faith.

The third quest has opened up the possibility for more fruitful historical research through its attentiveness to more precise criteria, its concern for the Jewish background of Jesus, and its ecumenical or interdenominational character (Catholic, Protestant, Jewish, and non-religious scholars working together). Yet these improvements in methodology and in the diversity of scholars engaged in the field have not yielded more stable results. In fact, the results of historical Jesus research are arguably more confused than ever. Perhaps the third quest's lasting contribution to historical Jesus research is a sense of humility concerning the results of this research as well as humility concerning its theological significance.

Conclusion

The quest for the historical Jesus has consumed vast amounts of ink, paper, and bytes over the last two centuries. Those who want to attack traditional forms of Christianity have appealed to the historical Jesus for vindication, while defenders of the faith have also appealed to these historical reconstructions to support their cause. It would appear, however, that both sides in the debate are asking too much of historical Jesus research.

Bultmann was indeed correct when he expressed fear about those who pursue historical Jesus research in order to prove Christian faith, but his abandonment of the quest was problematic for the Christian understanding of the Incarnation—"the Word became flesh and made his dwelling among us" (John 1:14). William Loewe, with much of the theological community, concludes that historical Jesus research has value in that it provides us with important insights and moves us away from mythological understandings of the New Testament, but it is limited in that Christian faith does not rest on an historical reconstruction. Christians do not put their faith in a critical sketch offered by historians; rather, Christian faith rests on the witness of the apostles and the ministry of the church in word and sacrament. Historical research on Jesus is legitimate and constructive, but its results are not normative.

Questions for Understanding

1. What were the defining concerns of the old quest?

2. Why did the old quest come to an end?

3. What was the major contribution of Albert Schweitzer to the quest for the historical Jesus?

4. Why did Bultmann reject the quest for the historical Jesus? What place does his project of demythologizing have in his theology?

5. On what grounds did Käsemann challenge Bultmann on the historical Jesus?

6. Describe three defining characteristics of the third quest.

7. Contrast the positions of Elizabeth Johnson and William Loewe on the theological significance of historical Jesus research.

Questions for Reflection

1. Can we overcome George Tyrell's parable about historical Jesus research? If so, how?

2. What do you think about the notion of myth used in this chapter? Given that Strauss used myth positively and Bultmann, negatively, what is the place of the concept in the study of the New Testament?

3. Is historical Jesus research foundational for Christian faith? If scholars could determine that Jesus offered a definitive teaching, would this teaching be binding for the church? Why or why not?

Endnotes

1 William P. Loewe, *The College Student's Introduction to Christology* (Collegeville, MN: Liturgical, 1996), 31–32.

2 Rudolf Bultmann, "New Testament and Mythology and Other Basic Writings," ed. Schubert Ogden (Philadelphia: Fortress, 1984; German original published in 1941).

3 Ibid., 9.

4 John P. Meier, "The Present State of the 'Third Quest' for the Historical Jesus: Loss and Gain," *Biblica* 80 (1999): 459–87.

5 Elizabeth Johnson, "The Theological Relevance of the Historical Jesus: A Debate and a Thesis," *Thomist* 48 (1984): 1–43. Johnson's position has developed considerably in the past twenty years.

6 William P. Loewe, "From the Humanity of Christ to the Historical Jesus," *Theological Studies* 61 (2000): 314–31.

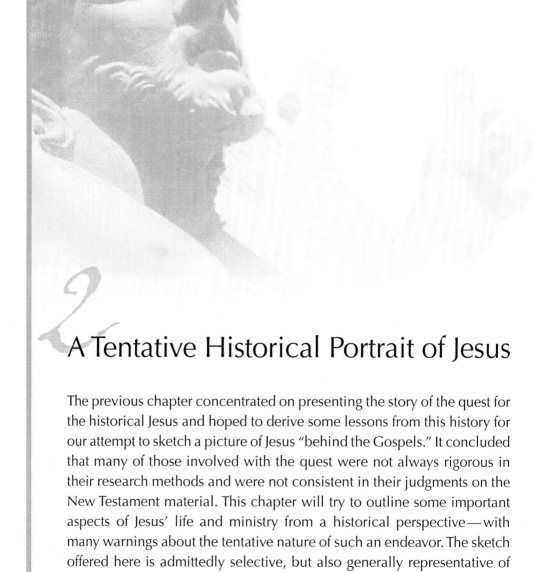

2 A Tentative Historical Portrait of Jesus

The previous chapter concentrated on presenting the story of the quest for the historical Jesus and hoped to derive some lessons from this history for our attempt to sketch a picture of Jesus "behind the Gospels." It concluded that many of those involved with the quest were not always rigorous in their research methods and were not consistent in their judgments on the New Testament material. This chapter will try to outline some important aspects of Jesus' life and ministry from a historical perspective—with many warnings about the tentative nature of such an endeavor. The sketch offered here is admittedly selective, but also generally representative of the state of scholarship on the historical Jesus in the first decade of the twenty-first century.

Selectively Sketching Jesus

As we noted previously when surveying the old quest for the historical Jesus, any account or sketch of the historical Jesus is going to reflect the location, the perspective, of the one who is doing the sketching or piecing together a portrait of Jesus behind the Gospels. Every account of the historical Jesus is subject to the criticism that it is self-serving. Listed here are four of the most respected and popular scholars who have written on the historical Jesus. The list is not an indictment of their selectivity or idiosyncratic approach to the historical Jesus; it merely points out that even among the best and most responsible scholars, the question of selectivity is always in play—even for the author of this book!

Scholar	Background	Sketch of Jesus
J. D. Crossan	A former Catholic priest from Ireland, Crossan is former chair of the Jesus Seminar, a non-orthodox, somewhat post-Christian community of scholars.	Jesus was a social critic and not an apocalyptic prophet. He was like many other social reformers who threatened those who were entrenched in the current system, and they killed him for it.
J. P. Meier	A Catholic priest trained in Scripture at the Pontifical Biblical Institute, Meier has taught at major Catholic seminaries in the U.S. and is now at the University of Notre Dame.	Jesus was a prophet in the tradition of Elijah and Elisha, who instituted an organized community around him. He understood himself to be intimately related to God and understood his mission, including his death, as redemptive.
E. P. Sanders	Progressive mainline Protestant scholar most noted for his work overcoming popular readings of Paul that pit him against Judaism. Sanders offers an alternative portrait of Judaism as a religion of grace. His seminal work has played an important role in addressing Christian anti-Semitism in biblical scholarship.	Jesus was a reform-minded Jew, interested in recovering and affirming Judaism in his ministry.
E. Schüssler-Fiorenza	A Harvard professor and perhaps the preeminent Catholic feminist scholar of Jesus.	Jesus was an egalitarian preacher who cut through distinctions of gender and religious difference to institute a new kind of community.

How Do We Decide What to Include?

One of the distinct merits of contemporary historical Jesus research is its emphasis on the importance of methodology (the set of operations or tasks one uses to produce results, in this case, how one identifies "Jesus behind the Gospels"). While such an emphasis cannot hope to produce an objective account of the historical Jesus, it can promote discussion and debate by providing common points of reference for those who disagree about particular matters. John Meier has suggested that historical Jesus research ought to be compared to a committee meeting. On this committee there are Jews, Catholics, Protestants, agnostics, atheists, and others. Each of these committee members is intelligent and honest, and all are scholars of the New Testament and early Judaism. Meier imagines sequestering such a committee in the basement of the Harvard Divinity school library until they can produce a consensus document on the historical Jesus. This invented study session in the basement of the Harvard library provides us with an interesting parable about the nature of committees and the limited scope of historical Jesus research. Meier uses this image to inject a sense of humor and humility into the sometimes raucous debates on historical Jesus research. But some have been troubled by Meier's parable; they suggest that such an image of historical research automatically surrenders the process to the atheist and the agnostic since their skepticism regarding the existence of God would skew the portrait of Jesus away from any religious or theological interpretation. But Meier's parable is not meant to surrender the project in that way; rather, it is meant to emphasize the importance of consensus in historical Jesus research. Meier is, therefore, willing to accept the non-theological parameters of historical Jesus research.

Meier has outlined five major, or primary, criteria for historical Jesus research.[1] **Criteria** are principles used for making a judgment. In the case of historical Jesus research, these criteria are the principles scholars use to make judgments about whether a given biblical story, or parts of a story, are historical. You will recall from the previous chapter that (1) all such judgments are tentative because they are open to revision given further evidence, and (2) not all scholars agree about how to use any set of criteria. In fact, some, like the Anglican scholar N. T. Wright, believe that criteria such as these are not appropriate. However, a substantial number of New Testament scholars are favorably disposed to the use of the following criteria, which are based on the study of the history of the Gospels and their formation. Ironically, some of these criteria have their roots in the work of Rudolf Bultmann, the great opponent of historical Jesus research!

The criteria presuppose an understanding of how the early traditions (or stories) about Jesus developed. This general consensus affirms that Jesus of Nazareth's life and ministry form the basis of the tradition: this is stage one. With the death of Jesus (and his Resurrection) the tradition took a distinct turn in that the one who had made the proclamation (Jesus) became the object of the early church's preaching or kērygma: this is stage two. For example, instead of Jesus proclaiming the kingdom of God, Paul proclaimed Christ as risen from the dead. Finally, in stage three, we have the emergence of full written Gospels, which combine elements of stage one in the form of the memory tradition of the earliest Christian communities with the experience of the risen Jesus—Jesus alive and present in those communities. So for the earliest Christians there was not always a neat and clean separation between stage one and two. Moreover, the creation of the Gospels themselves raises some questions about their genre and purpose. The Gospels were created not simply as records of what Jesus said and did; rather, in addition to preserving the memory tradition of the earliest church, they are also faith proclamations

Stages in the Formation of the Gospel Tradition

Stage One (prior to 30 CE)	In this stage Jesus lived and taught about the coming of the kingdom of God.	There is no written material from this stage, but the criteria help to sift later material to determine what sayings and traditions attributed to Jesus in the New Testament can be assigned to stage one.
Stage Two (30 CE–68 CE)	Following the death of Jesus, his followers made a proclamation (kērygma) that focused on their experience of the Resurrection of Jesus and his presence within the community of believers.	Paul's authentic letters and portions of Acts and the Gospels contain examples of the primitive apostolic kērygma.
Stage Three (68 CE–100 CE)	At this point the memories of Jesus' life and ministry are incorporated into the kērygma along with a variety of other material from various sources to create the canonical Gospels.	The Gospels

that speak the truth of the Christian faith to a community of believers at a particular place and time. Given this understanding, one would expect to find a large amount of material in the Gospels that does not come from stage one. The criteria discussed below are meant to help distinguish what material indeed comes from stage one and what material is the product of stage two or three.

One basic indicator of historicity is the criterion of embarrassment. According to this criterion, one begins with the assumption that the New Testament—and the Gospels in particular—were created to promote faith in Jesus as God's definitive agent of salvation and reconciliation and even God's own self-expression. The New Testament would, therefore, quite naturally try to present Jesus in the best possible light. The authors of the New Testament, if they were going to add, clarify, or embellish the material they were presenting, would naturally try to present a picture of Jesus that would inspire rather than detract from faith. Therefore, the criterion of embarrassment decrees: if there is a story or saying of Jesus in the New Testament that might compromise or embarrass the early church and its proclamation regarding Jesus, it stands to reason that it is probably not an embellishment or fabrication of the early church. Rather, the material in question should be attributed to a memory about what Jesus actually said or did. One example of material that would satisfy the criterion of embarrassment is Jesus' baptism by John: it is not easy to explain why Jesus undergoes a baptism "for the remission of sins" (see below for a historical explanation that does not contradict Christian faith). Another example is that Jesus was reported to have been crucified by the authorities. It's hard to imagine a less-attractive image for a savior, God's "settler of scores" and defender of Israel against oppression. This aspect of the gospel was no doubt a hard sell to those earliest apostles trying to evangelize the Roman world (see 1 Corinthians 1:23–24). The point of the criterion of embarrassment is that the early church would not likely have gone out of its way to create material that weakened its own tenuous position in the plethora of religious movements of the first century. Thus difficult or potentially embarrassing stories in the New Testament may be attributed to stage one (Jesus' life and ministry) rather than to the concerns and theology of the early post-resurrectional church (stages two or three).

The criterion of multiple attestation of forms and sources is perhaps the most objective, though still not without some controversy in its application. This criterion focuses on the principle that material found in more than one independent source or in several different literary forms is more likely to be rooted in stage one. For example, assuming that the basic two-source hypothesis is correct (that Mark's Gospel was the source

The Markan Hypothesis, the Two-Source Theory, and Q

If one reads the Gospels of Matthew, Mark, and Luke together, one cannot help but notice that at times they are almost identical—word for word—while at other times they could not be more dissimilar. John's Gospel, in contrast, is very different. Matthew, Mark, and Luke are called the synoptic Gospels ("synoptic" means to see together), and accounting for the similarities and differences in them requires one to posit a literary relationship: some material in one Gospel was copied from another. The problem of accounting for the relationship among these three synoptic Gospels is called the synoptic problem. For centuries most Christians assumed that Matthew's Gospel was written first, especially since he was thought to have been one of the Twelve, while Mark and Luke were considered versions of Matthew. In the nineteenth century, many scholars (e.g., K. Lachmann, C. Weisse, and C. Wilke) began to question this approach and to argue for the priority of Mark—this is the Markan hypothesis. There were several reasons for this: Mark leaves out so many important stories (e.g., the birth of Jesus, resurrection appearances, the Sermon on the Mount), which more convincingly explains that Mark was original and Matthew added these stories rather than positing reasons why Mark would have left them out. Additionally, both Matthew and Luke regularly agree with each other when they agree with Mark, but they agree only sporadically where they depart from Mark. It seemed, therefore, to many scholars in the nineteenth century that Mark represented the most basic form of the gospel story. Yet there remained the problem of accounting for the material that Matthew and Luke had in common with one another but was not found in Mark. C. Weisse, J. Holzmann, and later B. H. Streeter presented the theory that Matthew and Luke had two different copies (or versions) of a document that contained many sayings of Jesus. He abbreviated this source with the letter *Q* and thus was born the two-source hypothesis: two sources, Mark and Q, account for the differences and similarities among the three synoptic Gospels along with special source material that accounts for material unique to Matthew and Luke (abbreviated *M* and *L*, respectively).

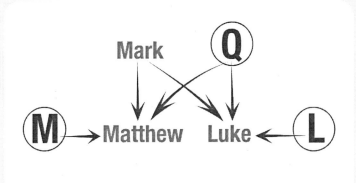

for both Matthew and Luke's Gospels, along with Q; see chart on page 33), if we were to find a story or saying attributed to Jesus in Mark and Q, then that material may go back to stage one—it was probably not created by the early church. Additionally, if one finds two different literary forms (e.g., a parable and a miracle story) agreeing on a mode of behavior or a pattern of speech, then that also may be judged historical. For example, we find in the Gospels many stories of Jesus healing people, but we also have a conflict story (the German word *streitgespräche* is often used to designate such stories) in which Jesus talks about the significance of his healings. Because we have two different types of stories or different literary forms that report that Jesus healed people, we can then say with some confidence that Jesus at least had the reputation of a healer during his lifetime.

The criterion of rejection and execution stems from the indisputable fact that Jesus died on a Roman cross; he was executed by those in power. It stands to reason that he must have done something to disturb or threaten those in power, otherwise they would merely have mocked or ignored him, not tortured him to death. This criterion seeks to isolate material in the Gospels that might help to explain why Jesus caused people in power to become upset or threatened (e.g., he claimed a kind of sweeping authority, he spoke or acted against the temple, or he questioned social norms that carried political overtones). If Jesus was simply a philosopher who preached love of neighbor, he would have been ignored, not killed.

The criterion of discontinuity or dissimilarity is perhaps the most controversial of all the primary criteria in historical Jesus research. For Bultmann, as well as for those involved in the new quest, this was the defining criterion of historical Jesus research, the surest criterion for isolating material from stage one. However, beginning with the work of Morna Hooker and others, criterion has rightly been tempered.[2] The criterion originally sought to isolate sayings and deeds of Jesus that could not be derived from the Judaism of the time or from the practice of the early church at the time of the Gospel's composition. For example, the Gospels depict Jesus as including women among his close friends and associates (without their husbands), which was unusual for a first-century Jew. It is unlikely that the early church would have created such stories in the New Testament given that its own practices were moving in a different direction—the early church was already reaffirming sex-role distinctions (cf. the Pastoral Epistles). Jesus' practice of inviting women into his closest circle of friends and disciples (though the Gospels never call women "disciples"; see below) stood in contrast, or was dissimilar, to the practices of early Judaism and the early Christian church.

The criterion of coherence rounds out the so-called five primary criteria. This criterion looks for material that strongly echoes patterns of speech or behavior identified by the other criteria. For example, if the use of other criteria establishes that Jesus exercised special concern for the marginalized in his ministry (the poor, the sick, and women), and we have another passage that depicts Jesus reacting favorably when he was approached by a woman with a public reputation as a sinner (e.g., John 7:53—8:11), then one may call the story historical even though the passage in question does not satisfy any of the other four criteria. It coheres well with the pattern of behavior exercised by Jesus during his lifetime, and it is "the kind of thing Jesus said and did" during his ministry. This is considered particularly reliable where we have identified both sayings and corresponding actions that were characteristic of Jesus.

These five primary criteria represent an important advance in historical Jesus research. Although not all scholars would agree on the use or importance of individual criteria, most scholars have recognized the significance of these five in helping to introduce some rigor in the attempt to reconstruct the life and ministry of Jesus. John Meier has fondly pointed out that whether someone affirms or denies that a particular New Testament story comes from stage one, we can at least understand why they have made that judgment. We are thus at a moment in historical Jesus research that, at least in principle, should help create more consensus and move historical Jesus research away from the proverbial dark well in which every scholar simply sees his or her own reflection.

Applying the Criteria: A Tentative Sketch of the Historical Jesus

The application of the criteria is not as simple as it might at first appear. Some would have you believe that once you have the sources defined and the criteria delineated the "historical Jesus machine" can go to work to render a definitive portrait of the historical human being Jesus. Yet the cri-

Primary Criteria for Historical Jesus Research

Embarrassment

Assuming that the early church was trying to promote faith in Jesus, the criterion of embarrassment focuses on the sayings or deeds of Jesus that would have created difficulty for the early church's efforts. The point of the criterion is that the early church would not likely have gone out of its way to create material that weakened its own tenuous position; rather, the criterion points to sayings or deeds of Jesus that were inconvenient or potentially embarrassing, but nonetheless part of the memory tradition of the church regarding Jesus' story. Some examples of material affirmed as historical by this criterion include Jesus' baptism by John and his execution by the authorities as a criminal.

Discontinuity or Dissimilarity

This criterion seeks to isolate sayings and deeds of Jesus that cannot be derived from Judaism of the time or from the practice of the early church at the time of the Gospels. It is a controversial criterion because, on the one hand, it seems to vilify early Judaism by suggesting that the important characteristics of Jesus are those things that are definitively not Jewish. On the other hand, the criterion isolates Jesus from the movement that takes him as its founder: the Christian church. One example might be Jesus' celibacy, since celibacy is discontinuous with early Christianity and did not become common practice until centuries after the time of Jesus.

Multiple Attestation of Forms and Sources

As in a courtroom where the testimony of witnesses who have no connection to one another is stronger than the testimony of witnesses who are in collusion with one another, the criterion of multiple attestation looks for sayings or deeds of Jesus that are reported in more than one independent source or more than one form. A saying or deed found in Paul and Mark has multiple attestation, whereas one found in Matthew and Mark may not. Similarly, a characteristic of Jesus found in a parable and a miracle story has multiple attestation. One example of multiple attestation of sources is the Last Supper, which is reported in Mark 14:22–25 and in 1 Corinthians 11:23–26.

Rejection and Execution

The historical fact that Jesus died on a Roman cross with the support of at least some of the Jewish leadership suggests that something within Jesus' ministry was seen as a threat to those in power. This criterion seeks to isolate those sayings and deeds of Jesus that would help explain why some people in power found Jesus to be worthy of public execution. One example is the story of Jesus' triumphant or messianic entry into Jerusalem—such a demonstration helps to explain why people in power thought Jesus was dangerous.

Coherence

This criterion in some ways supplements the rest. It operates by examining material that otherwise would not enjoy historical credibility (material that does not satisfy the other criteria listed above) and suggests that such material may be admitted as historically plausible if it coheres well with other material that has been judged historical. For example, if through the use of the other criteria we determine that Jesus expressed a preference for outsiders, strangers, and foreigners and also enjoyed offering parables and example stories regularly, then the story of the Good Samaritan, which does not satisfy any other criterion of historicity, may be admitted as historical, albeit in a loose sense, on the grounds that it coheres well with what we already know about Jesus. In effect, the story of the good Samaritan is the kind of story Jesus would have told.

teria do not work apart from the intelligence, reasonableness, and responsibility of those who are engaged in historical research. In other words, criteria do not make the historical Jesus, people do.[3] In what follows, the contours of what scholars claim to know about Jesus of Nazareth are given. Although such contours are not set in stone, they are substantiated by rigorous research and argumentation and can be revised through further research and argumentation.

Birth and Lineage

Speculation about the family of Jesus has dogged the Christian tradition since the first century! The Gospels themselves suggest that Jesus' contemporaries questioned his parentage (John 7:41), and Jesus' own attitude toward his family does not always seem positive (e.g., Mark 3:21; John 7:5). By the second century, the writer Celsus retold a story about the mother of Jesus having been raped by a Roman soldier. The only source of information on the birth and lineage of Jesus comes to us from the first two chapters of Matthew and Luke. But again, what can the historian say about Jesus' family, and what criteria could help isolate material that would shed light on such questions? Based on the criteria mentioned above, only a small portion of the material in the New Testament that purports to give us information on the family and background of Jesus is helpful. In fact, the block of material found in Matthew and Luke, the stories of Jesus' family and genealogy, are historically problematic, since both **infancy narratives** are examples of an established literary genre of the ancient world (cf., for example, the infancy stories of Sargon the Great, Moses, and Samuel). The historian, therefore, is left to sort through rather meager evidence.

The name Jesus (Yeshu in Hebrew), an abbreviated form of the name Joshua (Yehoshua), as well as the names of other family members (Joseph, Mary, James, Joses, and Simon) are all names of important figures in the Pentateuch (the first five books of the Bible: Genesis, Exodus, Leviticus, Numbers, Deuteronomy). Meier believes this suggests that it is possible the family was caught up in the reawakening of Jewish nationalism occurring in Galilee in the first century. Many Galileans were fed up with Roman domination. Hope simmered just beneath the surface; this hope was oriented to the near future for God's decisive intervention in Israel's history to bring about deliverance from Gentile oppression and the restoration of the Davidic monarchy, which was a sign of God's presence and favor (2 Samuel 7:16). This may help to explain the tradition of Jesus' Davidic descent recorded throughout the Gospels and even in Paul (Romans 1:3–4). According to Meier, such emphasis is not necessarily the product of the early church since it dates from the mid-50s CE and needs to be taken seriously as part of a very early tradition about Jesus. The criterion of multiple attestation, not necessarily establishing the descent of Jesus from David as a biological fact, does suggest that Davidic descent was a staple of the Christology of the earliest Christian community, and perhaps goes back to the ministry of Jesus.

Scholars generally agree that the formative years of Jesus are virtually unknowable, though some reasonable general conclusions about these years may be inferred. For instance, it is most probable that Jesus spoke Aramaic. Perhaps he knew some Hebrew in order to read the sacred texts, but as a layman he would not have had the opportunity or the necessity to study Hebrew in any depth. In Mark 6:3 Jesus is called a *tektōn* (woodworker), so Jesus was not among the many destitute in Galilee but was a craftsman. Although he was not the poorest of the poor, he surely knew what it meant to struggle for one's existence.

Like the issue of the virgin birth, the issue of Jesus' brothers and sisters touches upon significant theological issues in the history of the Christian tradition. Catholics take the position that Jesus had no true brothers or sisters (brothers and sisters who shared the same set of biological parents), whereas many Protestants argue that the plain sense of Scripture means that Jesus did have brothers and sisters (although both Martin Luther and John Calvin, great champions of the Reformation, supported the doctrine of the perpetual virginity of Mary). The argument offered by Jerome, to which Catholics have long appealed, suggests the brothers and sisters of Jesus mentioned in the Gospels are really cousins *(Against Helvidius)*. Meier insists that this position carries little exegetical or philological weight, especially since clear evidence shows that Josephus, Paul, and the evangelists are all able to distinguish *anepsioi* (cousins) from *adelphoi* (brothers). It must be said that concern over the identity of these brothers and sisters and their precise relationship to Jesus, though found as early as the second century in the *Protoevangelium of James* (a non-biblical book that describes Joseph as having had children by a previous wife), is not a concern that is reflected in the pages of the New Testament. Rather, the safeguarding of the perpetual virginity of Mary is a concern of the early church. The linguistic evidence and the text of the New Testament favor the so-called Helvidian position: the brothers and sisters of Jesus mentioned in the Gospels were his true brothers and sisters born after Jesus.[4] But this evidence does not necessarily exclude those who want to hold the position that the brothers and sisters mentioned in the New Testament were the half-brothers and sisters of Jesus from a previous marriage by Joseph (the so-called Epiphanen solution) since the New Testament does not explicitly exclude this interpretation. Those who take the latter position (which includes the vast majority of Christians) do so not on purely historical grounds but on the long-standing Christian belief regarding the perpetual virginity of Mary.

Did Jesus Have His Own Family?

Questions about Jesus' family of origin lead quite naturally to questions, popularized lately by books like *The DaVinci Code*, about whether Jesus had a wife and children of his own. Some have made the argument that the silence of the New Testament on the issue of Jesus' marital status should lead one to conclude that Jesus in fact was married, since marriage was the all-but-universal practice within first-century Palestinian Judaism. These scholars argue that without any evidence to the contrary, we must assume that Jesus thought and behaved like the vast majority of other Palestinian Jews (notice how the criterion of discontinuity or dissimilarity is problematic in this instance). This position fails on three points. First, the context of the New Testament is much more biographical than some want to admit. The silence of the Gospels on the question of Jesus' wife and children cannot necessarily be regarded as evidence in favor of marriage. The names of women with whom Jesus had been associated have been preserved in the New Testament texts. It would be very odd for the New Testament to eliminate any reference to Jesus' wife and children while other family members are mentioned frequently. Second, Josephus and Philo both contend that at least some of the Essene community remained

The Family of Jesus and the Government of the Church

The New Testament tells us that two members of Jesus' family played a role in the early church: Mary, the mother of Jesus, and James, "the brother of the Lord." One would think that Mary would have had a prominent role in early Christianity, but the New Testament simply tells us of her presence at the crucifixion of Jesus (John 19:25–27) and places her with the other disciples (along with Jesus' "brothers and sisters") as part of the early church (Acts 1:14). James receives far more attention in Acts and Galatians as an active force in the government of the early church.

James is counted among the three "pillars" of the Jerusalem church in Galatians 2:9, and he plays a central role in the early disputes over Gentile Christians in Acts 15:13–21. James probably had a family, though we do not know this. Yet no one in his family plays a similar role in the early church. It is possible, however, that another "brother" of Jesus,

Simon (Mark 6:3), also was the leader of the church in Jerusalem until 107 CE (see Eusebius, *Ecclesiatical History*, 4.5.3).

It is evident, therefore, that family members (or at least one member of Jesus' family) played an important leadership role in the early church. But the role of James stands out as the exception rather than the rule—it is expressly stated throughout the New Testament that one's family status does not determine one's place within the church. Time after time the New Testament portrays Jesus as distancing himself from family relations (e.g., Luke 11:27–28; Mark 3:31–35). It appears from several passages in the New Testament that one's status as a relative of Jesus was not relevant to the exercise of authority within the community, and no battle arose in the early church, as it did in Islam, over hereditary succession of leadership.

celibate (*Jewish War* 2.8.2 and *Every Good Man Is Free* 12–13). Third, the prophet Jeremiah is a good biblical example of the celibate life for the sake of a vocation. Jeremiah's prophetic career was dominated by political events that created an atmosphere of tension and desperation, and Jeremiah's celibacy seems to have been a sign to his fellow Jews that any idea of "business as usual" (such as making plans to marry and start a family) were out of place given the events that were beginning to transpire—God's judgment was falling upon Judah in the form of the Babylonian army and its conquest of Jerusalem. It is possible Jesus could have modeled his life and ministry on this important figure (even Moses in some rabbinic traditions was portrayed as a celibate), and in the context of his eschatological ministry, celibacy seems an appropriate symbol in the first century. This is further supported by evidence that Jesus' predecessor, John the Baptist, was celibate.

John the Baptist

Like the evidence for the existence of Jesus, the evidence for the existence of the Baptist is overwhelming in many ways. Corroborating texts from Origen and the fourth-century Christian historian Eusebius help to buttress the historical credibility of the testimony offered by the first-century Jewish historian Josephus in the *Jewish Antiquities* (18.3.3). In this text Josephus is not aware of any purported relationship between John and Jesus (contrary to Luke's portrayal of John and Jesus as distant relatives) and portrays John not as an eschatological prophet but as a moralizing philosopher. In the end, historians can easily affirm the existence

Person of Interest

Josephus

Josephus (ca. 37 CE–100 CE) was a Galilean who may have been a Pharisee, though many scholars are unsure of this. During the first revolt against Rome, Josephus became a leader of the Jewish army in Galilee, but his forces were destroyed quickly by the Roman legions. After the destruction of his army, Josephus tried to ingratiate himself with his Roman captors by presenting himself as a prophet. He even went so far as to predict that the Roman general, Vespasian, would become emperor and that he was the Messiah whom Israel had long awaited. Remarkably, Vespasian did indeed become emperor amid the chaos that surrounded Rome in 68 and 69 CE. Josephus's star was on the rise, and he was well rewarded when he was adopted by the Flavians. Josephus thus became known as "Flavius Josephus." In the last years of the Jewish war, Josephus assisted the Roman general Titus, the son of Vespasian, and even translated for him in negotiations over the siege of Jerusalem. He was derided as a traitor by his fellow Jews and was forced to watch as the Romans breached the walls of the city and eventually destroyed it along with the temple. Following the war, Josephus went to Rome and began to write a history of the Jewish rebellion against Rome (*The Jewish War*). It appears to be a pretty even-handed account of events, but it had a moral to it: don't mess with Rome (after all he knew who his patron was). After improving his Greek he began writing a massive work explaining the history of the Jews to the general non-Jewish audience of Rome (*Jewish Antiquities*); most of the book is a paraphrase of the Bible. Both works, but particularly his account of the war, are important sources for our knowledge about first-century Judaism.

of John the Baptist but questions remain as to the content of John's message and his relationship to Jesus.

The Gospels portray John as an anti-establishment figure who conducted his ministry in the wilderness. In Luke 1:80 his ministry was exercised in the wilderness of Judea near the Jordan. This is geographically near the Essene settlement at Qumran. Many parallels with the literature discovered at Qumran appear to have some relevance for understanding John. In particular, John's baptizing activity is remarkably similar to Essene water purification rituals and raise interesting questions about how much John focused on the corruption of the ruling classes in Jerusalem, a favorite topic for the Essenes (see, e.g., 1QpHab).

In the initial part of the first block of material on the Baptist in the sayings source Q (that source common to both Matthew and Luke; see Matthew 3:7–10), John does not describe his ministry with any reference to Jesus. He is a fiery eschatological prophet calling those who have come to him for baptism a "brood of vipers." He calls on them not simply to run in fear of God's coming judgment but to *metanoia*, corresponding to the Old Testament prophetic cry of *shuv* (repent). John is also in line with the Old Testament prophets in saying, "Already the axe is laid to the root of the tree" (cf. Isaiah 10:33–34; 32:19). What is striking about the quote is that John is delivering his message to those who have come out to the desert to be baptized by him. The Baptist appears to demand more than simple curiosity; rather, he demands a swift decision to be baptized and a radical reformation of both inner attitudes and external conduct. Q provides further insight to the Baptist's ministry. The material in Matthew 3:11–12 is as fiery as that of the previous passage. John looks to the future when someone "stronger" than him will come and exercise judgment. The phrase is interesting because it has no specific christological content, but this "stronger one" cannot be the God of Israel (**YHWH** or Yahweh) given the strong anthropomorphic image (i.e., an image of God as a human being) of "untying his sandal." The question then arises as to the identity of the "stronger one." John Meier argues that John was deliberately ambiguous; this "stronger one" functions as a judge, whereas the actual destruction of the wicked is left to YHWH. The righteous, that is the repentant, can be spared this if their repentance is sincere, and baptism is the appropriate sign of this repentance.

The Major Sects in First-Century Palestinian Judaism

Sect	Composition	Theology	Politics
Sadducees	mostly priestly aristocracy	The strict observance of the written Torah and the operation of the temple cult were the necessary and sufficient grounds for maintaining Israel's relationship (covenant) with God.	The Sadducees sought to make accommodations with the Romans in order to ensure that the temple could function and the Torah could be observed.
Pharisees	mostly laymen, though with supporters from among the priests	For the Pharisees, the Torah and its demands for purity had to be at the heart of all Jewish life, not just the cultic life of the temple. They were the great democratizers of Judaism and introduced the importance of Torah study for all laymen. In addition to the written Torah, the Pharisees adopted oral traditions connected to the Torah that they insisted were equally valid. The Pharisees held some apocalyptic beliefs like resurrection and final judgment that were not held by the Sadducees.	The Pharisees, or "separate ones," objected to the accommodations made by the Sadducees and generally resented Roman rule.
Essenes	mostly disenfranchised priests	These priestly figures separated themselves from the temple when it had become defiled by illegitimate priests and corruption. They retreated to the desert, though they had members and supporters in towns and villages. In the desert they prepared for the apocalyptic battle that would bring an end to the temple and its corrupt priesthood.	The Essenes were separatists and did not form political alliances.
Zealots	laymen, primarily in Galilee	The Zealots believed that foreign domination had to end in order for Israel to be faithful to God. They adopted the tactics of modern terrorists, including assassinations, insurrections, and theft. They did not proliferate until the middle part of the first century, well after the death of Jesus.	The Zealots were highly suspect in the eyes of other Jews, and they formed no alliances.

John's baptism shared some common traits with other Jewish rituals of water purification performed by those who dwelt in the Judean desert: (1) there was the belief that all Israel had gone astray, (2) purification was offered to those who seek it through repentance, and (3) this repentance offered hope for salvation on the day of reckoning. John was unlike others in that his baptism was a one-time action, and John was the one who performed the ritual, thereby accentuating his role in the playing out of the eschatological drama. John saw his ministry of baptism as the final pouring out of the Spirit on the repentant for their salvation, though not as a rite of initiation into some new group or "church," though baptism was used as a ritual of initiation by the Essenes at Qumran as well as for those who converted to Judaism in the first century.

The question of the meaning of John's baptism is confused with the phrase "for the forgiveness of sins" in Mark 1:4 and parallels. The issue is whether this phrase reflects early Christian practice or John's own (pre-Christian) understanding of baptism. The case against a Christian interpretation is threefold: (1) the New Testament never applies the complete phrase to Christian baptism, (2) it is highly unlikely that the early church would invent such an understanding of John's baptism and then describe how the sinless Jesus received this baptism (criterion of embarrassment), and (3) the New Testament does connect baptism with forgiveness of sins, yet never with this phraseology. When one avoids the anachronistic sacramental questions, it is best to interpret the phrase in line with the rest of the data on John. John understood his baptism as a dramatic acting out of the candidate's repentance while anticipating and announcing the definitive action of God in the outpouring of the Holy Spirit by "the one stronger" than himself.

Jesus' Baptism

The question of Jesus' baptism by John (Mark 1:9–11) is of some significance for any attempt to piece together the relationship between John and Jesus. The criterion of embarrassment suggests that it is a piece of historical data. Why would Christians who claim that Jesus was sinless invent a story in which he participates in a ritual that in Christian practice was associated with the forgiveness of sins? This would seem to create unnecessary problems; it is more likely that there was a pervasive memory of Jesus' baptism by John. There is also multiple attestations for this since both Mark and Q give witness to Jesus' baptism, as does 1 John 1:5–6. Additionally, the criterion of discontinuity authenticates this material because elsewhere in the New Testament Christian baptism is understood and legitimated in light of Jesus' death and Resurrection (e.g., Romans 6:3–11) and not through an appeal to Jesus' own experience of baptism. The meaning of Jesus' baptism is distinct from the theology of Christian baptism. Meier stresses four points regarding the religious mindset of Jesus at the start of his ministry. First, like John, Jesus believed that the end of Israel's history was approaching. Second, he believed Israel had gone astray and was in need of repentance. Third, the only way to escape the coming wrath was not to claim descent from Abraham, but to undergo a change in mind and heart. Fourth, his baptism was a way for him to acknowledge John's role as an eschatological prophet.[5] So Meier contends that Jesus submitted to John's charismatic ritual because he believed it was necessary for salvation from God's judgment. But this seems to attribute to Jesus' consciousness of sin—a real problem for Christians because we confess that Jesus "has similarly been tested in every way, yet without sin" (Hebrews 4:15). As Meier points out, however, Jesus' consciousness of sin does not equal "personal sin" in first-century Judaism.[6] Ezra and Nehemiah offer examples of how Jews of the Second Temple period could identify themselves as sinners without necessarily identifying sin with personal transgressions (Ezra 9:6–7; Nehemiah 9:36–37; cf. 1QS 1:18—2:2). In the example of Ezra and Nehemiah, they associate themselves with the generations that brought about the destruction of the nation two hundred years earlier, in addition to their contemporaries who are unrepentant. So there is the possibility, and even the likelihood, that Jesus envisioned his baptism "for the remission of sins" as part of a corporate act of penance: it would be like anti-war activists fasting as an act of penance for the war. Though they have always been opposed to the war, they nonetheless recognize that as Americans they must do penance for what they see as national sin.

Jesus and His Relationship with John the Baptist

Having wrestled with the meaning of John's baptism for Jesus we should try to determine the nature of the relationship between John and Jesus. Much of the evidence (e.g., Matthew 11:2–3 and Luke 7:18–19) suggests that the relationship between the two figures was ambiguous. Meier believes that Jesus was a disciple of John the Baptist. It is apparent from the Gospels that John did in fact have some followers, although not all who were baptized were disciples (i.e., not all those who were baptized left their families and work to live with John and join in his ministry). The only direct evidence we have regarding Jesus' association with John comes from the Fourth Gospel. For example, in John 1:28–45 Jesus appears on the scene with the Baptist in the desert near the area by the Jordan where John was engaged in a ministry of baptism. In John 3:22–36 Jesus spends some time with his disciples baptizing, while John continues to baptize nearby. In John 4:1 the **Pharisees** learn that Jesus' disciples are baptizing and gaining more followers than the Baptist. The criterion of embarrassment helps to substantiate that Jesus and his first disciples came from John's circle since there is a tendency within the Fourth Gospel to suppress any direct connection between the ministry of John and the ministry of Jesus. This same material also seems to cohere with what has been established, i.e., that Jesus was baptized by John and that this baptism was interpreted by Jesus as an important event in his own ministry.

The "second Baptist block" in Q (Matthew 11:2–19 pars.) gives us some evidence of what Jesus thought of John. In Matthew 11:2–6 John sends disciples to ask if Jesus is "the one who is to come." There is no indication that this functioned as any kind of messianic title in first-century Judaism; rather, like "the stronger one," "the one who is to come" is deliberately ambiguous. Jesus' response is thoughtful in that it focuses on the point at which Jesus' ministry diverges from John; it sounds a note of hope and joy not prominent elsewhere in the sayings of the Baptist. In the Old Testament images he cites (Isaiah 35:4; 29:20; 61:2), Jesus basically tells John that the *eschaton* (end) has arrived. The lack of any response of faith or acknowledgment on the part of the Baptist argues, through the criterion of embarrassment, in favor of the historicity of the episode since if it were a creation of the early church (i.e., part of stage two or three), it would most likely contain some sort of affirmation about Jesus from John.

The absence of that affirmation on John's part does not help the Christian cause as well as a bold affirmation would.

The thin sketch historians are able to offer of Jesus' background stands in sharp contrast to the wild stories that have circulated over the centuries and have become popular in recent years. There is no evidence that Jesus went to India or Britain. Nor is there any evidence that Jesus was married or had a family. What we can affirm about Jesus' background squares well with the material we have from Jesus' life and ministry. It seems that Jesus' entire life was directed toward the ministry he undertook—a ministry that would lead him to a brutal death. The formation of that ministry and the formation of Jesus' own self-identity took place in the context of great ferment and unrest in Galilee and Judea, at the feet of his family, and in relationship to the fiery message of John the Baptist.

The Kingdom of God

The New Testament uses the Greek expression *he basileia tou theou*, which is usually translated "kingdom of God." Most scholars agree, however, that the phrase demands a translation and an interpretation that moves away from any spatial or temporal notion. Many insist on a translation like "reign of God," since the phrase envisions a state of affairs or relationship rather than any geo-political entity. But others, including John Dominic Crossan and Stephen J. Patterson, both members of the controversial group of scholars known as the Jesus Seminar, have insisted that the image of the kingdom was meant in reference to the empire of Rome, which was oppressing the poor of the region. They would argue that translating *basileia* as "empire" best brings out the politically and socially subversive character of Jesus' ministry.

Scholars unanimously assign this phrase to stage one and interpret it against the backdrop of first-century Palestinian Judaism. The average Jew in the first century would have understood it as evoking Israel's story and its hope for God's decisive intervention in history. The Old Testament provides the basic myth or story line upon which the concept rests. Cultic, or priestly, and prophetic proclamations of YHWH's kingship as past, present, and future reality are found throughout the Old Testament, and during the **Babylonian Exile**, this hope for God's kingship becomes bound up with Israel's hope for liberation from Gentile oppression. The phrase, therefore, brought together religious, political, and social ideas.

Debates have raged for decades concerning the best understanding of what Jesus meant by this symbol. At issue is the relevance of apocalyptic eschatology for understanding the kingdom of God. Since the late nineteenth century the kingdom of God in the teaching of Jesus has been understood in terms of a future reality that would obliterate the present world order through a demonstrable and terrible act of divine intervention (this is often called consistent eschatology). In the middle part of the twentieth century C. H. Dodd formulated the idea of a realized eschatology from his reading of the Fourth Gospel. According to Dodd, the realization of the kingdom is something that happens in the person of Jesus as he confronts people. The kingdom is an interior and spiritual reality more than an extrinsic dramatic reality. A third position understands the kingdom in terms of a proleptic (or "inaugurated") eschatology—an already and not-yet eschatology. According to this position, the kingdom is present in the person of Jesus and in the response of conversion and faith made by those who encountered him, but the definitive, cosmic arrival of the kingdom in which all opposition of God would be destroyed is something for which the faithful must still wait. One may identify even a fourth position emerging in the 1980s, which sought to understand the kingdom of God as a social reality and not a religious reality. The kingdom of God was the reversal of oppression and an undoing of the patronage system that kept the poor oppressed and marginalized. This position, advocated by groups like the Jesus Seminar, is difficult to label, but perhaps it is best termed "social eschatology."

These competing interpretations of the kingdom, as well as how best to understand when it may arrive, are not necessarily mutually exclusive. The apolitical and social dimension of Jesus' proclamation need not be sacrificed for a more "religious" interpretation. Additionally, the kingdom seems to be both present and future realities in Jesus ministry, though some sayings and deeds of Jesus place greater emphasis on one than the other. William Loewe offered what many consider to be the proper alternative or perhaps even a synthesis of these apparently rival interpretations of the kingdom when he focused on a functional definition. For Loewe, a functional definition of the kingdom cuts to the heart of the matter because it addresses the question, what does the kingdom accomplish, or what is it for? The answer: the kingdom of God is meant to bring human and cosmic fulfillment and an answer to the problem of evil.[7] The solution to the problem of evil is not a cosmic mythical battle but a response to God's love and mercy uniquely present in Jesus as he summoned his contemporaries to "be converted and believe."

The Greek word **metanoia** literally means "to change one's mind." The word must be understood in the context of the prophetic call to repentance (*shuv*, in the prophets). William Loewe argues that Jesus is after "a transformation of persons on the level . . . of what we will call spontaneous felt meaning." He suggests that we all have a coherent set of meanings and values that manifest themselves in our dealings with the world. Another word for this is a *horizon*. Loewe states that the horizon of human experience is an experience of mistrust, abuse, and exploitation. What Jesus offers is a "shake up" of the world whose horizon is so disturbed by these experiences by making available a source of "acceptance, healing and liberation."

Several related questions come to mind at this point: How does Jesus make this transformation possible? Is it merely an exhortation or rhetorical flourish? Bernard Lonergan has written at length about the response Jesus sought from those he encountered, and characterizes it as "religious conversion." In religious conversion one's vision of the world and self-understanding in that world are radically transformed. For Lonergan, this happens as human beings perceive themselves as being loved and accepted, or to use the biblical language favored by Lonergan, we feel our heart flooded by God's love (Romans 5:5) and therefore have no need to feel threatened by any forces or power. Since we experience God's boundless love and the gift that is our life, we no longer need to pile up possessions or condemn others to protect ourselves; we can forgive others and bear their burdens. The experience of religious conversion is made available through Jesus' words, actions, and in his very person. An exploration of how Jesus proclaimed the kingdom and empowered religious conversion will help us gain a fuller understanding of Jesus' ministry.

Some Modern Approaches to New Testament Eschatology

Name	Theologians	Brief Description
Consistent Eschatology	Weiss and Schweitzer	The world as we know it is coming to an end rather soon. God will intervene in history to bring this end about, and at that time also bring about the defeat of evil. This is what Jesus meant when he announced the impending arrival of the "kingdom" or "reign of God."
Realized Eschatology	C. H. Dodd	The kingdom of which Jesus spoke is an interior reality. The arrival of the kingdom occurs when one is confronted by the person Jesus and responds to this encounter with conversion and faith. The believer thus renewed has experienced the arrival of God's *basileia* (reign) as Jesus described it.
Proleptic Eschatology	O. Cullmann, W. G. Kümmel	Both Weiss and Dodd were accurate in their respective descriptions of the coming of God's reign: many sayings of Jesus point to a future in-breaking of the *kingdom*, while in others it appears as though God's reign is present in Jesus.
Social Eschatology	Jesus Seminar (Crossan, Funk)	Jesus used religious symbols and religious language to unmask the unjust and dehumanizing conditions of first-century Palestine. His proclamation of the *kingdom* is primarily about social transformation and the creation of a different kind of counter-cultural and counter-imperial community.
Functional Eschatology	William Loewe	Rather than attempting to figure out when the *kingdom* is to arrive, this approach seeks to understand how the kingdom functions, what it is supposed to accomplish. For Loewe, the reign of God solves the problem of sin and brings about cosmic fulfillment. Such an approach has the benefit of affirming the insights of all four approaches listed above.

The Parables

Jesus' **parables** have long intrigued interpreters. Modern research into the parables of Jesus began with Adolf Jülicher's dismissal of the previous history of interpretation, which viewed them as allegories. For Jülicher, **allegory**—where each element within a story has a corresponding meaning or represents something outside the story—clouds the simple meaning of the parables. For many decades scholars attempted to recover the simplicity of Jesus' message. However, there has been a remarkable turn in parables research that has recovered allegory, complexity, and play in Jesus' parables. As a basic starting point for approaching Jesus' parables, we will use C. H. Dodd's definition. A parable is "a metaphor or simile drawn from nature or common life, arresting the hearer by its vividness or strangeness, leaving the mind in sufficient doubt about its precise application to tease it into active thought."[8] For Dodd, parables had a certain "play" in them, which required the response of those who heard Jesus. Dodd's agenda was somewhat limited: he wanted to show that Jesus simply inaugurated the kingdom through these parabolic invitations to faith. Yet Dodd did see the dialogical character of the parables by recognizing that parables required something from the respondent.

Recent research has also tried to understand Jesus' parables in their Jewish literary context. For example, David Stern argues that the rabbis often mentioned *meshalim* (singular *mashal*, the Hebrew word for parables) that were understood as playful encounters with the audience.[9] In the *mashal*, individuals in the audience were roughly connected to the agents or characters in the *mashal* so that there was always a powerful and even dangerous edge to these stories—you cannot be sure how the audience will react once they see themselves in the story! Stern also rejects the distinction between metaphor and allegory, arguing that such a distinction is blurred in rabbinic *meshalim*. The *nimshal*, or explanation of a parable, was quite often a necessary part of the *mashal*, so the allegorical interpretations of parables may not be unauthentic, as Jülicher believed. There is room for both disclosure and concealment in parables. This is part of the "play" that is so important to the interpretation of parables as well as an understanding of their role in the ministry of Jesus, a role that perhaps differentiates Jesus' use of parables from the rabbinic *meshalim*.

The parables are not merely tools to communicate information; rather, they necessarily conceal their meaning to provoke a dynamic response from the hearer. Jesus' parables in the synoptic Gospels (Matthew, Mark, and Luke) call for a radical reversal of societal roles and expectations. The social challenge in Jesus' parables is evident and is at the heart of his summons to *metanoia* (conversion). Additionally scholars like N. T. Wright have argued that Jesus, as the central feature of his ministry, retold Israel's story through the parables in ways that subverted Israel's temptation to embrace violent nationalism (Israel's desire to solve its problems through an armed struggle against Rome, or the contemporary situation in Palestine where many groups on both sides of the fence appeal to violence as inspired and even commanded by God).

An example of Jesus' parables may serve to illustrate the formal aspects we have just described. To be sure, identifying individual parables as stage-one material is immensely difficult. John Meier is convinced that the parables, for the most part, were thoroughly reworked by the early church so that any ascription of a parable to stage one is tenuous at best. But that Jesus spoke in parables seems clear. While not definitively from stage one, Joachim Jeremias regarded the parable of the lost sheep (Matthew 18:12–14; Luke 15:3–7) as authentic. This parable, though put in different contexts by each of the evangelists, was originally meant to vindicate Jesus' association with sinners and other marginalized figures. In its original context, the parable would have been addressed to those who objected to the fellowship Jesus offered. The dynamic of the parable is pretty straightforward: those who listen to it would immediately identify with the ninety-nine sheep rather than the lost one. After all, who would leave the sheep in the wilderness to be ravaged by animals and thieves while he went to look for the lost sheep? For those of us who have worked in retail situations we recognize this as "shrinkage"—a certain percentage of merchandise will be damaged or stolen, which will cut into profits. This is factored into the pricing of the merchandise. But Jesus startlingly reverses his audience's expectations and describes the joy of the shepherd at finding the lost sheep and his lack of concern for those he left in the wilderness! Those who have identified themselves as the ninety-nine obedient sheep are now identified as lost. The only solution for Jesus' audience is then to self-identify with the one who was lost. Such identification opens the door for recognizing God's love and mercy, but also removes the barriers between the righteous and the sinners that had occasioned the parable in the first place. The parable provokes; it invites Jesus' opponents to understand themselves as "found" and their lives as God's gift. This self-understanding is a revelation of God's love overflowing the hearts of those who hear the parable and respond.

The Kingdom in Action

Jesus' proclamation of the kingdom also includes provocative actions. The most obvious actions are often referred to as **miracles** in the Christian church. The Latin word *miraculum* literally means "something to be wondered at." In our common parlance we understand a miracle as something that cannot be explained according to the laws of nature but must be attributed to the direct activity of God (Thomas Aquinas in *Contra Gent.*, 3.102 defines a miracle as an event "done by divine agency outside the commonly observed order of things"). Today the Catholic Church often holds official inquests into the allegation of a miracle. At places like Lourdes in France, medical tribunals are set up that adjudicate these claims. The reason for this is obvious: the church does not want to have frauds running around the world claiming that "God did x or y" when it was really the work of a new therapy or a new drug. While the tribunals certainly have a place in the life of the church, especially if one wants to define a miracle as "an event that subverts the laws of nature," such a system is not appropriate for understanding the miracles of Jesus. First, we must realize that there were many people in the ancient world who claimed and were recognized as having extraordinary power. Whether they did, in fact, have these powers is beyond the ability of the modern historian to determine, but that others believed they had the power is unquestioned. For example, Apollonius of Tyana was a remarkable contemporary of Jesus. He was regarded by some as a "divine man" (*theios anēr*) and even had a popular narrative of his life and healings written some time later by an admirer (Philostratus, *Life of Apollonius*). While many features of Jesus' ministry differentiate him from Apollonius, the relevant point is that for the ancients the fact that some individuals could perform such works or miracles was a given—even

Jesus' opponents believed that his exorcisms and other deeds were effective. In Mark 3:22, for example, his opponents do not claim that Jesus cannot exorcise demons; rather, they claim that this is a sign of Jesus' own demonic possession ("'He is possessed by Beelzebul,' and 'By the prince of demons he casts out demons'"). So the question concerning Jesus' miracles was not whether he could do amazing things, but what was the meaning of the things he did.

The New Testament uses Greek words like *dynamis* (power), *ergon* (work), or *sēmeion* (sign) to describe what we call Jesus' miracles. These terms have a certain pregnancy, something inside waiting to emerge. These signs or works function on a variety of levels to differentiate Jesus from his contemporaries—including Apollonius. According to John Meier, the ideal type of miracle in the Gospels has seven characteristics:[10]

1. A Relationship of Faith and Love Between the Human Being and the Deity/Divine Agent

2. The Person in Need Is a Disciple or Worshiper

3. The Miracle is Performed with a Brief but Intelligible Set of Words

4. There Is No Indication that the Deity is Coerced into Acting on Behalf of the Human Being

5. Miracles Are Done in Obedience to Jesus' Father and in the Context of His Mission

6. Miracles are Understood as Symbolic Representations of the Kingdom

7. Jesus' Miracles Do Not Directly Punish or Hurt Anyone

The uniqueness of Jesus' miracles, for lack of a better term, rests in the way these actions supported his claim to authority in announcing the in-breaking of the kingdom.

Like the parables, Jesus' miracles offer his audience an opportunity to see God's mercy and love in the lives of people who are marginalized. In the first century, disease, infirmity, and demonic possession were all often considered signs of God's absence from the life of the sufferer. The possessed, the hungry, the suffering, and even those written off as dead were all excluded from the common life and from common meals. However, Jesus' ministry reincorporates these people into the life of the community, bringing about a dramatic reconciliation or reconstitution of a humanity that is whole, complete, and without exclusion. However, this is all done in the service of Jesus' proclamation of the kingdom, a reign that comes about through the experience of conversion to God. Jesus' dramatic actions here are, in essence, parables in action that empower a kind of love that is possible when people understand and experience themselves as loved unrestrictedly. But this conversion is never quite complete, for people are always looking for ways to exclude.

A New Community

Jesus announced an inclusive kingdom, a new community, a new fellowship made possible by the experience of conversion. He then gathered around himself a group of followers (this appears to echo the tradition of the Old Testament prophet Elijah in 1 Kings 19:20).[11] A wide range

Person of Interest

Apollonius of Tyana

Apollonius of Tyana (ca. 1 CE–100 CE) was a contemporary of Jesus and engaged in a ministry or career similar in some ways to that of Jesus. He was a countercultural critic, an ascetic (someone who engages in acts of self-denial), a philosopher, and a miracle worker; in this way Apollonius established himself as an important religious figure in the first century. The Greek writer Philostratus, through his biography of Apollonius (*Life of Apollonius*), sealed his legacy in the third century and, in the minds of some people (e.g., the French philosopher Voltaire), created a rival for Jesus. Philostratus was commissioned to write the biography by the Roman empress Julia Domna, wife of the emperor Septimius Severus (reigned 194–211). The empress was a lover of religious traditions and avidly collected the teachings and accounts of various religious figures. She came into possession of the diary of a man named Damis, a disciple of Apollonius. Intrigued by what she read, she commissioned Philostratus to write a full biography based on the account of Damis. The resultant *Life of Apollonius* contains several stories that echo biblical accounts, particularly when it comes to exorcisms and healings. Some have suggested that the example of Apollonius marginalizes Christian claims about the uniqueness of Jesus' miracles, while others suggest that Philostratus relied on Gospel stories to create his account of Apollonius's career and present him as an alternative to Christ.

of people were attracted by Jesus, and the Gospels depict large crowds following after him, but only a small portion of these admirers are called *mathētai* (disciples) in the New Testament. Discipleship, or following Jesus, was the special place of a group of people who met certain criteria. First, disciples did not choose their status; rather, Jesus called them. He initiated and established the parameters of the relationship. Jesus' invitation cut across social divides and included a wide swath of first-century Jewish society—including both impoverished, public sinners, as well as more "respectable" members of society. This inclusiveness may also be inferred from other figures closely associated with Jesus but who are not called disciples. The Gospels cite a number of well-to-do individuals, including Zacchaeus the publican, Lazarus and his sisters, and the anonymous host of the Last Supper. Although the Gospels do not use the word *mathētēs* to describe the many women who followed Jesus (probably because there was no feminine form of the word in Aramaic), there can be little doubt that they were in fact disciples.[12] Second, Jesus' call to discipleship required a radical break with personal and social ties that defined one—including family, friends, and livelihood. Additionally, those who were called disciples needed to be prepared to endure danger and hostility. Jesus also gave his disciples several distinguishing "marks"—the practice of baptism, special instructions about simplicity in prayer, and the practice of feasting rather than fasting. The marks, along with the commands to imitate Jesus and participate in his ministry, created among Jesus' followers a new kind of family—what many call fictive kinship (the process of granting someone who is not a member of a family the title, the rights, and the obligations normally given to family).[13] This family and the people it included posed problems for some first-century Jews.

The Jewish people, especially within the first century, were concerned with maintaining the covenantal identity of the nation (the identity of Israel as YHWH's chosen people, a people set apart). To do this the law of Moses had to be observed and the cult of the temple maintained. Those who did not consistently and appropriately observe the law and use the system of sacrifices in the temple not only put in jeopardy their own relationship with God but also compromised the national identity, the Jewish people's relationship with God. The reasons for this are numerous, and they are not as superficial as many modern people might think. Recall the prophets of the eighth century BCE who berated the people of Judah and Israel for their violations of **ethical monotheism**, for the abuse of the poor and needy while maintaining a superficial spirit of worship (e.g., see Isaiah 1:12–23). Scripture often associated the failures of Israel and Judah with their willingness to adopt the customs, religious practices, and lifestyles of their neighbors (e.g., 2 Kings 17:7–18). So while we might be horrified at those who questioned Jesus' association with public sinners, they believed that they were responding to the history of Israel and the admonitions of the prophets. Jesus' actions in this area certainly caused controversy and disturbed many of his contemporaries. But what was Jesus up to when he created these controversies? Did Jesus intend to call into question Israel's status as God's chosen people?

One may cite Jesus' designation of a group known as "the Twelve" as evidence that he did not call into question Israel's chosen status; rather, through this symbolic act, Jesus sought to renew or reconstitute Israel. Though we know little about most of these twelve individuals (note that the lists of the Twelve in the Gospels differ somewhat), they symbolized a reconstituted Israel around the ministry of Jesus as they embodied what it meant to be a disciple. For Jesus and his Jewish contemporaries, any understanding of God's rule over the world—the kingdom—is unthinkable without the fulfillment of the hopes of Israel. Although these hopes and expectations were radically redefined by Jesus and his followers, he nonetheless acted within the framework of first-century Judaism.

Within that framework, however, Jesus also stretched some social and religious boundaries, particularly in his practice of eating with outsiders, or table fellowship. In first-century Judaism, those with whom one ate was a matter of great importance. One either shared a blessing or a curse depending on the company one kept at the dinner table. The fact that Jesus chose to eat with outsiders (e.g., public sinners and tax collectors) raised eyebrows and caused consternation among his coreligionists. Yet the practice of table fellowship is more than just an example of Jesus' keeping dangerous company, or his propensity to shock and annoy "the establishment"; rather, through table fellowship Jesus signaled an offer of community, forgiveness, and salvation. The offer of fellowship to "tax collectors and sinners" rather than the demand for a change of life characterizes Jesus' ministry in the Gospels. In other words, the offer of forgiveness and fellowship precedes the call for repentance and conversion—in fact it is the fellowship that makes such conversion possible. Jesus' practice of table fellowship thus signaled the in-breaking of the kingdom in ways that many in Israel would have found familiar as well as challenging.

Jesus and Judaism

It is a distortion of early Judaism to suggest that there was a dichotomy between the Torah and love or mercy. The idea of "covenantal love" (*chesed*) was and is at the heart of Judaism. The relationship between covenantal love and "righteousness" (*tsedeqah*) can be problematic for Christians as they attempt to discern the attitude of Jesus toward the practices of early Judaism. Suffice it to say that the ideal of love and mercy is in tension with the pursuit of righteousness in practical religion. Just think about Christian history or Islamic history—the examples are almost too numerous. The ideal of covenantal love as the origin and end of the pursuit of righteousness often does not meet up with the reality of religious living, and there are constant efforts at reform (Amos, Hosea, and the rest of the prophets in the Old Testament; Francis of Assisi, Catherine of Siena, or Mother Teresa of Calcutta in the history of Christianity). Now one should not simply lump together these figures and list Jesus as "one of the prophets," but to better understand Jesus' attitude toward the Mosaic law and religious living, one should see Jesus' teaching not as an abrogation of the Torah but as a prophetic critique of religious practice.

The ministry of Jesus must be understood as a ministry to Israel. Jesus was a Jew, and his ministry is intelligible as a religious renewal or reform movement. Some scholars have registered concern regarding this interpretation of Jesus' sayings, that portraying Jesus as a reformer or renewer of Judaism implies something was amiss with Judaism in the first century. While concerns over Christian misinterpretations of Judaism are generally well founded, to say that Jesus was concerned about religious reform does not imply **anti-Semitism** or a dismissal of Judaism. Rather, traditions are vital to the extent that they can inspire reformers. As decadent as late medieval Catholicism was in so many ways, the tradition could still produce

The Battle to Understand Judaism in the New Testament

Christian faith has long presented itself as a religion of "grace" in contrast with Judaism as a religion of "works" or personal achievement—in Judaism one has to work hard to earn God's favor and blessing. Such an attitude often appears when Christians read the letters of Paul, especially Romans and Galatians. From the earliest centuries of the Common Era, Christian writers and preachers attacked Judaism and the Jewish people as corrupt and petty. Such charges became engrained in Christian consciousness and provided the soil from which sprang anti-Semitism. Even the great theologians of the twentieth century were largely complicit in the anti-Judaism (bigotry oriented toward the religion) if not the anti-Semitism (racial bigotry) so prevalent in Europe and the U.S. at the time.

George F. Moore was one of the first modern scholars to identify the problem of a Christian reading of Judaism in the New Testament. In an essay titled "Christian Writers on Judaism" (*Harvard Theological Review* 14 [1921]: 197–254), Moore documented how late nineteenth-century writers portrayed Judaism as the antithesis of Christianity: Judaism was a legalistic religion; God was inaccessible; one must earn salvation by good works or personal merit. This view dominated much New Testament scholarship. Moore began to put some holes in the façade of this position, but it was not until the Canadian scholar E. P. Sanders came on the scene that a drastic reappraisal of Judaism began to take place in the twentieth century. While some may disagree with his reading of Paul's letters—the "new perspective on Paul"—his contribution to an understanding of Judaism in the first century has been revolutionary. His two major works are *Paul and Palestinian Judaism: A Comparison of Patterns of Religion* (London: SCM, 1977) and *Jesus and Judaism* (Minneapolis: Fortress, 1985). In the former, Sanders outlines his understanding of the concept that ties first-century Palestinian Judaism together: covenantal nomism (the Greek word *nomos* means "law"). Sanders's point was this:

(1) God has chosen Israel and (2) given the law. The law implies both (3) God's promise to maintain election and (4) the requirement to obey. (5) God rewards obedience and punishes transgression. (6) The law provides for means of atonement, and atonement results in (7) maintenance or re-establishment of the covenantal relationship. (8) All those who are maintained in the covenant by obedience, atonement, and God's mercy belong to the group which will be saved. An important interpretation of the first and last points is that election and ultimately salvation are considered to be by God's mercy rather than human achievement. . . .

By consistently maintaining the basic framework of covenantal nomism, the gifts and demands of God were kept in a healthy relationship with each other, the minutiae of the law were observed on the basis of the large principles of religion and because of commitment to God, and humility before God who chose and would ultimately redeem Israel was encouraged. (*Paul and Palestinian Judaism*, 422, 427)

a Martin Luther. Though Roman Catholics do not agree with everything Luther taught, he is rightly viewed in Catholic circles as someone interested in reforming the church precisely because he valued it, not because he hated it or wanted it destroyed. While the comparison between Christ and Luther is incongruent in many ways, it may prove helpful for understanding that the disputes Jesus had with religious authorities revolved around important principles on which both parties agreed.

The Torah, the first five books of the Bible, was at the heart of Jewish life. These books narrate the story (*haggadah*, Hebrew for "telling" or "narrating") of Israel's ancestors and offer instruction (*halakah*, Hebrew for "instruction," literally "walking") for responding to Israel's God. The stories provide Israel with its self-understanding as God's beloved, chosen, and redeemed people. This election was gratuitous, Israel did nothing to deserve it, and in fact the Old Testament points out time and again the ways Israel turned away from God's election. The instruction, the law, provided Israel with the appropriate response to God's gracious election.[14] Divorced from the narratives, the instruction could take on a life of its own and be used to brutalize and marginalize people. One can interpret many of Jesus' disputes with Jewish officials (often stereotyped with the expression "scribes and Pharisees," or "chief priests and Pharisees") as stemming from Jesus' desire to protect the traditions of Israel by connecting them with the story of God's mercy and love.

A good example of this is the late Christian story of the woman caught in adultery (John 7:53—8:11), though the story probably does not go back to stage one (it appears to be a scribal addition to John's Gospel). Yet the episode illustrates how Jesus, amid what appears to be a legal dispute, appeals to the story of Israel to call for an expanded and deeper interpretation of the demands of *halakah*. A woman caught in the act of adultery is brought before Jesus (one may fairly wonder what happened to her partner). The Pharisees ask Jesus whether they should stone her as the Torah seemed to require. In response Jesus writes with his finger on the ground and invites anyone who is without sin to cast a stone at her. Jesus then bends down to write a second time. John Paul Heil has rightly pointed to Jesus' writing as the *crux interpretum* of the passage. For Heil, this act recalls God's giving of the Commandments on Sinai. The tablets that are given to Moses were inscribed with letters that came from God's finger (Exodus 31:18; Deuteronomy 9:10; 10:2), but these tablets had to be rewritten because Moses smashed them when he descended the mountain and found the people of Israel, who had just sworn loyalty to

YHWH, in a drunken orgy around the golden calf. The Old Testament tells us that despite Israel's sin, disobedience, and failure, God gave them another chance. The Commandments were rewritten, and Israel remained chosen, even though they deserved to be forsaken by God.[15] Thus, when Jesus writes with his finger on the ground, and particularly when he writes the second time, he is reminding the Jewish community of their own story. They, the entire people of Israel, like the adulterous woman, have sinned. Jesus thus challenges those who would use the Commandments to play a game of "gotcha" apart from the story of God's love, mercy, and fidelity.

If the story of the woman caught in adultery has any resonance within the life of Jesus—and a case can be made through the criterion of coherence—it provides an example of how Jesus, faithful to the prophetic and best rabbinic traditions, sees the story of God's love and the value of the human (made in God's image) as the determining factor for the interpretation and application of any commandment. Jesus' summons to conversion, however, did not make Jesus a libertine; rather, the demands of the covenant are properly understood and lived when interpreted as part of the story of YHWH's love for Israel.

The Death of Jesus

Mel Gibson's film *The Passion of the Christ* raised several important and controversial issues surrounding the execution of Jesus. Many scholars and theologians believe that Gibson erroneously portrayed the Jewish authorities as being primarily responsible for the death of Jesus and portrayed them in an exceedingly negative light. The extent to which these charges against Gibson are valid is a matter of debate, but there is little disagreement about the way controversy surrounding the film highlighted the historical question of who was responsible for the death of Jesus. One point of agreement that has emerged among scholars is that Jesus provoked opposition, yet the identity of his opponents remains at least partly uncertain. The fact that Jesus is often portrayed in the Gospels as fighting with "the scribes and the Pharisees" or even "the Jews" does not clarify the matter, for the Gospels also contend that the Jewish **Sanhedrin**, led by the Sadducees at the time, was responsible for "handing over" Jesus to the Romans. The Sanhedrin was a group of clerics who were responsible for the administration of the temple and ensuring the observance of Jewish law. Since 6 CE, when Herod's son Archelaus was deposed and a Roman prefecture was instituted in Judea, the Sanhedrin had to work under a watchful Roman eye. It is apparent that some arrangement existed between the Roman governor (Pontius Pilate) and the Sanhedrin. The leader of the Sanhedrin was confirmed by the Roman governor and allowed to exercise his office only with the support of Rome. It is interesting to note that the High Priest (the head of the Sanhedrin) at the time of Jesus (Joseph Caiaphas) was elevated to that office shortly before Pilate became governor, and remained until Pilate was recalled to Rome in 36 CE. This is remarkable given that there was rapid turnover in the high priesthood before Caiaphas. We can reasonably deduce from this that Caiaphas was generally willing to cooperate with the Roman authorities.

The cooperation between Pilate and Caiaphas does not answer the question of responsibility for the death of Jesus; nor does it address the irregularities one finds in the Gospel accounts of Jesus' trial. From the evidence at hand, it appears that the Jewish trial narrated in the Gospels is not reliable: there could not have been a trial at night, for such a thing was forbidden by law and good sense; additionally, the Sanhedrin handled matters only within its jurisdiction, but a charge of sedition or any charge calling for the death penalty could not have involved the Sanhedrin since it did not have the *potestas gladii* (power to execute).[16] It seems that the hearing before Caiaphas was not a trial but merely a kind of interview that provided a transition to the real trial before Pilate the following morning. But what could have caused the Sanhedrin, controlled by the Sadducees and not the Pharisees at this time, to see Jesus as a threat? In Mark 14:64 the Sanhedrin charged Jesus with blasphemy (*blasphemeō*, "to speak against God"). Is this a Christian "spin" on the death of Jesus? What could Jesus have said or done that could be construed as blasphemous?

In the Gospel tradition the hearing before Caiaphas appears to center on Jesus' activity in the temple and the question of Jesus' self-understanding. Jesus' stay in Jerusalem, and particularly his symbolic activity in the temple (Mark 11:15–19), present us with a crucial piece of data for grasping Jesus' self-understanding. The temple action—driving the money changers and vendors out of the temple—is to be viewed in the context of the prophetic literature, particularly Zechariah, whom Jesus evokes with his messianic entry into Jerusalem (Mark 11:1–10; cf. Zechariah 9:9). Questions about Jesus' attitude and his activity in the temple focus the charge of the high priest at the hearing. The charge is answered by Jesus in the affirmative with an appeal to Daniel, chapter 7 (the "Son of Man") and Psalm 110 ("seated at the right hand" of God) and tells the high priest that he will be a witness to the events that will vindicate Jesus' claim to be Messiah (even though he uses the phrase "Son of Man": Mark 14:62 pars.).[17] Although the response Jesus gives in the Gospels is suffused with later Christology, the basics of the dispute seem plausible: if Jesus spoke against the temple and offered a form of reconciliation to sinners apart from the temple, he was implicitly claiming an authority for himself that rivaled the authority of the ruling elite.

Jesus' entry into Jerusalem and his prophetic action in the temple both portray Jesus as understanding himself as having divine authority. Many New Testament scholars are understandably hesitant to identify Jesus' self-understanding since it smacks of historical psychology, a highly suspect discipline. After all, do we have a good sense of even our own motivations and self-understanding? Many hours of expensive therapy can help one to gain some understanding of these issues, but how can one accurately answer such questions for figures from the distant past? Other scholars insist that one can infer the basic contours of Jesus' self-understanding from his actions. N. T. Wright, for example, even goes so far as to argue that Jesus understood himself to be Israel's Messiah, a point with which many scholars would disagree. Wright is careful to nuance his presentation of the Messiah in first-century Judaism, which he deems a highly complex idea,[18] and offers some basic ideas and tasks associated with the Messiah that cut across the sectarian literature of the time: the Messiah was to defeat Israel's enemies in battle, and the Messiah was to rebuild, restore, or cleanse the temple.[19] Wright contends that Jesus envisioned himself as the king, the Messiah, God's anointed, through whom YHWH was at last restoring his people.[20] This definition, or redefinition, of Messiah emerges within the context of Wright's presentation of Jesus' prophetic "kingdom praxis," (the stories Jesus told), and the worldview created by these stories and **praxis**.

Jesus' announcement of the *kingdom* was meant to embody and enact the hope that God would visit and restore the people of Israel. This is apparent in the synoptic Gospels, where Jesus, from the earliest days of his ministry to the time of his death, is portrayed as conscious of his status as Messiah and never misses an opportunity to express that self-understanding.[21] Yet one must also reconcile that the Gospels present a clear gap between the authority Jesus seems to claim through his actions and the level at which Jesus is prepared to accept the designation "messiah." Jesus' reluctance to use the title may account, in part, for his use of the self-designation Son of Man. In the hearing before Caiaphas, Jesus' use of this self-designation causes dismay within the Sanhedrin because the Son of Man figure is best situated and understood within the context of Israel's nationalistic hope for restoration. From the Jewish perspective, Jesus' subversion of Israel's story and symbols were the heart of the matter. Both the Pharisees and the Sadducees believed Jesus was a false prophet who led the people away from the true worship of YHWH. For the Sadducees, Jesus was troublesome because he stirred up sentiment against those who controlled access to YHWH through the temple. Though Jesus did not lead an army, his messianic pretensions could become the focus of a real revolution, for which Rome would hold the entire nation responsible. Additionally, Wright contends that Jesus committed blasphemy by placing himself beside YHWH. Quite simply, from the Jewish perspective, Jesus was a false prophet and deserved death (Deuteronomy 13:1–11).

Jesus' own attitude toward his death is best grasped through a reading of his last supper with his disciples. There Jesus blends the story of his life with the story of Israel so that Jesus' life is understood as the climax of Israel's story.[22] The symbolic activity in the temple makes it clear that Jesus is replacing the system of sacrifice with himself; his own death was to bring about a new exodus, an end to Israel's oppression.[23] This fits in well with Jesus' prophetic ministry—reinterpreting the nationalistic and violent symbols of Israel with nonviolent resistance. Jesus' own life would be the symbol of the new people of YHWH, a people defined by their suffering and the suffering of their Messiah. N. T. Wright goes further, however, and contends that the death of Jesus was understood by him as vicarious substitution—Jesus would suffer in place of the people of Israel.

In doing so, Jesus was using the tradition established in the stories of **Maccabean** martyrs as well as the theology articulated in Isaiah's **Suffering Servant**.[24] Jesus' death would bring about a victory:

> Jesus believed it was his [G]od-given vocation to identify with the rebel cause, the kingdom cause, when at last that identification could not be understood as [an] endorsement [of violent nationalism]. . . . He would go ahead of his people, to take upon himself both the fate that they had suffered one way or another for half a millennium at the hands of pagan empires and the fate that [many of] his contemporaries were apparently hell-bent upon pulling down on their heads once for all. The martyr tradition [as embodied in the Maccabean literature in particular] suggested that this was the way in which Israel would at last be brought through suffering to vindication. (N. T. Wright, *Jesus and the Victory of God* [Minneapolis: Fortress, 1996], 596)

This victory and vindication was to be accomplished in Jesus' mind through the two central tasks of the Messiah: purification of the temple and victory in battle. We have seen the purification of the temple and Jesus' interpretation of his death as sacrificial in the Last Supper. Jesus' messianic task was completed with the victory in battle over Israel's enemies—yet these enemies were not those defined by violent nationalists in Jerusalem or Galilee. Rather, Jesus' proclamation of the kingdom and his call to conversion redefined Israel's enemy as Satan rather than Rome, as sin rather than as the presence of a Gentile government in Israel. His confrontation with power, particularly Roman power, and the love he demonstrated in the face of that power, were evident in the story of his life and his death.[25]

Conclusion

An historically reconstructed portrait of Jesus, no matter how intriguing or provocative, is not the norm or foundation for Christian faith. Yet a sketch like the one provided here is useful for gaining an account of the way Christian faith developed from the life and ministry of Jesus. It forces us to wrestle with the historical particularities of Jesus' ministry and self-understanding. This sketch also highlights the importance of Jesus' call to conversion in response to his proclamation of the kingdom. It is apparent from the brief sketch offered here that this conversion and the kingdom are complex realities that can only be sketched partially from the historical point of view. The experience of religious conversion, anticipated in the initial faith of Jesus' followers during his lifetime, nonetheless cannot substitute for the centerpiece of the Christian faith: the Resurrection of Christ and his victory over death.

Questions for Understanding

1. Which of the five primary criteria discussed at the beginning of the chapter is likely to be most controversial? Why? Which is arguably the most objective? Why?

2. From the perspective of the historian, did Jesus have brothers and sisters? Is there any room for believing in the perpetual virginity of Mary? Explain.

3. By getting baptized by John, was Jesus admitting personal sin? Explain.

4. How should one translate (and understand) the expression "the kingdom of God"? Is this simply an alternate way of describing heaven?

5. What is a parable, and how does it relate to Jesus' proclamation of the kingdom?

6. Who was Apollonius of Tyana, and why is he important for understanding Jesus' miracles?

7. Did Jesus do away with the Mosaic or Jewish law? Did he seek to establish a new religion? Explain.

8. Why was Jesus executed? How did Jesus understand his death?

Questions for Reflection

1. Identify two important areas of historical Jesus research that show evidence of anti-Semitism. Are Christians and Christianity inherently anti-Semitic? What can Christians do to address and correct anti-Semitism?

2. If conversion (*metanoia*) is the response sought by Jesus to his proclamation of the kingdom, how should we understand the relationship

between politics and religious conviction? Did Jesus' message have political implications? What does this mean for the political involvement of Christians today? Explain.

3. Historians generally believe that Jesus included women among his closest disciples but did not include women among the Twelve. Is this significant for understanding the role of women in the Christian church today? Is Jesus' exclusion of women here sufficient to justify contemporary church practice? Explain.

Endnotes

1 John P. Meier, *A Marginal Jew: Rethinking the Historical Jesus*, ABRL (Garden City, NJ: Doubleday, 1991), 1:297.

2 Morna Hooker, "On Using the Wrong Tool," *Theology* 75 (1972): 570–81.

3 For a good discussion of this issue in relation to John Meier's work, see the following essays: Tony Kelly, "The Historical Jesus and Human Subjectivity: A Response to John Meier," *Pacifica* 4 (1991): 202–28; Ben Meyer, "The Relevance of 'Horizon,'" *Downside Review* 386 (1994): 1–15; Christopher McMahon, "The Historical Jesus and Frankenstein's Monster: The Historical Jesus According to John P. Meier," *New Blackfriars* 83 (2002): 505–13.

4 Meier, *Marginal Jew*, 1:318–32; idem., "The Brothers and Sisters of Jesus in Ecumenical Perspective," *Catholic Biblical Quarterly* 54 (1992): 1–28; idem., "On Retrojecting Later Questions from Later Texts: A Reply to Richard Bauckham," *Catholic Biblical Quarterly* 59 (1997): 511–27.

5 Meier, *Marginal Jew*, 1:109.

6 Ibid., 113.

7 William P. Loewe, *A College Student's Introduction to Christology* (Collegeville, MN: Liturgical, 1996), 47–48.

8 C. H. Dodd, *Parables of the Kingdom* (New York: Scribners, 1936), 5.

9 David Stern, *Parables in Midrash* (Cambridge, MA: Harvard, 1994).

10 Meier, *Marginal Jew*, 2:548–49.

11 Ibid., 3:48, 50–54; see also Günther Bornkamm, *Jesus of Nazareth*, trans. Irene and Fraser McLuskey with James M. Robinson (New York: Harper, 1960), 145.

12 The discussion of female disciples does not touch directly on the Catholic Church's argument against the ordination of women. Part of that argument involves the fact that women are not numbered among "the Twelve" or the contention that they were not "apostles" (cf. Romans 16:7, which some see as a reference to a woman apostle in the early church). See John Paul II, *Ordinatio Sacerdotalis*, and The Congregation for the Doctrine of the Faith, *Inter Insigniores*, for the arguments against women's ordination.

13 N. T. Wright, *Jesus and the Victory of God* (Minneapolis: Fortress, 1996), 430–32.

14 This is at the heart of E. P. Sanders's notion of "covenantal nomism."

15 John Paul Heil, "The Story of Jesus and the Adulteress (Jn 7:53—8:11) Reconsidered," *Biblica* 72 (1991): 182–91.

16 The only exception appears to be by way of concession: if a Gentile were to enter the temple he would be subject to stoning. We have at least two inscriptions from the temple area that attest to this (see, e.g., Josephus, *Antiquities* 15.427).

17   For Wright, Psalm 110 plays a significant role in Jesus' self-understanding in Mark
     12:35–37 pars. On the use of Psalm 110 in early Christianity, see David Hay, *Glory
     at the Right Hand: Psalm 110 in Early Christianity*, Society of Biblical Literature
     Monograph Series 18 (Nashville: Abingdon, 1973).

18   N. T. Wright, *The New Testament and the People of God* (Minneapolis: Fortress,
     1992), 307–20.

19   N. T. Wright, *Jesus and the Victory of God* (Minneapolis: Fortress, 1996), 481–86.

20   Ibid., 481–86.

21   Ibid., 487–88. Wright cites Wrede and Bultmann as two influential figures who
     advocated the identification of Jesus as Messiah as a post-resurrection event.

22   Ibid., 553–63.

23   Ibid., 558.

24   Ibid., 576–92. In early Judaism there were stories that envisioned salvation from the
     present evil age through the sufferings of certain figures who embodied the suffer-
     ings of Israel.

25   Ibid., 606–9.

3

The Resurrection

The last two chapters concluded with some provocative ideas about how Jesus lived his life and understood his death. But these questions were pursued from an historian's perspective. At this point, we leave the basement of the Harvard library and our friends who have been working so hard to produce their consensus document on the historical Jesus, and turn to the question of the origin of Christian faith. This will certainly involve historical questions (we may consult the basement group on occasion), but in this chapter we will entertain theological questions, questions that treat the religious experience of the followers of Jesus and the genesis of the Christian church. Specifically, we will focus on the stories and the theology of the Resurrection. This theology is so central to the Christian expression of faith that in 1 Corinthians 15:14 Paul writes, "And if Christ has not been raised, then our proclamation has been in vain and your faith has been in vain." Such a sharp statement helps to delineate the importance of the present chapter, and puts into perspective those who find discussion of the Resurrection narratives so challenging.

The Old Testament Period

The Afterlife in the Deuteronomistic Tradition

There is no uniform belief concerning an afterlife in the Old Testament. In fact, for most of the Old Testament, an afterlife is never acknowledged. For many modern students this seems quite perplexing. Why would one believe in God if there is no heaven? One of the most stirring responses to this question is found in Deuteronomy 30. In this part of Deuteronomy, Moses speaks to the Hebrew people at the end of their long journey out of slavery in Egypt and just before they cross the Jordan River to occupy the land promised to Abraham in Genesis 15. Moses gathers the people and challenges them to embrace the covenant—to bind themselves to YHWH who brought them out of Egypt and slavery. Moses spells out the terms of the covenant and addresses the people in Deuteronomy 30:16–20:

> If you obey the commandments of the LORD, your God, which I enjoin on you today, loving him, and walking in his ways, and keeping his commandments, statutes and decrees, you will live and grow numerous, and the LORD, your God, will bless you in the land you are entering to occupy. If, however, you turn away your hearts and will not listen, but are led astray and adore and serve other gods, I tell you now that you will certainly perish; you will not have a long life on the land which you are crossing the Jordan to enter and occupy. I call heaven and earth today to witness against you: I have set before you life and death, the blessing and the curse. Choose life, then, that you and your descendants may live, by loving the LORD, your God, heeding his voice, and holding fast to him. For that will mean life for you, a long life for you to live on the land which the LORD swore he would give to your fathers Abraham, Isaac and Jacob.

For the **Deuteronomist** (i.e., the author[s] of Deuteronomy and the Deuteronomistic history that runs from Joshua to 2 Kings), the rewards for covenantal obedience and fidelity are life, prosperity, and security in the land. Breaking covenantal fidelity brings with it famine, war, and death. So the choice is just that straightforward: life versus death, blessing or curse in "the here and now." This outlook is shared by most of the authors of the Old Testament; for them, there is no discernable afterlife. To the extent that an afterlife is envisioned at all, it is described by the Hebrew word **Sheol**, the abode of the dead. In *Sheol* the dead sleep; they forget life and do not praise God (e.g., Isaiah 38:18; Psalm 88:10–12; Job 7:9; 31:3–19).

This bleak picture of blessing for the righteous faithful and curses for the wicked often ran against the experience of the suffering righteous and the prosperity of the wicked. Even Jeremiah, who was closely associated with the Deuteronomistic outlook, wondered how YHWH would address the apparent inconsistencies in this theology (Jeremiah 12:1–4). In the prophets there is a pervasive pessimism about an afterlife, but this pessimism is bracketed by deep questions and concerns about how to understand God's covenantal love and fidelity, YHWH's *chesed*, beyond death, beyond the destruction that befell the nation in the eighth and sixth centuries BCE.

The Babylonian Exile and the Afterlife

Perhaps the most dramatic event in the history of Judah was the destruction of Solomon's temple and the exile of the leading citizens of Jerusalem in 587 BCE by Nebuchadnezzar, king of Babylon. The Hebrew prophet Ezekiel heard of these events while he was in Babylon and offered prophetic messages to reassure the people of YHWH's fidelity. Perhaps the most dramatic image of consolation from Ezekiel is found in 37:1–14, the famous passage in which Ezekiel prophesies to the dry bones.

> The hand of the LORD came upon me, and he led me out in the spirit of the LORD and set me in the center of the plain, which was now filled with bones. . . . He asked me: Son of man, can these bones come to life? "Lord GOD," I answered, "you alone know that." Then he said to me: Prophesy over these bones, and say to them: Dry bones, hear

the word of the LORD! Thus says the Lord GOD to these bones: See! I will bring spirit into you, that you may come to life. . . . I prophesied as he told me, and the spirit came into them; they came alive and stood upright, a vast army. Then he said to me: Son of man, these bones are the whole house of Israel. They have been saying, "Our bones are dried up, our hope is lost, and we are cut off." Therefore, prophesy and say to them: Thus says the Lord GOD: O my people, I will open your graves and have you rise from them, and bring you back to the land of Israel. Then you shall know that I am the LORD, when I open your graves and have you rise from them, O my people! I will put my spirit in you that you may live, and I will settle you upon your land; thus you shall know that I am the LORD. I have promised, and I will do it, says the LORD.

This is an early passage. Though we find similar passages in other biblical books that, at first glance, appear to be written before Ezekiel, many of those passages are properly regarded as later additions to the biblical books (e.g., Isaiah 26). The passage from Ezekiel is undoubtedly from the sixth century BCE and is not a late addition. But the question remains, does Ezekiel envision "resurrection from the dead" as a hope for Judah, or is this passage a vivid way of consoling the exiles from Jerusalem and promising that YHWH will return the people to their land? In other words, is the death described in this passage a metaphorical death coming from Judah's exile from the land and the destruction of the temple, or is Ezekiel talking about personal and literal death, the cessation of biological activity? Most scholars would argue for the former, not the latter. But this passage and the events that gave rise to it are decisive for the development of Jewish belief in an afterlife, and particularly in resurrection.

The Afterlife and the Maccabean Crisis

The crucial event for the development of an afterlife tradition is the Maccabean rebellion in the second century BCE. Following the return from the Babylonian Exile and the rebuilding of the temple in Jerusalem by Joshua and Zerubbabel in 515 BCE, the Jewish people enjoyed relative peace. They were no longer an independent and autonomous nation as they had

The Afterlife in History and Tradition

Here is a sampling of various positions on the afterlife from around the world. These accounts are highly simplified and meant as an invitation to further explore the afterlife in other religious traditions.

Ancient Egypt

Egyptian attitudes toward death can be gleaned from the practice of mummification. An examination of such Egyptian burial practices as the inclusion of household goods and servants in the tombs of the nobility suggests an expectation that life would continue after death in much the same manner as before death. In other words, there was no great change. There was certainly no expectation of corporate judgment or cosmic battles.

Ancient Greece and Rome

In ancient Greece and Rome, Hades or Pluto was a place where the dead were confined and judged by three judges. Heroes who exhibited virtue in battle could earn a place in the Elysian Fields; recall the visions of Maximus in the film *Gladiator* (although the Greek hero Achilles from the Trojan wars is not placed in Elysium in Book XI of Homer's *Iliad*). Additionally, Tartarus was reserved for those who had offended the gods. Originally Tartarus was seen as a place of confinement for those who endangered the gods, but it later became a place for punishment. The vast majority of the dead, who were neither virtuous nor evil, were consigned to the Fields of Asphodel where they existed as shadows or ghosts.

Hinduism

Human existence is defined by *samsara*, or the cycle of rebirth. According to the *Code of Manu*, for instance, one's rebirth is determined by the degree to which one abides by the obligations of the caste system (the hierarchical system by which families are given certain roles within society). Certain duties define castes, and those who remain faithful to those duties can be released from their caste (recall the conversations about this between Arjuna and Lord Krishna in the *Bhagavad-Gita*). Yet the cycle of rebirth is not permanent; one seeks union with the divine and liberation from *samsara*.

Buddhism

Like Hinduism, Buddhism envisions a cycle of rebirth called *samsara*. One can be reborn into a heavenly, godlike existence, but that existence is still within *samsara*, as is rebirth into a region of "hell." The goal is not union with the divine but liberation from *samsara* through recognizing the nature of reality and its inherent emptiness (*anatman* and *sunyata*). Nirvana is the name given to the state of perfect rest and nothingness that one finds with enlightenment and the practice of the Noble Eightfold Path. Some forms of Buddhism (e.g., Pure Land) envision a "western land" of bliss into which devotees of Buddha will be reborn, but this is merely an intermediary stage in which one practices the Noble Eightfold Path, the only path to Nirvana.

Islam

In contrast to the traditions mentioned above, Islam is younger than Judaism and Christianity; it emerged in the seventh century CE. Its vision of the afterlife roughly coincides with apocalyptic visions within Judaism and Christianity. Within Islam, the afterlife is divided into two abodes: one for those who have done good deeds and followed the commandments of God, and one for those who have done evil. The former is called Jannah or Firdous (the "garden" or "paradise"; see Qur'an 18:107; 23:11). The abode for the evildoers is called Jahannam. There is some uncertainty as to whether Jahannam is a place of eternal punishment or of remedial, temporary punishment meant to bring about repentance.

been from the time of David up through Zedekiah, but were now incorporated into the great Persian Empire. The Persians generally allowed the Jewish people to worship YHWH as they saw fit, so long as good order was preserved. But with the demise of the Persian Empire under pressure from Alexander the Great and his Greek armies in the fourth century (around 332 BCE), the situation began to change. Alexander and his immediate successors who controlled Judah and Jerusalem (what came to be known as the **Ptolemaic Kingdom**) generally allowed the Jews to worship in peace. Alexander's wars had a number of goals, however, and prominent among them was a form of **cultural imperialism**. Alexander was convinced that Greek culture and the Greek way of life were far superior to all others, and wherever he went he established Greek cities (often named for himself: Alexandria). His successors increasingly pressured the local populace to assimilate to a Greek lifestyle and worldview. When the **Seleucid Kingdom** (also founded by Alexander's successors) came to control Jerusalem, the Jewish people were put under great duress.

The Seleucid king Antiochus IV Epiphanes outlawed the Jewish religion (1 Maccabees 1:41–64; 2 Maccabees 6:1–11) and erected an altar to (and perhaps even an image of) the Greek god Zeus in the Jerusalem temple (2 Maccabees 6:2). Antiochus intended to enforce the full assimilation of Jews to the dominant Greek culture. His plan received support from many prominent priestly families and even some of the high priests, but the majority objected vehemently. This touched off a widescale rebellion led by a family known as the Maccabees. In the deuterocanonical books that bear the name Maccabees we find harrowing accounts of devout Jews who were willing to suffer torture and die rather than forsake the covenant and its obligations. This turn of events raised the question of YHWH's fidelity in an increasingly sharp way: if faithfulness was supposed to bring peace and prosperity, why are the righteous suffering and dying for their faithfulness to YHWH? When are they going to see the rewards promised them in Deuteronomy 30? Amid this crisis we see an important shift in Jewish theology. As YHWH's people suffer, their cries reach to heaven; they are now told to wait, to be patient and endure in faith, for God is coming soon and will vindicate the righteous and punish the wicked. But what will this vindication look like? How will it happen?

The Canon, the Apocrypha, and the Deuterocanonicals

The word *canon* comes from the Greek word *kanōn*, meaning "rule" or "measure." The word has come to be associated with the collection of books recognized as the rule or measure of the Christian faith. Scripture certainly provides us with the principles of our faith, but one must ask the further question regarding how these books in particular were recognized as a "rule" or "measure" of the faith.

The Old Testament

The Old Testament or Hebrew Bible was developed in several stages. The Law was the first group of books recognized as authoritative (around the year 400 BCE). In Hebrew it is called the Torah (instruction) and in Greek, the Pentateuch (five scrolls). By the year 200 BCE the Prophets (*Nevi'im*) were recognized as an authoritative and fixed collection so that in the New Testament the expression "the Law and the Prophets" occurs frequently, describing the Old Testament (e.g., Matthew 5:17). The Writings (*Kethuvim*) represent a fairly eclectic collection of books. Even though much of the material is quite ancient, this was the last group to achieve canonical status (in the late first or second century CE).

The issue of canonicity in the Old Testament is complicated by the fact that what has been stated above refers mainly to the Palestinian canon. One must remember that large Jewish communities outside Palestine often had their own collections of books. Specifically, a large contingent of Greek-speaking Jews lived in Egypt, especially in the city of Alexandria, in the second century BCE. These Jews used a Greek translation of the Old Testament, which they found more accessible than the original Hebrew. This translation is known as the Septuagint ("seventy," abbreviated LXX) because of a legend surrounding its origin. The Letter of Aristeas to Philocrates tells how a ruler of Egypt commanded seventy-two scholars (six from each tribe of Israel) to make a translation of the Torah into Greek. According to the legend, the project was completed in seventy-two days. The term Septuagint, however, began to be used to describe the entire collection of books translated into Greek.

The Septuagint raises serious questions for Christians. While the canonical status of both the Law and the Prophets were fixed before the advent of Christianity, the last group of books (the Writings) remained open: a number of Greek-speaking Jews in Egypt and elsewhere included books among their Writings that were not included in that collection in Palestine. Greek-speaking Christians of the first and second centuries, making extensive use of the Greek translation of the Old Testament used by Greek-speaking Jews, included these writings in their lists of Old Testament books. The subsequent definition of the Palestinian canon had little effect on the Christian use of books that the Palestinian canon had excluded, specifically Judith, Tobit, Wisdom, Sirach, Baruch, 1 and 2 Maccabees, as well as Greek additions to Daniel and Esther.

These books are often called **deuterocanonical** in Catholic circles because their canonicity has at times been called into question. From the time of Melito of Sardis (second century) through that of Jerome (fifth century), a great number of people favored limiting the Christian Old Testament to the thirty-nine books accepted in the Palestinian canon. Some prominent proponents of this position include Cyril of Jerusalem, Athanasius, and Gregory Nazianzen. In the Western (Catholic) church, the consensus was to accept these books as canonical until the sixteenth century, when the Protestant Reformation greatly complicated the matter. In his debates with Catholic apologists over the doctrine of Purgatory in the sixteenth century, Martin Luther attacked the deuterocanonicals, partly because 2 Maccabees 12:45 seemed to justify the practice of buying and selling indulgences. The Reformers successfully excluded

The Canon, the Apocrypha, and the Deuterocanonicals *(continued)*

the deuterocanonicals from the Protestant canon of the Old Testament. Today these books sometimes appear in a separate section of Protestant Bibles labeled apocrypha, along with other books, some of which are recognized as canonical by eastern orthodox churches but not by Catholics.

Many books were written during the intertestamental period that never became part of either the Catholic or Protestant canon. Some of these books nonetheless exercised considerable influence. Examples include the sectarian documents from *Qumran, Jubilees, Enoch,* and *The Testaments of the Twelve Patriarchs.*

The New Testament

The canon of the New Testament is as complicated an issue as that of the Old Testament, although its development occurred over a much shorter period of time. Within the New Testament itself, references to "scripture" refer to the books of the Jewish Bible, principally the Law and the Prophets: there was no understanding of scripture apart from the Old Testament at that time. The issue of a canon of Christian Scriptures was not raised until the second century with the rise of **Gnosticism** and other heresies (false teachings). The Gnostic religious movement came to the Greco-Roman world from the East. It quickly blended into the Hellenistic environment of early

Christianity and adopted elements of the Jesus story, creating serious problems for the early Christian church and its identity. The Gnostic blending of Christian tradition with their own (heretical) beliefs appears in their writings, termed *apocrypha,* from the Greek word for "hidden"; such works were supposedly "found" after having been hidden away for centuries. Many of these works were examples of pseudepigrapha, writings that falsely claim to have been written by some important figure, in this case, early followers of Jesus. Examples include the Gospel of Mary, the Gospel of Thomas, and the Gospel of Truth. These gospels often contained bizarre or novel stories of Jesus' life. Irenaeus of Lyons, a great bishop and writer in the second century, responded to the Gnostic threat in his work *Against Heresies.* He also laid out several criteria by which books might be judged as authentic or spurious. These criteria were (1) usage in important Christian communities and churches, (2) apostolic origin, and (3) conformity with "the rule of faith." Even with these criteria, several different canons emerged within the early church.

In the final analysis, the Bible is a collection of books put together over a long period of time and containing many different theologies. We need to be aware of this as we seek to interpret the Bible. The Bible can only be read faithfully when read as part of a community of faith.

At this time (the second century BCE), a genre of literature and theology emerged that sought to address the crisis facing many Jews: apocalyptic eschatology (see chapter 1). Apocalyptic eschatology attempted to answer more directly the questions that were raging at the time about YHWH's fidelity and justice. A comprehensive definition of apocalyptic eschatology has proved elusive, but the following reflects a general consensus on the subject in current scholarship.

Apocalyptic eschatology is a genre of revelatory literature with a narrative framework, in which a revelation from God is given to a human being, usually through an intermediary, making known a transcendent reality which envisages eschatological salvation and the existence of another, supernatural world, and usually intended for a group in crisis with the purpose of exhortation and/or consolation by means of divine authority.[1]

We could fill out this definition by including several additional themes and characteristics common to the apocalyptic genre: dualistic views, signs of the coming end (*eschatology* comes from the Greek word *eschaton*, for "end" or "culmination"), emphasis on the end of the world, and final judgment. One of the earliest and most important Hebrew examples of apocalyptic literature is the book of Daniel. Though it purports to be an account of events and visions during the Babylonian Exile (587–539 BCE), it is really a product of the Maccabean crisis (ca. 167–164 BCE) and should be read as such. Daniel's late date is evident from several factors. The Hebrew of Daniel is not that of the sixth century but of the second century and includes long sections written in Aramaic. Additionally, the theology of Daniel is apocalyptic and not prophetic: it uses highly developed symbolism; envisions a parallel, unseen universe; and anticipates the (literal) resurrection of the dead. Moreover, the description of historical events from the Babylonian period—supposedly events contemporary with the setting of Daniel—is weak and hazy, but the supposed forecast of the temple's desecration in 167 BCE is clear, specific, and accurate (9:27; 11:30–35).

The book of Daniel tells the story of Israel suffering at the hands of an unjust king and the heroic acts of a young man named Daniel who receives special visions and messages from heaven that console him and his compatriots amid their great suffering. One of the most important consolations described in Daniel is the expectation that those who die will be raised up to receive the payment due for their behavior—blessedness for the righteous and innocent, and a lake of fire for the wicked. Daniel 12:1–3 offers a classical statement of Jewish apocalyptic hope for resurrection:

At that time there shall arise Michael, the great prince, guardian of your people; It shall be a time unsurpassed in distress since nations began until that time. At that time your people shall escape, everyone who is found written in the book. Many of those who sleep in the dust of the earth shall awake; some shall live forever, others shall be an everlasting horror and disgrace. But the wise shall shine brightly like the splendor of the firmament, and those who lead the many to justice shall be like the stars forever.

For Daniel, YHWH's fidelity and love for Israel will be definitively vindicated when, at the end of time, evil will be defeated, the wicked will be punished, and the faithful will rise up from their graves and be transformed and taken into a new heavenly existence. It is this expectation that the New Testament presupposes when it describes Jesus' resurrection and the hope Christians have for a general resurrection of the dead. However, it is important to understand that belief in or hope for a Resurrection was not universal in first-century Judaism.

The Afterlife in the Intertestamental Period

In the intertestamental period (from the close of the Old Testament period to the beginning of the Christian writings, ca. 150 BCE–50 CE), Second-Temple Judaism entertained a wide range of opinions about the afterlife. Prominent among these options was resurrection, but this was not the only possibility. In fact, the options included (1) the denial of any afterlife, (2) a disembodied afterlife, and (3) resurrection. We find a denial of the afterlife behind the controversy between Jesus and the **Sadducees** in Mark 12:18–27. The Sadducees mockingly ask Jesus about a woman who has been the wife of several husbands, all now deceased. At the resurrection, to whom will she belong? Jesus hurls the mockery and ignorance back on his questioners as he describes the radical transformation that takes place in the resurrection. The point for us as interpreters of the Christian faith is that many of those in first-century Jerusalem did not believe in any afterlife. Some commentators, like Alan Segal, believe that the Sadducees denied an afterlife because they enjoyed power and privilege in this life. There was no need to hope for a reward in the afterlife, the issue at hand was managing the covenantal relationship with YHWH here and now.[2] While Segal may be guilty of reducing the Sadducees' theology to a materialistic principle, materialistic principles probably do play a role in their denial of the afterlife.

Person of Interest

Philo

Philo (ca. 25 BCE–45 CE) was a contemporary of Jesus and a major philosopher. A Greek-speaking Jew, Philo was born and lived in that ancient center of Hellenistic culture, Alexandria. He was an admirer of Greek philosophy (especially Platonic) and used it to interpret Judaism. Although he was viewed with suspicion by some fellow Jews, he became highly influential within early Christianity through his writings, which interpret Scripture allegorically, and his appropriation of the notion of the divine Logos (Word).

Philo embraced a dualistic understanding of reality, particularly the duality of God and the world, the infinite and the finite. This dualism, familiar for centuries in Greek philosophy, informed his reading of Scripture. The materialism of Scripture, its earthy narrative, needed to be unlocked through allegorical interpretation, i.e., by interpreting each element in Scripture as referring to a spiritual reality. For example, he interprets the narratives of Genesis as depicting the soul's relationship to God rather than a literal account of the origins of the universe. His interpretation of the Jewish Law (Torah) centered on the moral life and the union of the soul with God. For Philo the value of the Scriptures rested in their capacity to promote spiritual union with God and not in their power to describe events in history.

Philo's dualism also influenced his account of God. Although he did not go as far as many Greek philosophers, who separated God from human beings, he did adopt the notion that God related to the created order and to human beings through the Logos, the divine Word of God. Philo's understanding of the divine Logos was decisive for early Christianity in its attempts to articulate their understanding of the relationship between Jesus and God, as will appear in the next chapter.

The second attitude toward afterlife in first-century Judaism—hope for a disembodied existence with God—was expressed in **Platonic** terms (i.e., borrowing from the philosophical school begun by Plato). The best example of this Platonic or Hellenistic position is found in Philo of Alexandria, an Egyptian Jewish philosopher who lived around the same time as Jesus. For Philo, the righteous dead, "who deserves so high a title, does not surely die, but has his life prolonged, and so attains to an eternal end" (*Questions and Answers on Genesis*, 1.16). A similar position is also found in the nonbiblical book **Jubilees**, a **midrash** or commentary on and expansion of Genesis. In *Jubilees* 23:30–31 we read:

And at that time the Lord will heal His servants,
And they shall rise up and see great peace,
And drive out their adversaries.
And the righteous shall see and be thankful,
And rejoice with joy for ever and ever,
And shall see all their judgments and all their curses on
    their enemies.
And their bones shall rest in the earth,
And their spirits shall have much joy,
And they shall know that it is the Lord who executes judgment,
And shows mercy to hundreds and thousands and to all that
    love Him.[3]

The passage describes the joy of the righteous at the demise of their enemies. The righteous, however, are dead: "their bones rest in the earth" while "their spirits have much joy." There is no apparent hope for the transformation of the body after death. Rather, hope is expressed in terms of a disembodied happiness, a spiritual joy with God.

The origins of the third option, resurrection from the dead, have already been described. For the Jews of the first century, resurrection was not simply a form of life after death. Resurrection was an event for which people hoped. When loved ones died they were not assumed to have immediately been resurrected; rather, they were thought to endure an "in-between" period where they await the resurrection and YHWH's definitive breakthrough in history. So resurrection was not simply "life after death," but "life after life after death!"[4] The Jewish people developed a variety of ways to describe the in-between state of the righteous who had died. The Persian word *paradise* was borrowed to describe this condition—a garden where the righteous existed before the resurrection (e.g. *1 Enoch* 37–70). Others described the righteous as resting in God's hands (Wisdom 3:1–8), and still others described them as angelic beings or spirits. But this in-between state was not the goal; resurrection was not merely a pious way Jews described the way one endures after death. Resurrection is the reversal of death and involves the transformation of the dead body. For example, the Maccabean martyrs of the second century BCE taunted their executioners and boldly declared their confidence that God would restore their tongues when they were cut out, their hands when they were cut off, etc.[5] While the Maccabean martyrs offer one prominent example, it should be noted that there was no uniformity of expectation on the issue of resurrection. In Daniel 12 the resurrected body is "star-like," in contrast to the simple material body envisioned by the Maccabean martyrs.

For Jews of the first century, resurrection was not primarily about the individual; it was about the people of God. Resurrection was a primary way many Jews envisioned the vindication of YHWH's *chesed* because this was how God intended to restore Israel and punish the wicked (usually Gentiles and their Jewish collaborators). So the resurrection was a cosmic event, bringing the righteous and the wicked together so that the great reversal could take place. The oppressed would find prosperity, while the powerful would be cast out and despised. Resurrection was for all people.

Among at least a segment of the Jewish population, belief in the *eschaton* and resurrection had an important corollary: the Messiah. You will recall from the previous chapter that Jewish expectations concerning the Messiah were hardly uniform, so it is not surprising that the precise relationship between the Messiah and resurrection is not entirely clear or

Some Messianic Figures in Judaism

Cyrus the Great (576 BCE–529 BCE)

This great Persian king defeated the Babylonians, sent the Jews back to Jerusalem from their exile in Babylon, and gave them funds to rebuild the temple. For this reason, the Bible hails Cyrus as "the Lord's anointed" (i.e., "messiah"; Isaiah 45:1). He is the only Gentile (non-Jew) to be given that title.

Zerubbabel (sixth century BCE)

Zerubbabel was the grandson of King Jehoiachin (Jeconiah). When the Babylonian king Nebuchadnezzar took hostages after his first conquest of Jerusalem in 598 BCE, Jehoiachin was among his most prized captives. He quickly became quite respected and popular with his Babylonian captors, and his family was well cared for. When the Jews were returned to Jerusalem to rebuild their temple, Jehoiachin's grandson, Zerubbabel, became a prominent leader of the efforts to restore the nation after the Exile. As the political ruler of the city, many hoped that he would reestablish the Davidic monarchy; thus many began to recognize him as God's anointed one (or messiah). Possibly for political reasons, Zerubbabel was removed from his position by his Persian overlords, and the high priest Joshua became the symbol of national rule. As the Second Temple period unfolded, the high priest rather than a descendant of David ruled the affairs of the Jews in Jerusalem, yet many continued to expect that God would raise up one of David's descendents to restore the kingdom.

Some Messianic Figures in Judaism *(continued)*

Simon ben Kosibah (also Simon Bar Kokhba or "Son of a Star," referring to Numbers 24:17, which was viewed as a messianic prophecy; †135 CE)

Simon was the last independent Jewish ruler of Judea. Following the first revolt against Rome (66–73 CE), the people of Judea, the territory around Jerusalem, continued to chafe under Roman rule. When the emperor Hadrian attempted to erect a pagan altar on the site of the temple in Jerusalem and curtailed the practice of circumcision, the Jews revolted again. Simon became the military and political leader of the revolt and was designated by several rabbis as "messiah" (see *Midrash Rabbah*

Lamentations, 2.2.4). Through the use of guerilla tactics he was able to defeat the Roman soldiers garrisoned in the region in 132 CE and succeeded in establishing an independent Jewish state. The Romans sent more troops and new leaders to put down the revolt and, following a brutal two-year military campaign, successfully destroyed the state in 135 CE. Following the Roman victory, the emperor decreed that Jews were not to be admitted to the region or even look upon Jerusalem from a distance. Hadrian renamed the province "Syria Palestine"—Palestine being the name of Israel's much-despised enemy the Philistines—and built a Roman city (Aelia Capitolina) on the remains of Jerusalem.

consistent. Generally, the Messiah would establish YHWH's kingdom by defeating YHWH's enemies and rebuilding or cleansing the temple. Like the resurrection, therefore, belief in the Messiah was necessarily social and political as well as religious, since YHWH's kingdom and the great reversal at the *eschaton* meant that those now in power would be thrown out.

The New Testament Period

The Language of Resurrection

Among those Jews of the first century who held an apocalyptic outlook (e.g., the Pharisees and their supporters) talk of resurrection would have resonated nicely with the account of Jesus' proclamation of the kingdom in the previous chapter. The resurrection was intelligible. It made sense within the context of Jesus' life and ministry as well as within the larger context of Israel's history. Yet when one turns to the narratives of Jesus' Resurrection, one finds a lack of clarity and consistency that has troubled many who have encountered those narratives. In an effort to understand the issues, let's look at the evidence to see what can be gleaned. We will begin with the earliest proclamation of Jesus' Resurrection as repeated by the apostle Paul, a self-described Pharisee, and thus one who was predisposed to the theological importance of resurrection.

In 1 Corinthians 15:1–8 Paul reminds the Corinthian community of the message he proclaimed to them. This message is some of the oldest material in the New Testament, dating to the period of Paul's conversion and association with the Jerusalem community (late 30s CE).

> Now I am reminding you, brothers, of the gospel I preached to you, which you indeed received and in which you also stand. Through it you are also being saved, if you hold fast to the word I preached to you, unless you believed in vain. For I handed on to you as of first importance what I also received: that Christ died for our sins in accordance with the scriptures; that he was buried; that he was raised on the third day in accordance with the scriptures; that he appeared to Kephas, then to the Twelve. After that, he appeared to more than five hundred brothers at once, most of whom are still living, though some have fallen asleep. After that he appeared to James, then to all the apostles. Last of all, as to one born abnormally, he appeared to me.

This proclamation of the Resurrection has several interesting features. First, notice that Paul's account includes no narrative of the discovery of the tomb, only a list of those to whom the risen Christ appeared. Second, Paul includes his own experience of the risen Christ some years after Jesus' Crucifixion. Was Paul's experience of the risen Christ the same as that of the women at the tomb, Peter, and the others? Third, two key phrases appear in this passage: "he was raised" and "he appeared." These two phrases provide us with a direction for exploring the New Testament proclamation of Jesus' Resurrection.

When Paul declares "he was raised," notice that the verb employs the passive voice—it describes what God did to Jesus. Jesus, therefore, is the recipient of the action of the verb and God the actor. Additionally, the action described by the verb is metaphorical. While the word *resurrection* has a particular religious meaning for us in English, in the Greek of the New Testament the expressions are part of the common language of everyday life and not specifically religious. The Greek words *egeirō* and *anistēmi* used in this context are quite ordinary, and can refer to the quite normal activity of standing up or waking someone out of their sleep, though neither of these meanings is appropriate for understanding resurrection in a literal sense. Any description of God's activity requires us to employ metaphor or analogy. Positively, Paul also offers something definite about what it means to be raised from the dead, namely that in the resurrection all that is negative about our current condition will be removed. He contrasts the "natural body" (sōma psychikos) of our current life with the "spiritual body" (sōma pnuematikos) of the resurrection. The resurrection is not mere resuscitation, but a final or eschatological transformation of a human life as it encounters God.

The second phrase from First Corinthians that demands attention is "he appeared." What does Paul mean by this? The use of the verb "to see" (horaō) is used throughout Scripture to describe ecstatic and visionary experiences. All of these experiences share two components: (1) the initiative rests with the revealer, i.e., the one who discloses; and (2) the recipient of the revelation has a prior involvement with the one who does the disclosing and usually emerges from the encounter with some sort of mission.[6] In light of the metaphorical character of the appearance language in the New Testament, one might wonder about the objectivity of the experience of the Resurrection. In other words, if a casual observer was walking along the road that Sunday morning, would she have looked to the right and wondered, "Who is that man talking to Mary? His clothes are amazingly white. I wonder what kind of detergent he uses." In other words, was the risen Christ visible to the casual observer, or was an encounter with the risen Christ a highly personal, privileged revelatory event?

Paul's early testimony regarding the Easter proclamation reaffirms that resurrection language uses analogy and metaphor—after all we are not talking about a zombie coming out of the grave. Rather, the Resurrection of Jesus is a transcendent event that is only accessible or describable through metaphor, by comparing the experience of the Resurrection to more common experiences. Yet the Gospels do not suggest that the Resurrection itself is a metaphor.

The Gospel Accounts of the Resurrection

The Gospel accounts of Jesus' Resurrection and appearances, like Paul's testimony, also use metaphor, but strongly emphasize the relational and revelatory character of the Resurrection.

The earliest Gospel account is found in Mark 16:1–8. You will notice in your Bible that Mark contains three different conclusions. The first ending (Mark 16:1–8) is the ending we find in not only the oldest but the most reliable manuscripts of Mark's Gospel (older does not always mean more reliable). The so-called shorter ending was added in the fourth century CE, and the longer ending (16:9–20) was added in the second century CE; both are secondary. The original ending of Mark's Gospel in 16:8 gives us no account of Jesus' appearing to the disciples. Rather, it is simply a narrative of Mary Magdalene, Mary the mother of James, and Salome discovering the empty tomb and hearing a messenger declare, "He is risen!" They are told to instruct the other disciples to go to Galilee, where Jesus will appear. It is in many ways a strange ending. Yet for Mark the story of the women at the tomb directs the reader to the experience of Jesus' Resurrection common to all Christians. Such an experience is accompanied by misgivings, doubt, and even fear.

Matthew 28:1–20 reports the discovery of the empty tomb, but it also includes an appearance of the risen Christ to the women in Jerusalem and an appearance to the Eleven ("the Twelve" become "the Eleven" after the departure and death of Judas) in Galilee. The account of the Resurrection in Matthew is accompanied by some remarkable scenes, including the story of the guards at the tomb and their being bribed to spread a rumor that Jesus' body had been stolen by his disciples. Even more remarkable is the account of other resurrections coinciding with that of Jesus. In Matthew 27:51–53 we are told that at the moment of Jesus' death, "the veil of the sanctuary was torn in two from top to bottom. The earth quaked, rocks were split, tombs were opened, and the bodies of many saints who had fallen asleep were raised. And coming forth from their tombs after his Resurrection, they entered the holy city and appeared to many." The scene evokes both Isaiah 26 and Daniel 12, but if this is a historical recollection, it is strange that it would not make its way into the other Gospel accounts. This detail in Matthew helps to situate the resurrection of Jesus within the expectation of a general Resurrection from the dead. In other words, the resurrection of an individual made little sense in first-century Judaism, and Matthew's reference to other resurrections is an overt attempt to address such questions. One should note, however, that Matthew's account is still not a general resurrection, only a foretaste or anticipation of the Resurrection.

Luke's account of Jesus' Resurrection and appearances runs in a unique direction. He records the appearance of the risen Christ in and around Jerusalem and not Galilee. Perhaps most distinctive, however, is Luke's account of the encounter between the risen Christ and two disciples on the road to Emmaus. These disciples know full well the story of Jesus and the reports of the empty tomb, but they fail to recognize Jesus as they meet and speak with him at length. It is only when they sit together and share a meal (with obvious Eucharistic overtones) that they recognize the risen Christ in their midst, but at that moment he disappears.

In John's Gospel we have a highly complex account of the finding of the empty tomb. Mary Magdalene tells Simon and "the other disciple" about the tomb, and the two disciples race back to the tomb. The "other disciple" comes to believe as soon as he sees the empty tomb, but the rest wait to see the risen Christ, particularly Thomas. Meanwhile, Mary Magdalene sees the risen Christ and is sent to the other disciples to announce the good news. The story in John bears a number of similarities to the synoptics, though always with a Johannine spin (e.g., the intimacy of Jesus and the Father is emphasized, the coming to belief of "the other disciple," and the doubt of Thomas).

The New Testament offers a wide range of accounts. Needless to say, these discrepancies are viewed with great suspicion by those who would contend that the Resurrection narratives are mythological, the products of vivid imagination or simple credulity. New Testament scholars suggest that these discrepancies in the account of Jesus' Resurrection and his appearance to the disciples can be attributed to the existence of two distinct traditions in the proclamation of the Resurrection. One tradition focused on the appearance of Jesus to the disciples, while the other narrated the story of the empty tomb. Along with other apologetic and theological interests, this helps to account for the wide variations among the Gospels. For other scholars, however, the discrepancies between Gospel narratives raise serious questions for the authenticity of resurrection stories. If the New Testament narratives are demonstrably unreliable, then one is free to speculate about what actually happened that might have given rise to such stories.

The Variant Accounts of Jesus' Resurrection in the Gospels

	Mark 16:1–8	Matthew 28	Luke 24	Mark 16:9–20	John 20
Time of Day	very early; first day of the week	first day of week; growing light	first day of week at dawn	early first day of the week	still dark on first day of the week
Women Present at the Tomb	Mary Magdalene, Mary, the mother of James, and Salome	Mary Magdalene and "the other Mary"	Mary Magdalene, Mary, the mother of James; Joanna; others	Mary Magdalene	Mary Magdalene and another
Purpose for the Women's Visit	bringing spices to anoint the body	to see tomb	bringing spices they had prepared on Friday	none	none
The Stone Seal on the Tomb	The women find the stone rolled back and a youth sitting inside the tomb.	There is an earthquake; an angel descends and rolls back the stone and sits on it while the guards sleep.	The women find the stone rolled back; two men in dazzling robes appear and speak to them.	none	The women find the stone rolled away; later two angels appear sitting inside the tomb.
Conversation at the Tomb	Youth says not to fear, Jesus is risen; women are told to go and tell the disciples that Jesus is going to Galilee.	Angel says not to fear, Jesus is risen; women are told to go and tell the disciples that Jesus is going to Galilee.	Men ask question; recall prophesy made in Galilee.	none	Angels ask: "Why do you weep?" Mary thinks the body was stolen.
Reaction of the Women at the Tomb	They fear and tremble, tell no one.	They quickly depart in fear to tell disciples.	They return and tell the Eleven and the rest.	They go and tell Jesus' followers.	They go and tell Peter and the "other disciple."
Appearances of Jesus at or Around the Tomb	none	Jesus meets the women, and they touch his feet; he repeats the message about Galilee.	"The Lord appeared to Simon."	Jesus appears to Mary Magdalene.	Jesus appears to Mary Magdalene; he speaks of ascending; Peter and other disciple run to tomb.
Appearance of Jesus in the Country	none	none	road to Emmaus	two men walking in the country	none

The Variant Accounts of Jesus' Resurrection in the Gospels *(continued)*

	Mark 16:1–8	Matthew 28	Luke 24	Mark 16:9–20	John 20
Appearance of Jesus in Jerusalem	none	none	Jesus appears to the Eleven at meal Easter night.	Jesus appears to the Eleven at table.	Jesus appears to disciples Easter night at a meal, and again a week later (Thomas absent Easter, present later).
Appearance of Jesus in Galilee	none	appeared to the Eleven on a mountain	none	none	appeared to seven disciples at Sea of Tiberias

(Adapted from *The Virginal Conception and Bodily Resurrection of Jesus*, by Raymond E. Brown, copyright © 1973 by the Missionary Society of St. Paul the Apostle in the State of New York. Used by Permission of Paulist Press, Inc., New York/Mahwah, NJ. www.paulistpress.com.)

The Contemporary Debate

Edward Schillebeeckx on the Resurrection

Beginning with the work of the famous Flemish theologian Edward Schillebeeckx, modern Roman Catholic biblical scholars and theologians have taken a well-worn path in the pursuit of understanding Jesus' Resurrection, focusing on the symbolic or metaphoric value of resurrection language for expressing the religious experience of the disciples.[7] This approach has walked a very fine line between **orthodoxy** and **heresy**. In fact, Schillebeeckx was asked to account for his position by the Congregation for the Doctrine of the Faith, the Vatican body responsible for overseeing, among other things, the teaching of theology. Schillebeeckx was asked to clarify several points he had made in his works on Christology, but Schillebeeckx was never condemned for his position on the Resurrection (though many have faulted him for it). Let's take a moment to present his position and get a sense of the issues at stake.

For Schillebeeckx, the story of the empty tomb is a late tradition from the Christian community in Jerusalem and not an historical recollection from the earliest disciples. The earliest disciples had met on a regular basis to venerate the memory of Jesus at the place where they believed he was buried. In fact, Schillebeeckx contends that the discovery of Jesus' bones would not have posed a problem for the earliest Christians and their conviction that Jesus had been raised from the dead. Rather than focusing on the empty tomb, Schillebeeckx focuses on Paul and his conversion as the paradigm for understanding the Resurrection (Acts 9, 22, and 26). The Easter experience is thus an experience of grace, an experience of conversion and forgiveness—the experience of Jesus' saving presence. The New Testament testifies to the way Jesus' disciples abandoned him in his hour of suffering. It also testifies that they reassembled after Jesus' death. Schillebeeckx latches on to this event as the genesis of the Resurrection stories. In the context of the reassembled disciples the presence of Jesus was felt, and a collective experience of grace and forgiveness overwhelmed the assembled disciples so that they could indeed proclaim the Resurrection. Schillebeeckx should not be read, however, as suggesting that the Resurrection experience was merely a psychological projection; rather, he asserts that God is at work here. But for Schillebeeckx there is also a fundamental similarity between the early disciples' experience of Resurrection and coming to faith and our own experience of Christ's presence. The two, however, are not identical: the first disciples bore special witness to their experience of the Resurrection by drawing on their memory of Jesus' life and ministry, whereas contemporary Christians must rely on the witness of the disciples.

The life and ministry of Jesus are decisive for any account of the Resurrection. Schillebeeckx does not agree with those who say that we can only know the risen Christ proclaimed by the early church; rather, he argues that our faith rests on the memory of Jesus, which provided the basis for identifying the risen Christ as Jesus of Nazareth. In telling us of the risen Christ, therefore, the disciples tell us something about the Jesus who lived among them. While the experience of the Resurrection was central for the early Christians, our faith is rooted in the life of Jesus. The Resurrection provided the catalyst that enabled the early disciples to know and appreciate Jesus' life among us and its saving significance.

Roger Haight on the Resurrection

The American Jesuit Roger Haight's account of the Resurrection agrees substantially with that offered by Schillebeeckx. Like Schillebeeckx, Haight has suffered severe criticism and rebuke from the Vatican, though not regarding his treatment of the Resurrection per se. For Haight, Jesus was taken up into the life of God—exalted—at the moment of his death; there was no interim period between his death and resurrection.[8] So what happened to Jesus happened at the moment of his death, and all narratives that report a series of events between the death of Jesus and his Resurrection are legendary and artificial. For Haight, the Emmaus story in Luke seems to be the best and most historical account of the genesis of faith in the risen Christ. Through the remembrance of Jesus, particularly in the table fellowship of those closest to him, the power of Jesus and the recognition of his vindication by God become apparent. Christian faith in the Resurrection of Jesus arises out of a more basic faith in God mediated by Jesus, and a lingering commitment to his person as the one in whom God was encountered. Following Jesus' death, the memory of his ministry, together with the work of the Spirit, are responsible for generating faith in Jesus' Resurrection. When we say, "Jesus is risen," this is an affirmation of what Haight calls "faith-hope," which expresses a religious commitment and trust in God on the part of both the individual and the community. It is pronounced partly on the historical grounds of Jesus' life and ministry but also on the grounds of the experience of the Spirit. Resurrection was, for Jesus, an intimate part of his life and not an add-on or an afterthought.

Wolfhart Pannenberg long ago issued some important cautions regarding overly symbolic interpretations of Jesus' Resurrection. Pannenberg stressed that the early Christians consistently affirm basic continuity between Jesus crucified and Jesus as he appeared to the disciples: it was Jesus who was transformed in the Resurrection. While the appearance stories and the empty tomb stories appear to be different traditions for proclaiming the Resurrection, the early disciples did suppose that the tomb was empty, for the empty tomb provided the necessary conditions for proclaiming the Resurrection of Jesus.

N. T. Wright's Defense of the Resurrection

In recent years a significant minority of scholars, led by the Anglican bishop N. T. Wright, have taken Pannenberg's caveats a step further and have begun to challenge the approach to Jesus' Resurrection powerfully argued by scholars like Schillebeeckx and Haight. Wright and others argue in favor of the basic historicity of the biblical narratives of the Resurrection particularly because of the way it helps to explain why Christianity emerged and took the form that it did. For Wright, early Christians retained a belief in resurrection, but modified it substantially. They also retained belief in a coming Messiah, but redefined that belief around their experience of Jesus. Why and how they redefined first-century Judaism points to the experience of the Resurrection, but not the experience as it is described by Schillebeeckx and Haight.

First, Wright believes that a set of fundamental assumptions corrupt the arguments of Schillebeeckx, Haight, and others who would insist that

Person of Interest

N. T. Wright

Tom Wright, as his friends call him, is one of the most innovative scholars and pastors the Anglican Church (Church of England) has seen in some time. Born in 1948, Bishop Wright earned his doctorate at Oxford University in 1981 and has worked diligently to offer a fresh understanding of the Apostle Paul. He argues against E. P. Sanders and the "New Perspective on Paul," which tries to harmonize or soften the lines that divide the apostle from first-century Palestinian Judaism. Wright has argued instead for a more "edgy" account of Paul that diffuses the anti-Judaism that has dominated the study of Paul over the centuries (by focusing on Romans 9–11) but that also sees in Paul a radical theology of justification through faith (by also focusing on Galatians). Additionally, Wright has played an important role in contemporary historical Jesus research. He has demarcated the limits of the "third quest" for the historical Jesus and has offered an account that has engaged many English-speaking Evangelical Christians in a debate that they had long found alienating. With a style that is combative but engaging, Wright's pastoral and Evangelical sensibilities have won for him a wide audience in England and North America.

resurrection language was merely an opportunistic way of describing the belief that the disciples were forgiven for their failings and given a mission to spread Jesus' message to the world. These scholars assume that the early Christians believed that God had exalted or vindicated Jesus in heaven, and expressed that belief using the language of resurrection. They further assume that the disciples came to believe in Jesus' divinity and then expressed that belief in resurrection language.

Wright argues that those who believe that resurrection language was simply a pious way of describing Jesus' exaltation have missed the point of resurrection language in the first century. As was noted previously, Jews at that time had sophisticated language for honoring the martyrs and describing their resting place as they awaited the resurrection. If, Wright argues, the earliest disciples thought Jesus had simply been lifted up to God (exalted) or had gone to a special place with God, resurrection language would have been out of place. But resurrection language makes sense if the earliest Christians indeed believed that Jesus had been raised from the dead and the tomb was empty. After he ceased to appear, then exaltation language (i.e., "he is seated at the right hand of God"), which we find throughout the New Testament, would make perfect sense to explain the cessation of the appearances but, according to Wright, it cannot account for the assertion that Jesus had been raised from the dead.

Those who argue that belief in the divinity of Jesus was the catalyst for the early Christian belief in the Resurrection likewise run afoul of the evidence, according to Wright. Even if belief in the divinity of Christ was generated as early as the first moments after Jesus' death (there is much evidence to the contrary in the New Testament), there is no logical connection between that affirmation and Resurrection. How would the Resurrection make sense? Wright affirms that belief in the resurrection acted as a catalyst for affirming the divinity and exaltation of Christ, not the reverse.

For Wright, the early Christians would not have regarded the empty tomb as theologically or religiously significant—tomb robbers were commonplace and early Christians did not expect that Jesus would rise from the dead (Gospel passages in which Jesus predicts his resurrection are not stage-one material). As was noted above, Resurrection was a communal, corporate, and even cosmic event within early Judaism. Additionally, a vision of the risen Christ, whether real or imagined, would not have produced talk of resurrection among those who had the vision. Visionary experiences were manifold in first-century Judaism, yet none of these employed resurrection language as the appropriate way to describe such an experience. Consider Acts 12, which narrates the story of an encounter with Peter, who was thought to be dead: those present assumed that they were seeing "his angel" and not the real Peter (Acts 12:15). This simply demonstrates that an encounter with, or a vision of, a dead person did not require a subsequent proclamation of resurrection in first-century Judaism.

Having poked holes in the arguments of Schillebeeckx and others, Wright offers what he thinks is a far more convincing narrative. He finds the best explanation for the Resurrection narratives as well as the best explanation for how and why Christian belief and practice emerged as it did was the early Christian belief that God had raised Jesus from the dead and that this same Jesus appeared to them. For the early Christians, Jesus really died, his tomb was empty, he really did meet with the disciples, but he appeared to them in a transformed state. Though this account of Jesus' Resurrection would never make it out of the basement of the Harvard Divinity School Library where our historians have been sequestered, it nonetheless represents the most probable conclusion for the historian, according to Wright. But the historian can affirm only the empty tomb and the convincing appearances of Jesus, nothing more. The disciples remained cautious, doubtful, and even confused in their experience of the Resurrection: Thomas was not alone!

Conclusion

The Resurrection of Jesus is an historic event; it was an event that changed things. Most obviously it changed the disciples. The same disciples who at the time of Jesus' arrest would rather flee naked into the night (Mark 14:51–52) would subsequently proclaim the name of Jesus and his Resurrection boldly, even though it cost them their lives. The disciples changed their relationship to Judaism, their own religion. Jesus and all of his followers regarded themselves as Jews—they lived as Jews and prayed as Jews. Yet because of Jesus' Resurrection they began to redefine Judaism in new ways. This redefinition, these new practices, had roots in the life of Jesus, but the new practices had power and became definitive for the community through the power of the Resurrection. To cite one practical example, this meant worship on the first day of the week rather than, or in addition to, worship on the seventh (Sabbath) day. These disciples did not just say that God had loved Jesus and took him to heaven. Rather, God had vindicated him in a totally unexpected way, but a way that resonated with Israel's hope. The Resurrection was not an afterthought; it was meaningful only in conjunction with his life. The power of Jesus' resurrection to transform lives, to make God's love available, is only disclosed and made effective to the extent that it is read through the life of Jesus, and it is to this that the evangelists bear witness in their accounts of the Resurrection.

Questions for Understanding

1. Describe the Deuteronomistic approach to life after death.

2. Explain the significance of the Maccabean crisis for the development of a theology of Resurrection.

3. Describe the spectrum of positions on the afterlife in first-century Judaism.

4. The New Testament affirms that Jesus "was raised" and "was seen." Describe how these phrases use analogies to describe the Resurrection and the appearances of Jesus.

5. Describe the position articulated by Schillebeeckx and Haight on the Resurrection of Jesus. What are the merits of this approach? What are some of the problems?

6. How does N. T. Wright challenge the approach of Schillebeeckx and Haight? Do you find any merit in Wright's approach? Explain.

Questions for Reflection

1. In the middle of the last century, the great Israeli archaeologist Eleazar Sukenik uncovered an ossuary (a box used to bury the bones of a deceased person) bearing the inscription "Jesus son of Joseph." It was

subsequently shown to be a forgery. If the ossuary had been authentic, would this nullify Christian faith? Explain.

2. Although Church law now permits it, for a long time cremation was not permitted in the Catholic Church because it was seen as a denial of the Christian hope for resurrection. If Christians proclaim a hope for future resurrection, is allowing cremation inconsistent? Explain. Would you feel comfortable with cremating the remains of your spouse, child, or family member?

3. It was apparent in this chapter that apocalyptic eschatology was heavily political in its outlook. Many Christians in our day, particularly in the western world, have abandoned the apocalyptic worldview that played such an important role in the New Testament. Has the abandonment of apocalyptic eschatology separated Christians from the world of politics? Why is it that the most obviously political Christians in the United States are those who hold tenaciously to an apocalyptic outlook? Should Christians become more politically active? How?

Endnotes

1 SBL definition emended by David Hellholm, "The Problem of Apocalyptic Genre and the Apocalypse of John," in A. Y. Collins, ed., *Early Christian Apocalypticism: Genre and Social Setting*, Semeia 36 (Decatur, GA: Scholars Press, 1986), 27.

2 Alan Segal, *Life After Death: A History of the Afterlife in Western Religion* (New York: Doubleday, 2004), 378.

3 Translation taken from R. H. Charles, *The Apocrypha and Pseudepigrapha of the Old Testament* (Oxford: Clarendon, 1913).

4 N. T. Wright, *The Resurrection of the Son of God* (Minneapolis: Fortress, 2003), 201.

5 2 Maccabees 7:11.

6 N. T. Wright challenges this by appealing to the case of James and Paul, both of whom were not among Jesus' followers and both of whom "saw" the risen Christ (1 Corinthians 15:7–8).

7 For what follows, see Edward Shillebeeckx, *Jesus: An Experiment in Christology*, trans. Hubert Hoskins (New York: Seabury Press, 1979), 320–97.

8 Roger Haight, *Jesus, Symbol of God* (New York: Orbis, 1999), 126. The material that follows is presented in ibid., chapter 5.

New Testament Christologies

Most Jews of the first century would have grown up hearing and praying the **Shema** (Deuteronomy 6:4–9), a prayer that boldly affirmed Israel's belief in one God. It begins: "Hear (*shema*) O Israel! The Lord [YHWH] is God, the Lord [YHWH] alone." This affirmation was central to the life of first-century Jews, including Jesus. Jewish men were accustomed to using leather straps to bind small boxes containing this prayer (*phylacteries* in Greek; see Exodus 13:9,16, Deuteronomy 11:18, and Matthew 23:5) on their foreheads and left arm as they prayed. Even today, on the doorposts of many Jewish houses are small cylindrical containers (called *mezuzah* in Hebrew) with the text of the *Shema* inside. Given these rituals reinforcing the Jewish commitment to the oneness of YHWH, it would be ridiculous and nonsensical for Jesus to show up in a first-century synagogue and say, "Hi, I'm YHWH." Yet in the eyes of the earliest Christians, the power of the Resurrection (interpreted through the life and ministry of Jesus) accomplished what many Jews of the time believed that YHWH would do for Israel: in the Resurrection they experienced God's presence with them, renewing their covenant relationship, empowering them in the face of oppression, and saving them from evil and destruction. The desire of Christians to speak about YHWH's presence in Jesus seemed to be frustrated by the unambiguous affirmation of YHWH's oneness in the *Shema*. However, Jewish thought had also long allowed speculation about how God's power might be experienced in the world. We will see in this chapter that first-century Jewish thought explored and expanded its own Scriptures and flourished under the influence of Greek ideas to articulate notions of YHWH's Word and Wisdom. These categories were ready at hand for early Christians to articulate the relationship between Jesus and YHWH in a way that was in keeping with Jewish belief.

The development of Christology in the New Testament—the attempt to articulate the religious significance of Jesus—involves the interplay of several factors: insight born of the resurrection experience, the memory tradition of Jesus' life and ministry, developments within apocalyptic Judaism, and tensions with the limits of Jewish monotheism. The results of this interplay yield profound yet somewhat uneven Christologies. We should be careful, therefore, about demanding full and clear doctrinal orthodoxy from the New Testament when such clarity was the product of subsequent generations. This does not mean that the New Testament offers us a Christology that is less than orthodox! All Christian interpretations of Jesus' religious significance rest on Scripture as the norm or guide for faith, but that faith has developed through time and circumstance to reach a state of formal clarity. As we shall see in later chapters, even that formal clarity demands further exploration.

The Growth of New Testament Christology: Titles, Roles, and Patterns

The Christology of the New Testament makes use of a variety of titles or roles that had been circulating within first-century Judaism to make sense of Jesus. First, let's clarify what is meant by "title," "role," and "pattern."

Titles are like proper names; they are characters in the story of Israel and were used by early Christians to confess their faith in Jesus. Two obvious examples include **Lord** (e.g., Philippians 2:11), used as a circumlocution for the divine name (YHWH), and **Messiah** (Greek *christos*, Christ; e.g., Matthew 16:16). A role, on the other hand, is more of a job description. For example, the Letter to the Hebrews identifies Jesus as "a great high priest" (4:14). To call Jesus a great high priest is to describe a manner in which he functions or a role he performs, and was never used as a profession of faith in early Christian prayer or worship.

New Testament Christology situates these titles and roles into narrative, sequential, or chronological patterns, thereby privileging certain moments that point to the identity and meaning of Jesus. For example, the title Lord was often associated with the exaltation of Jesus (e.g., Philippians 2:11) and not commonly associated with his life and ministry. The reader should be aware, however, that the relationship between these titles, roles, and patterns are not always stable; titles and roles overlap, and christological patterns can employ a variety of titles. In what follows, some basic aspects of New Testament Christology will be discussed using titles, roles, and patterns. All of this is somewhat artificial and certainly not part of the thinking of the early church as it wrestled with language about Jesus, but it may prove helpful for gaining an understanding of the christological language used in the New Testament.

As chapter 2 demonstrated, Jesus himself appears to be somewhat uncomfortable with self-description in the gospel tradition, since any such attempt might result in a misunderstanding of his ministry. If we can talk about a "Christology of Jesus" as the starting point for a discussion of New Testament Christology in general, then we must begin with Jesus' self-designation as **Son of Man**.

The Son of Man is a notoriously complex topic in New Testament Christology and historical Jesus research.[1] It is a self-designation, or self-description, often used by Jesus but not used by others to refer to Jesus (for a possible exception see Acts 7:56). The enigmatic phrase "son of man" (*bar nasha* in Aramaic) can be understood in at least three senses: (1) the indefinite sense (a human being or mortal, used thus throughout the book of Ezekiel), (2) the generic sense (a person in my position), and (3) the eschatological sense (referring to a specific eschatological figure prominent in the literature of Jesus' time). It appears as though Jesus used the phrase in the eschatological sense and connected it to his role as "Suffering Servant of YHWH," an enigmatic figure who would manifest YHWH's glory through suffering. The figure of the Son of Man is found in Scripture in Daniel 7:13, but also in non-canonical books of Jesus' time, such as *1 Enoch*. The Son of Man was interpreted by some Jews of the first century as a key figure in the story of Israel, a figure who vindicates YHWH's fidelity toward Israel and his judgment against the wicked. But the Son of Man, like Isaiah's Suffering Servant, is probably best understood corporately as a figure representative of righteous Israelites as a group, not an individual. In fact, the application of this role to an individual is a unique feature of Jesus' preaching and the preaching of the early church.

The Son of Man in both early Judaism and within early Christian writings is a figure who points to the future. When Jesus identifies himself with the Son of Man he often does so in regard to some future event, sometimes his suffering (as in Mark) but most often his coming vindication: "you will see the Son of Man seated at the right hand of the Power and coming with the clouds of heaven" (Mark 14:62). This passage also signals the importance of Psalm 110:1 for New Testament Christology ("The LORD says to you, my lord: 'Take your throne at my right hand, while I make your enemies your footstool'"). Through the Resurrection Jesus has been exalted to God's right hand, the place of intimacy, happiness, and power. In the future, he will come on the clouds as the vindicated Son of Man to execute judgment against the faithless and the unjust and to vindicate the righteous faithful. This orientation toward the future is an important pattern in New Testament Christology and often closely associated with the struggle to identify Jesus as the Messiah.

The title Messiah provides us with an appropriate point of transition from a "Christology of Jesus" to a Christology of the early church. It is apparent that Jesus himself had an ambivalent attitude toward the title Messiah, or "anointed one." It was customary in the ancient Near East to anoint people as they assumed important new positions in the community (king, priest, and prophet). Anointing had a wide range of meanings, but usually it served as a marking of divine protection, health, and mission. The term *messiah* gradually became associated with the kings of Judah, though not exclusively. Following the Babylonian Exile (586 BCE–539 BCE) it began to be used in conjunction with Israel's hope of future restoration and deliverance from oppression. While there was no uniform set of expectations concerning a messiah figure in first-century Judaism, his role generally included achievements like the inauguration of a new age, punishment of the wicked, general resurrection of the dead, defeat of Gentile (non-Jewish) oppressors, purification of the temple, and reestablishment of the Davidic monarchy. When viewed in this light, the applicability of the title Christ or Messiah to Jesus seems curious—Jesus did not envision himself as the one who would bring defeat to Israel's political enemies or vindicate the violent nationalism that often characterized first-century Palestine. Yet Jesus did identify himself with messianic expectations through a variety of symbolic actions and provocative pronouncements. In light of such statements, the earliest Christians identified Jesus as Messiah, even though Jesus had not performed many of the actions (performed the role) that many Jews in the first century expected of the Messiah. The earliest Christians, however, oriented themselves toward a future when Jesus would be vindicated as Messiah and perform the basic functions expected of that role. This future event was called the **Parousia**.

The Greek word *parousia* was often used to describe the visit of the emperor. One can imagine the joy—and horror—such a visitation might evoke in a particular town: those who were "good servants" of the empire might expect rewards and accolades, while those who were poor administrators would be fearful about the repercussions of such a visit. The word thus became an effective image for the apocalyptic expectations that played an important role in early Christianity; Jesus at his parousia would exercise his Lordship over all and execute judgment against evildoers. The expectation of the parousia, or second coming of Christ, effectively bridged the early Christian experience of Jesus as decisive for Israel's future and the Jewish expectation of final judgment and resurrection. The parousia would finally and definitively inaugurate the kingdom that Jesus had proclaimed as breaking into the world in his day, and thus would bring about the defeat of evil and the resurrection of the dead, thereby vindicating Jesus' role as Messiah. This future vindication contrasts with the earthly ministry of Jesus in which he is depicted as a lowly servant. The christological pattern that shifts between these two stages—first lowly, then exalted—is often called "two-step Christology."

Two-step Christology is thought to be the christological pattern characteristic of the early part of stage two, the decades immediately after the death and Resurrection of Jesus. In the letters of Paul, where we find evidence of the earliest Christology, there seems to emerge a diversity of Christologies, while in the Gospels Jesus is depicted as Lord and Messiah at earlier and earlier points along a time line. Raymond Brown used the expression **christological moment** to refer to scenes taken from the life and ministry of Jesus that became the vehicle for the expression of a post-resurrectional Christology.[2] Jesus' Lordship, recognized by his disciples

Some Titles, Roles, and Patterns in New Testament Christology

Term	Title	Role	Description
Christ / Messiah	x	x	Jesus vindicates Israel over and against the forces of evil and oppression; he fulfills the promises YHWH made to Israel through David and to the prophets.
High Priest		x	Jesus is able to offer the definitive sacrifice of himself; this sacrifice removes the sin of the faithful so that there is no further need of sacrifice.
Lord	x		Jesus has affected a union between YHWH and Israel; sin is destroyed.
Son of God	x	x	Jesus brings about the redemption of Israel from its period of oppression and servitude.
Son of Man		x	Jesus, through his suffering, will vindicate YHWH and act as cosmic judge, condemning the wicked and blessing the righteous.
Son of David	x	x	Like "messiah" this title signifies the continuity of Jesus with the promises made by YHWH through the prophets; Jesus is viewed as a figure of national hope for restoration and a sign of divine protection against oppression.
Suffering Servant		x	Through his suffering, Jesus brings to a close the era of Israel's sinfulness and separation from YHWH; the nation can find peace and union with God.
Word-Wisdom		x	YHWH's Word creates, destroys, judges, and preserves the universe, yet God's Word also dwells with Israel in the Torah, and now, through the teaching and person of Jesus.

Some Titles, Roles, and Patterns in New Testament Christology *(continued)*

Pattern	Titles and Roles Associated with this Pattern	Examples	Description
Parousia Christology	Lord, Christ, Son of Man	Acts 3:19–21; 1 Corinthians 16:22	At a point in the near future, Jesus will come in glory and power to judge the living and the dead and definitively inaugurate God's rule on earth.
Resurrection-Exaltation Christology	Lord, Christ, Son of God	Philippians 2:1–11; Acts 13:33	The Resurrection and the exaltation of Jesus through the suffering and humiliation he had undergone
Ministry Christology	Christ, Son of God, Son of Man, Suffering Servant, Lord	Mark 1:11	Moments in the life and ministry of Jesus provide glimpses of Jesus' true identity as he serves the marginalized, encounters resistance and hatred, and finally suffers to bring about the victory for God and God's people over sin and death.
Preexistent Christology	Lord, Word, Wisdom	1 Corinthians 10:4; Colossians 1:15–20; John 1:1–14	From the very origins of the universe and throughout the history of Israel, God's Wisdom, or God's Word, dwelt in the world and guided Israel; in Jesus, the Word of God has come to instruct and guide Israel to union with God.

in the Resurrection, is transferred to various points in the life of Jesus. These points, or moments, tend to emerge earlier in the narrative of Jesus in the progressive development of the New Testament. For example, the earliest Gospel, Mark, uses the scene of Jesus' baptism as an inaugural christological moment in the life of Jesus. But in Matthew and Luke, their birth or infancy narratives are the key early christological moments. This developmental pattern, however, should be read with caution; as we shall see in the case of some of the material from Paul's letters, the pattern is far from neat.

One of the more problematic titles for beginning students of theology is **Son of God**, often used to signify important christological moments (e.g., Mark 15:39). Most modern Christians immediately think of the doctrine of the Trinity (that God is three persons in one divine substance—Father, Son, and Spirit). But students should be cautious about reading late doctrinal developments back into the biblical texts, and since the doctrine of the Trinity is not defined until the fourth century CE, it ought not be read into the pages of the New Testament. On the other hand, having made a case for historical modesty about the development of Christian doctrine, we should not pretend that such a doctrine emerged out of a vacuum. Rather, these doctrinal developments have their roots in the witness of Scripture and the beliefs of the early church. We must be attentive to the way doctrinal development takes place: as a movement from experience, to question, to formal doctrinal statements. In the New Testament, we are at the point of experience and question; we have not yet arrived at formal doctrinal statements.

In the Old Testament the son of God is a role rather than a title. On occasion it designates angels, as in the case of Job 1:6 where even "[the] Satan" (Hebrew for "the adversary") is described as a son of God. In the Old Testament the people of Israel collectively or individually are designated as son(s) of God. Since the king could be called God's son, some have thought that this title may have come to be associated with the coming messiah, but even the Qumran literature does not unambiguously support this view. The dominant view in the Old Testament is that a son of God was someone who had received a God-given task. As such, the title is applied to Jesus to signify his unique God-given task: redemption. In the Fourth Gospel, as in many early Christian writings, the uniqueness of Jesus' task is emphasized when Jesus is called "the only begotten Son" *(monogenēs)*. But it would be a mistake to conceive of the uniqueness of Jesus' relationship with the Father simply in terms of mission or function. Rather, in the New Testament, the title of Jesus as Son reflects the special intimacy Jesus has with the Father and which, in his redemptive mission, he makes available to those who have faith: as we cry out to God we too call God *Abba* (Galatians 4:4–6). So while not Trinitarian per se, the title Son of God expresses the fundamental intimacy between Jesus and his Father that would eventually provide the foundation for the doctrine of the Trinity.

The title, roles, and patterns that comprise New Testament Christology are only partially understood when abstracted from the literature of the New Testament. In what follows, the preliminary considerations regarding New Testament Christology neatly presented above are given their proper form within their respective literary contexts. In that context Christology becomes much more fluid and complex but also more powerful and more precisely connected to the life of the early Christian community.

Christology in Paul

It is one of the strange facts of New Testament history that the earliest theological reflections on Jesus comes to us by way of a man who never knew Jesus personally during his lifetime. Paul of Tarsus was, by all accounts, a persecutor of the church who subsequently had a revelatory experience of the risen Christ, which he insisted was qualitatively the same as the experience of those who had been close to Jesus during his lifetime (1 Corinthians 15:1–11). His letters, while not christological essays, stand as important witnesses to the theological developments described above.

Paul's letters are highly occasional pieces; they do not offer a systematic presentation of his thought, but address questions in an ad hoc fashion. Nevertheless, one can piece together a pretty good idea of Paul's doctrine concerning Christ. For Paul, the religious significance of Christ can only be gained through reading his story in conjunction with the story of Israel. Yet, for Paul, the gospel is at the same time universal—it is meant first for the Jews and then for the Gentiles. God's love and fidelity, YHWH's *chesed*, are at the heart of the plan of salvation. This plan of salvation is historical; it unfolds through history. The history in which God acts to save humanity falls into three basic periods: Adam to Moses, Moses to the Messiah, and from the Messiah to the end of time. God's plan is not restricted to humanity, but encompasses the entire cosmos so as to reconcile all creation to God in Christ.

Paul freely makes use of christological titles to indicate the place of Christ in God's plan of salvation. Paul often uses "the Son" to designate

Person of Interest

Paul

Paul has always been a controversial figure. During his lifetime he was in conflict with other "apostles" and various groups within the Christian church (Galatians 1–2). After all, Paul had not known Jesus, but was a latecomer to the Christian movement. He was born in the Greek city of Tarsus in what is now southern Turkey, probably in the first century CE. His parents were Jewish, though he, like the other citizens of his hometown, all enjoyed the special status of Roman citizenship (Acts 22:25–29; 23:27) and were thus also thoroughly imbued with Greco-Roman culture. His upbringing with one foot in the world of Greek thought and the other in the world of Judaism is reflected in his two names—one Jewish (Saul) and the other Greek (Paul). Paul became an ardent supporter of the Pharisaic movement and even a persecutor of Christians (Acts 7:58, 22:20). Then he underwent a dramatic conversion, or call, which is famously narrated in Acts 9:1–19. There Paul was said to be on "the road to Damascus" when he encountered the risen Christ. The years following his call are somewhat murky. He seems to have spent time in "Arabia," Damascus, his home in Tarsus, and even made a brief visit to Jerusalem. He moved into the spotlight when he was sent to Antioch with Barnabas. The church at Antioch, which had for some time supported a community of both Jewish and Gentile Christians, commissioned Paul and Barnabas to spread the gospel among the Gentiles. Their success stirred many Jewish Christians from Jerusalem to question Paul's motivation, his authority, and his orthodoxy. The mission of inclusion, however, won the day. At the so-called Council of Jerusalem (49 CE; Gal 2:1–10, Acts15:6–21) the early church decided that circumcision was not required for Gentile Christians to enter the Christian church. Paul's martyrdom in Rome is commemorated by the famous basilica "St. Paul Outside the Walls."

the preexistence of Jesus, that period before his birth when Jesus existed with God in heaven. As already noted, in the Old Testament a son of God was someone who had received a God-given task. For Paul, God's Son is given the task of redemption by the Father and sent forth to earth to carry out that task.

"The Christ" was used in conjunction with Israel's hope of future restoration and deliverance. With this title Paul designates Jesus as the fulfillment of those hopes. In fact, Paul is so enamored with this title that it practically becomes a second name for Jesus: Jesus Christ, or Christ Jesus.

It signifies a re-understanding of God's plan for the restoration of Israel and the redemption of the Gentiles.

"Lord" is, for Paul, a way of referring to the glorified risen Christ's dominion over creation won through his obedience and death. When Paul calls Jesus "Lord," he expresses the belief that Christ was due the same worship and honor as God while always remaining distinct as the Son. One can easily see the potential danger here: Jesus appears to be equal to God in some sense. While Paul and the early church have not really violated the monotheism of the *Shema*, one can imagine what non-Christian Jews of the time thought when they heard Christians making such bold statements about the preexistence of Jesus as God's Son and his exaltation at God's right hand.

Two important poetic sections from Paul's letters are of considerable interest for addressing the question of Christ's preexistence. The first of these is the hymn in Philippians 2:6–11. It speaks of Christ,

> who, though he was in the form of God, did not regard equality with God something to be grasped. Rather, he emptied himself, taking the form of a slave, coming in human likeness; and found human in appearance, he humbled himself, becoming obedient to death, even death on a cross. Because of this, God greatly exalted him and bestowed on him the name that is above every name, that at the name of Jesus every knee should bend, of those in heaven and on earth and under the earth, and every tongue confess that Jesus Christ is Lord, to the glory of God the Father.

The hymn is to the exalted Christ, who is proclaimed Lord upon his exaltation, his taking a place at the right hand of God (Psalm 110). In the Philippians hymn Christ's exaltation came about because of his self-emptying (Greek *kenōsis*) to be born as a human being and his obedience as a human being to the point of a humiliating death.

The basic pattern of the Philippians hymn is obvious enough—descent and ascent, emptying and exaltation—but some major christological issues are signaled in the passage as well. The opening sentence envisions the preexistent Christ (i.e., before he was born) existing "in the form of God" (*en morphē theou*). What does that mean? And what does it mean to say that "he did not consider equality with God something to be grasped at" *(ouch harpagmon hēgēsato to einai isa theō)*? This passage has perplexed scholars for a long time. Some suggest that this passage refers to early Christian belief in the full divinity of Christ. Christ being "in the form of God" means he is God. But this phrase is not as simple and straightforward as it appears. After all, Adam and Eve are created in the image and likeness of God, yet we would not be inclined to say they are equal with God. Other scholars contend that Christ is the preexistent heavenly man who empties himself out of humility but is rewarded with the divine name (Lord) because of his obedience to God. In other words, he is rewarded with the divine prerogatives that Adam and Eve sought on their own (Genesis 3:5). It is noteworthy that Paul uses this hymn in a context where he reminds the Philippians that they are to have the mind of Christ, a humble mind (Philippians 2:1–5). There are many other issues and a wide variety of opinions on the interpretation of the Philippians hymn, but suffice it to say that more christological questions are raised in this passage than are answered.

Kenōsis and Buddhism

The contemporary world has become increasingly conscious of its religious diversity, and that diversity has helped to create both conflict and dialogue between religious traditions. Christianity and Buddhism have sustained a substantial dialogue for many decades. Two prominent figures who bear witness to the fruitfulness of this dialogue are the Buddhist monk Tich Nat Han and the late Christian monk Thomas Merton, OCSO, both of whom have produced numerous works that testify to common convictions about the nature of human existence and proper moral and spiritual responses to a world dominated by violence. In recent years other scholars have engaged in substantial dialogue (e.g., John Cobb and Masao Abe). Another important area of common exploration has emerged in conjunction with the Buddhist doctrine of *sunyata*, or the inherent emptiness of existence. The doctrine of *sunyata*

was advanced by the Buddhist scholar Najarguna in response to certain developments within early Buddhism. He envisioned it as a faithful recovery of the Buddha's own teaching on the three marks or qualities of reality *(laksanas)*. All reality is (1) *anitya* (all things in existence are transitory or passing), (2) *duhkha* (since all things are transitory, no thing really satisfies; thus, reality is unsatisfactory), and (3) *anatman* (just like all aspects of existence, the self is *anitya*; it follows that there is no self, no *atman*). Such an account of reality, on the face of it, contradicts the Christian understanding of creation and the affirmation of creation in the incarnation. In his popular book *Crossing the Threshold of Hope* (San Francisco: Harper Collins, 1994), the late Holy Father, Pope John Paul II gave voice to Christian concerns about the apparent contradictions between Christian and Buddhist understandings of the created

Kenōsis and Buddhism *(continued)*

world. He was criticized by many—including a number of Christian scholars—who thought that he did not give Buddhist doctrine its due. Through dialogue over the past several decades, some Buddhists and Christians have seized on Paul's Letter to the Philippians, particularly the hymn in chapter 2, as an important point of convergence between the two traditions. In that hymn, Paul asks the Philippians to adopt the mind of Christ, who "emptied himself" and thereby was exalted. The Greek work for "self-emptying" in this context is *kenōsis.* Some Christian theologians have begun to explore the possible similarities between Paul's moral exhortation to the Philippians and the Buddhist doctrine of the inherent emptiness of existence and its corollary doctrine of nonattachment to the transitory world. The goal of the Buddhist "path" is realized not by trying to attain a comprehensive view of reality, which has been the concern of Christian theologians, but by using what Buddhists call "right understanding" to abandon all "view-making" or reality-making habits of the mind. The point is to let reality be and for the human person to be unattached, to resist the desire to control and dominate. This metaphysics is anti-metaphysical but still profoundly moral.

Another key text in the Pauline literature is a hymn found in the Letter to the Colossians 1:15–20. Many scholars debate whether Paul actually wrote this letter, but we are not concerned here with the precise author of the text but with its Christology. The hymn reads as follows:

> He is the image of the invisible God, the firstborn of all creation. For in him were created all things in heaven and on earth, the visible and the invisible, whether thrones or dominions or principalities or powers; all things were created through him and for him. He is before all things, and in him all things hold together. He is the head of the body, the church. He is the beginning, the firstborn from the dead, that in all things he himself might be preeminent. For in him all the fullness was pleased to dwell, and through him to reconcile all things for him, making peace by the blood of his cross (through him), whether those on earth or those in heaven.

As in the Philippians hymn, this passage raises the question, what does "image of God" mean here? Once again, it is obvious that the hymn regards Christ as present at the creation of the universe, and all creation is sustained in existence through him. This thematic connection of Christ with creation will prove fruitful for further elaboration on the precise relationship between the Son and God as the first century comes to a close.

Christology in Paul bears witness to the ferment and complexity of the first decades of the Christian church. On the one hand, Paul seems to present a Christology that is focused on the future and Christ's parousia, but this pattern is challenged by his inclusion of material like the Philippians hymn, which present a christological pattern that envisions Christ as preexistent. In fact, the hymns in Philippians and Colossians resonate strongly with the Christology of the latest Gospel account, John (see section below). Paul, therefore, troubles any account of New Testament Christology that posits a neat linear path of development either through titles or patterns.

Christology in the Synoptic Gospels

The study of New Testament Christology, particularly in the synoptic Gospels, has moved away from an emphasis on titles and patterns to explore the distinctive christological portraits offered in the New Testament. The previous discussion of roles, titles, and patterns provides important background for understanding the Christology of the evangelists. Each of the evangelists acts as an artist, creating a distinctive portrait of Christ, though the portrait is made with words instead of paint. These portraits are designed to speak to a particular audience and to make the message of Christ's saving power apparent to those who hear the gospel.

The Gospel of Mark

Mark identifies Jesus as the Messiah, the Son of God, and the Son of Man, titles with which the reader is now somewhat familiar. But Mark thoroughly redefines these titles in light of Jesus' suffering and death. His death casts a shadow over the entire Gospel and causes the disciples to misunderstand and fail in their attempts to follow Jesus.

For Mark, the proclamation of the kingdom of God provides the framework for a presentation of a complex interplay between Christology and discipleship. "The kingdom of God" is a phrase by which Israel gave expression to its hope that God would "break through" and rule the world definitively. Jesus' own life is a proleptic, or anticipatory, realization of the kingdom. The climax of Jesus' life is his suffering and death.

This climax provides the interpretive key for his teaching and healing. Jesus' identity as Messiah is only realized at his death. This is the meaning of the so-called messianic secret in Mark. The disciples are generally depicted in the first part of the Gospel (through 8:27) as examples to be emulated. In the second half of the Gospel, they appear in a less than favorable light. In the end, the real disciple must imitate Jesus, whose identity and mission are revealed in his suffering and death (Mark 15:39). Failure to imitate Jesus is a rejection of Jesus. One of the most remarkable scenes in Mark is found in Mark 14:51–52, where a young man observes the arrest of Jesus from a distance. All of Jesus' friends have left him and fled. When this young man is discovered by the authorities, they try to arrest him only to find that the man is so desperate to escape suffering with Jesus that he runs out of his clothes and flees naked into the night! The failure of the disciples, particularly their refusal to suffer, and Jesus' religious self-definition as the suffering Son of Man stand in sharp contrast in Mark.

This disturbing portrait of Jesus and his disciples probably emerged from the Christian community at Rome shortly after the emperor Nero began a localized but brutal persecution.[3] Mark's emphasis on suffering and the failure of the disciples no doubt reflects aspects of Jesus' own ministry, but Mark's Christology of suffering is as much the product of the early church's concern to respond to the call of Jesus within its own circumstances.

The Gospel of Matthew

Matthew's Gospel is also framed by conflict, but the strife here is not with the Roman Empire; rather, it involves the relationship between the early Christian community and its relationship to Judaism. Many would argue that in this context it is anachronistic to talk about "Judaism" and "Christianity" as two different communities or religions since such a rigid distinction did not develop until the second century CE. Increasingly scholars have argued that Matthew understood himself and his community as a viable expression of Judaism in competition with other expressions of Judaism in the first century—another form of what has come to be called **middle Judaism**.[4] Others, however, would contend that the inclusion of Gentiles and emphasis on the messiahship of Jesus moved the Christian community of Matthew further and further outside of incipient "normative Judaism" toward the end of the first and into the second and third centuries. Whatever one's conclusions about the relationship of Matthew's community to first-century Judaism(s), it is evident from the text that a rift has developed between Matthew and some important elements within Judaism, and this rift has important implications for reading the Gospel and understanding its Christology.

The Christology of Matthew's Gospel is elegantly presented in summary fashion in the first two chapters. These chapters, often called an infancy

The Parting of Ways: Christianity and Judaism

Christians commonly read the New Testament with the assumption that Christianity and Judaism are two different religions and were understood as such from the time of Jesus. Yet history does not bear out such an assumption. Actually the parting of ways between Christianity and Judaism was a complex process.

Scholars vary in their interpretations of how and when the split between Judaism and Christianity occurred. Some scholars would place the split in the time of Paul, when Gentiles started to enter into the Christian community without having to observe the Mosaic (Jewish) law. Other scholars argue that not until at least the end of the second century CE is there a definitive break between Christians and Jews. In either case, during Jesus' lifetime and immediately thereafter there was no question about Christianity as a distinct religion. It was surely a distinct movement and certainly controversial, but so were many expressions of Judaism. The Pharisaic movement was not welcome everywhere, and the Essenes were viewed as a marginal group and perhaps as dangerous by the aristocracy in Jerusalem, but they were no less Jewish for that.

Jesus himself operated within the bounds of Jewish thought and practice. His controversies with established teachers within Judaism, though highly embellished or even invented by the early Christians,

was par for the course in Jewish circles. Arguing a point of Torah is a sign of respect for Torah and allegiance to the covenant—which might raise the question whether arguments about God, Christ, and morals are viewed as a sign of respect within contemporary Christianity. Jesus challenged Jewish violence and sectarianism, and this certainly would have annoyed many people in first-century Palestine, but it was hardly a denial of Judaism. Moreover, Paul's insistence on grace and faith rather than Torah observance ("works of the law") is a reformulation of the basic covenantal formula—after all, Torah was a gift (grace) from God.

The differentiation between Judaism and early Christianity, the parting of ways, was accelerated by the destruction of the temple in Jerusalem in 70 CE. Following that event Judaism began a long process of transformation into a more homogenous or normative religious tradition. The diversity that had characterized it earlier in the first century began to give way under the pressure of political and cultural circumstances. This process continued well into the second and third centuries CE, and while alternative expressions of Judaism continued in some ways, modern Judaism began to form out of what many scholars call the middle Judaism that existed after the destruction of the temple.

narrative, tell the story of Jesus' birth. In some ways the story acts like a theological overture to the rest of the Gospel. Like a musical piece at the start of a play or opera, the overture sets the mood and offers the audience some important musical signals for interpreting the story. In Matthew, the evangelist begins with a ***toledot***, a list of generations. This is a common device for linking seemingly disparate stories, particularly in Genesis (see Genesis 5, where the stories of Adam and Noah are connected in this way). Matthew traces the lineage of Jesus from Abraham to David, through the kings of Judah, down to Jesus. The genealogy concludes with a note on its perfect symmetry: fourteen generations from Abraham to David, fourteen from David to the Babylonian Exile, and fourteen to the birth of Jesus. It is no coincidence that the numerical value of David's name was fourteen—note that letters were used to represent numerical values in the ancient Roman world; Arabic numerals arrived much later. Jesus, therefore, is born at the perfect time; but when the king of the Jews (Herod the Great) learned of this auspicious birth, he arranged to have the child killed. Matthew deftly weaves his narrative so that Herod is foiled by the three astrologers *(magoi)* who, without the aid of the Scriptures and having only the stars to guide them, are able to locate the messianic child and worship him with symbolic gifts. These Gentiles respond to the Jewish Messiah while the officials that rule Jerusalem see Jesus as a threat to be destroyed.

Matthew's infancy narrative presents Jesus as the fulfillment of Israel's messianic hopes, but his arrival also lays bare the fact that many who had waited for the Messiah were unprepared to welcome him and unable to respond to his call to conversion and repentance. Matthew depicts Jesus as the royal, eschatological, and covenantal agent of God in human history, a portrait that unfolds throughout the course of the Gospel.

The Gospel of Luke

Luke's historical and social context is not defined by strife, but by circumstances that require the Gospel to adopt an apologetic tone. It seems that Luke's audience is composed mainly of Gentiles, who are concerned with two important questions. The first is, what does a Jewish Messiah have to do with the salvation of Gentiles? In other words, how can a religious figure from a tradition so apparently suspicious of foreigners be the way of salvation for these outsiders? Luke responds by pointing out that Jesus is the friend of the outsider, the neglected, and the weak. The marginalized become the focus of Jesus' proclamation to an extent not found in the other Gospels, and this proves to be the key for understanding the Gentile mission. The second question involves the destruction of Jerusalem which, coupled with the rejection of the Christian message by most Jews, seemed to suggest that God had abandoned the covenant with Israel. But how can this God be trusted if he can break his covenant? Isn't God faithful to the promises made to Israel? Luke's response emphasizes the continuity of the covenant Jesus announces and the covenant between YHWH and the people of Israel. This continuity with the Old Testament is essential for Luke's overall argument: God is faithful to his promises.

The infancy narrative in Luke is remarkable, especially when compared to Matthew's version. First, when one compares the genealogies in each Gospel one notices at least two important differences: Luke traces Jesus' ancestry back to Adam, all humanity's common ancestor, and to David, but through a line that does not include any of the kings of Judah (Luke 3:28–31; cf. Matthew 1:6–11). Luke thus portrays Jesus as a commoner like everyone else, universally identified. This theme of universalism is accentuated by Luke's propensity to have socially marginalized figures—like a young virgin and shepherds—figure prominently in the birth story. These figures attend to the advent of Jesus as the first to hear and respond to the gospel, for he is their Savior and has come to despoil the rich and the mighty (Luke 1:51–53, 6:20–26).

Luke portrays Jesus, however, not simply as a social contrarian, but as one led by the Spirit, whose actions are informed by a deep prayerfulness (e.g., 11:1) and intimacy with God. It is out of this intimacy with God that Jesus reaches out to those on the margins, particularly women. Perhaps the most poignant example of this is the familiar story of the woman who interrupts a meal at the house of Simon the Pharisee by anointing and kissing Jesus (a similar story is found in Matthew and Mark). The woman is described as a "sinner," but we are not told what sin she has committed. Simon, the host, grows increasingly uncomfortable and annoyed with the extravagance of her gesture. Jesus' response emphasizes the workings of forgiveness: her love is great because her sin was great. Luke's special source collection (L) also emphasizes this theme, particularly his parables. The familiar example story of the good Samaritan depicts Jesus as offering a

Gospel Portraits of Jesus: For Particular Audiences

Evangelist	Approximate Date	Circumstances of the Evangelist	Christological Portrait
Mark	Around 70 CE	Rome The emperor Nero, for political and economic reasons, had set fire to part of the city of Rome (or at least permitted the fires to go unchecked). People blamed Nero for the destruction, and he in turn accused the Christians (they were easy scapegoats). The resulting persecutions exposed the faith of many Roman Christians as shallow. Mark is written to this suffering church in the years following.	The climax of Jesus' life is his suffering and death. This climax provides the interpretive key for his teaching and healing. Jesus' identity as Messiah is only realized at his death (Mark 15:39), the so-called messianic secret. The disciples are depicted in the first part of the Gospel (through 8:27) as examples to be emulated. In the second half they are depicted in a less-favorable light. In the end, the real disciple must imitate Jesus.
Matthew	Around 85 CE	Syria-Palestine The Gospel seems to reflect a state of turmoil within Jewish Christianity that would be characteristic of the period in which the rabbis gathered in Jamnia and began to reform Judaism after the destruction of the temple. In this reformation a form of normative Judaism began to emerge, which increasingly excluded other expressions of Judaism (such as the Sadducees and Essenes). One of the groups that came under suspicion was the Christian community of Matthew. The dispute centered around the question of who was the authoritative interpreter of the Mosaic law: Jesus or the rabbis?	Matthew depicts Jesus as Son of God, Davidic Messiah, and supreme teacher, or a new Moses. Matthew demonstrates continuity between Jesus and the story of Israel by using several devices including the *toledot*, or list of generations at the beginning of the Gospel. Jesus' ministry begins with a great sermon (the Sermon on the Mount), where Jesus lays out a demanding interpretation of Torah.
Luke	Around 80 CE	Greece or Asia Minor Luke's Gospel is not defined by crisis as are Mark's and Matthew's; rather, Luke's concern is to make Jesus—the Jewish Messiah—intelligible in a non-Jewish context.	Jesus is depicted as the universal Savior and the fulfillment of all of Israel's aspirations. As such, Jesus is a friend to the outcast and the marginalized (especially women).

Gospel Portraits of Jesus: For Particular Audiences *(continued)*

Evangelist	Approximate Date	Circumstances of the Evangelist	Christological Portrait
John	Around 95 CE	Asia Minor (Ephesus?) The history behind the Fourth Gospel is notoriously complex, but its parent community was apparently torn by internal and external strife concerning the person of Jesus.	John's Gospel emphasizes the role and identity of Jesus as God's Word or "Logos." As such, Jesus is explicitly given divine status. This is further reflected in the "I AM" statements found in the Gospel. "I AM" is meant to evoke in the reader the identification of YHWH in the burning bush scene found in Exodus 3:14. Jesus is, in a sense, identifying himself with YHWH.

Samaritan, a member of a community despised by "orthodox" Jews of Jerusalem and Galilee, as an example of what it means to love one's neighbor. Both of these stories illustrate Luke's fundamental interpretation of Jesus as God's universal offer of salvation. Such a portrait cannot be captured by a single title but requires the complex narrative offered by Luke.

Together, the synoptic evangelists created powerful narrative portraits of Jesus, portraits that do not focus on titles or definitions but tell a story. Through the story of Jesus' life, told in light of the Resurrection, the kērygma of the early church comes to life. Yet none of these christological portraits address the nagging question raised in the christological hymns in the Pauline letters: what is the precise relationship between God and Jesus?

Wisdom and Logos: The Confluence of Jewish and Greek Ideas

The titles, patterns, and christological portraits discussed in the previous sections culminate, to some extent, toward the end of the first century and the close of the New Testament period with the flourishing of **Wisdom Christology**. The **wisdom tradition** helped the early church more adequately understand the intimacy between Jesus and God and was decisive for subsequent doctrinal formulations. Like the prophetic tradition and the priestly tradition, the wisdom tradition was a form or expression of the varied Judaisms that existed in the centuries up through the time of Jesus. As its name suggests, the wisdom tradition placed a heavy emphasis on the wisdom of God and God's communication with the created world, and strove by this means to understand the convergence of the divine and the human in Israel's story. Roland Murphy, one of the foremost experts in the literature, outlined some of the main features of the wisdom tradition.[5]

Embodied as it is in wisdom literature, the wisdom tradition has to do with both a particular theological content and a literary style. Its origins are in the life of the clan or tribe, the courts of royalty (note the tradition's connection with the great King Solomon), and in the temple services (embodied in numerous Psalms). Wisdom is of different kinds (judicial, natural, theological, and experiential), it is not conscious of tradition but concerned with the "here and now," and it is not restricted to Israel but includes all nations. This last feature makes the wisdom tradition important in early Christian attempts to articulate its significance beyond the confines of Judaism. Most important for early Christology is the tendency of the tradition to personify divine Wisdom, particularly by associating the wisdom of God and the word of God. Both expressions—wisdom and word—signify the active presence of God in the world. This presence creates, communicates, sustains, and guides Israel.

Psalm 33:6 is a strong starting point for understanding the importance of God's word in creation: "By the LORD's word the heavens were made; by the breath of his mouth all their host" (cf. Genesis 1:1—2:4). God's word is also powerful and effective, healing the dead in their graves (Psalm 107:20) and changing the course of nature (Psalm 147:15–18). Perhaps the best illustration of the dynamic power of God's word is found in Isaiah 55:10–11:

> For just as from the heavens the rain and snow come down and do not return there till they have watered the earth, making it fertile and fruitful, giving seed to him who sows and bread to him who eats, so shall my word be that goes forth from my mouth; It shall not return to me void, but shall do my will, achieving the end for which I sent it.

In Wisdom 18:14–16 we find another powerful statement on God's word; the author describes the presence of YHWH in the actions of the "angel of death" in Exodus through his word:

> For when peaceful stillness compassed everything and the night in its swift course was half spent, your all-powerful word from heaven's royal throne bounded, a fierce warrior, into the doomed land, bearing the sharp sword of your inexorable decree. And as he alighted, he filled every place with death; he still reached to heaven, while he stood upon the earth.

Notice that the word of God is given the role of the warrior, defeating the enemies of YHWH and connecting heaven and earth as the plan of YHWH is enacted.

The notion of heaven and earth being connected through the word of God is further developed in the thought of the great Alexandrian Jew Philo. A contemporary of Jesus, Philo used Greek philosophy to interpret the Hebrew Scriptures—or perhaps the reverse! Drawing upon Greek philosophy, he emphasized the utter perfection of God and therefore God's remoteness and separation from the created world. If God were to be directly connected to the world, then God's perfection and immutability would be compromised; the picture of God that would emerge would be far too similar to the mythological images of the old Olympian gods of the Greeks. For the Greeks, reason had long been thought of as a divine principle, a spark of divinity, in the created world (often called the *logos spermatikos* or "seminal word"). For Philo, as for the Greeks, the **Logos** stood between God and the created order as a conduit or a point of connection:

> And the Father who created the universe has given to his archangelic and most ancient Word a preeminent gift, to stand on the confines of both, and separated that which had been created from the Creator. And this same Word is continually a suppliant to the immortal God on behalf of the mortal race, which is exposed to affliction and misery; and is also the ambassador, sent by the Ruler of all, to the subject race. And the Word rejoices in the gift, and, exulting in it, announces it and boasts of it, saying, "And I stood in the midst, between the Lord and You." (Philo, *Who is the Heir of Divine Things?* 42.205–6)

The Logos is divine; it is the thought of God coming to expression. As such it connects the world of ideas (the real world for Greek philosophers like Plato) with the material world of the senses. The Logos thus connects God to the world, but it also acts as a barrier between the contingent material world and the infinity of God. It is from this milieu that the early Christian fixation on a Christology of the divine Word, or **Logos Christology**, emerged.

Wisdom and Logos in John's Christology

Perhaps the most obvious example of Logos Christology in the New Testament can be found in the prologue to the Fourth Gospel. The first three verses of the prologue give us ample evidence of this Logos Christology:

> In the beginning was the Word, and the Word was with God, and the Word was God. He was in the beginning with God. All things came to be through him, and without him nothing came to be. (John 1:1–3)

From this simple passage we can begin to identify some obvious benefits of this perspective for New Testament Christology. First, Jesus is more clearly identified with God. Second, the life and ministry of Jesus, as well as his death and Resurrection, are not innovations in the history of Israel. Rather, the life, death, and Resurrection of Jesus were viewed as an extension of God acting on behalf of humanity from the first moment of creation. Through the Word, the Logos, God has created the universe, spoken to Israel, and fought on their behalf against the forces of evil and destruction.

While the first chapter of John may help to clarify the precise nature of the relationship between Jesus and God, it also creates several problems. If one examines closely the Greek text of John 1:1, the apparent clarity of the verse is clouded. The Greek reads as follows (with a slavishly literal translation in parentheses):

> 1a en *archē ēn ho logos,* (In the beginning was the Word)
> 1b *kai ho logos ēn pros ton theon,* (and the Word was with the God)
> 1c *kai theos ēn ho logos* (and God was the Word)

The commas in the above passage separate three clauses. Our concern here is with the second and third clauses. The Greek term for *Word*, as already noted, is *logos*, and the word for "God" is *theos*. Additionally, the words *ho* and *ton* are different forms of the definite article *the*. Note

Person of Interest

Origen

Origen (185 CE–254 CE) was one of the three or four greatest Christian writers prior to the fourth century, yet some of his doctrines came under suspicion in later centuries and were condemned as heresies. Thus Origen is not termed a church father or a saint, even though many of his writings are read by Christians who pray the Liturgy of the Hours (the "official" daily prayers of the church, which include Psalms, Scripture passages, and devotional readings from great Christian writers). Origen was a prolific writer and the leader of the great Christian school of instruction (the catechetical school) in Alexandria. He devoted himself to a strict disciplined life, which unfortunately included self-mutilation—he took Jesus' admonition in Matthew 19:12 literally! He suffered from church politics in Alexandria in the third century and was eventually tortured by the Roman imperial authorities during the persecution led by the emperor Decius. Origen's most important contributions lie in his ability to synthesize Greek philosophy with the Christian Scriptures. Although many insights were gained through this endeavor, many would argue that Christian doctrine began to suffer distortion and corruption with the introduction of such influences. His most celebrated work is *On First Principles* (*Peri Archōn*) in which, like Philo, he offers an allegorical understanding of Scripture. For Origen, nothing is what it appears to be; the literal sense of the text is only a figure or shadow of a spiritual reality. Origen also wrote an influential commentary on John in which he subordinated the divinity of the Son to that of the Father on the basis of John 1:1. He also popularized the idea that all things, even Satan, would be restored to God in the end of time (the Greek work for this is **apokatastasis**). These innovative speculations would result in many problems for generations of theologians after Origen.

that the Word was with "the God" in 1b, but 1c states that "God," with no definite article, was the Word. Most commentators agree that the prologue makes a distinction between "the God" that the Word is with and the "God" the Word is. This is occasionally rendered into English as "the Word was with God and the Word was divine."[6] Although Christians today are unanimous in affirming that the Word is fully divine, and read John 1:1 as reflecting this, it was not so clear to many ancients. The apparent distinction offered in this passage would be cited by luminaries like Origen and would fuel the fires of christological speculation in the years after the writing of the New Testament.

Conclusion

The New Testament made use of a variety of images and symbols to explore the experience of God in Jesus. These efforts culminated in the development of Logos Christology, which emphasized the creative and redemptive power of God's self-communication. But these efforts did not settle the precise question of Jesus' relationship to God. The New Testament offers the Christian faithful a set of stories and symbols that communicate and help us appropriate the proclamation of God's salvation in Christ, narrative creations that early Christians regarded as decisive for Christian life and worship. Following the close of the first century CE, the canon of the New Testament began to achieve a fixed form and exercised an increasingly normative role for the Christian community, but the limitations of its christological formulations would become apparent.

Questions for Understanding

1. What is the *Shema*, and how does it complicate the Christology of the earliest Christians?

2. What is the difference between a christological title, a christological role, and a christological pattern?

3. What is the origin of the phrase "Son of Man," and what does it mean?

4. Why might it have been difficult to convince first-century Jews (or, indeed, anyone) that Jesus of Nazareth was God's *messiah*?

5. List some of the titles and roles associated with Paul's Christology.

6. Does the hymn in Philippians 2 state unequivocally that Jesus is God? Explain.

7. How do the infancy narratives in Matthew and Luke function as christological moments?

8. What is the Logos, and why is it important for understanding the development of New Testament Christology?

9. Who was Philo, and what is his connection to the development of New Testament Christology?

10. Does John's prologue proclaim that Jesus is God? Explain.

Questions for Reflection

1. Christians read the Hebrew Bible (the Old Testament) as their own Scripture and see in it many pointed references to Christian doctrine. Given what you have read in this chapter, is such a practice legitimate? Are there limits to such a practice? (See *The Catechism of the Catholic Church*, 121–23; also the PBC document, *The Jewish People and their Scriptures in the Christian Bible.*)

2. If the Bible does not present answers to all of our questions about Jesus, must Christians simply embrace theological ambiguity, or can they find clarity beyond the language of the Scriptures? Are there benefits to such ambiguity? Are there dangers? Explain.

3. If the New Testament offers primarily narrative accounts of Jesus' identity, are Christians therefore wedded to narrative (stories) in a unique way? What are the implications of this for understanding Christian worship or Christian moral theology?

Endnotes

1 For a good summary of the major points in the discussion of the "Son of Man," see John R. Donahue, "Recent Studies on the Origin of 'Son of Man' in the Gospels," *Catholic Biblical Quarterly* 48 (1986): 484–98, and John Collins, "The Son of Man in First-Century Judaism," *New Testament Studies* 38 (1992): 448–66.

2 Raymond Brown, "Aspects of New Testament Thought," in *The New Jerome Biblical Commentary*, ed. R. Brown, J. Fitzmyer, and R. Murphy (Englewood Cliffs, NJ: Prentice-Hall, 1990), 1357.

3 Some scholars have tried to argue for a Palestinian or Syrian setting for Mark, but a majority of scholars still identify Rome as the place of composition (for a complete discussion, see Francis Moloney, *The Gospel of Mark: A Commentary* [Peabody, MA: Hendrickson, 2002]).

4 E.g., Anthony J. Saldarini, *Matthew's Jewish-Christian Community*, Chicago Studies in the History of Judaism (Chicago: University of Chicago, 1994).

5 Roland E. Murphy, "Wisdom Literature," in *The New Jerome Biblical Commentary*, ed. R. Brown, J. Fitzmyer, and R. Murphy (Englewood Cliffs, NJ: Prentice-Hall, 1990), 447–50.

6 The New English Bible translates the passage as "the Word was what God was," though other commentators have argued that "the Word was divine" is appropriate. Scholars such as R. Brown have argued that while there is an important distinction between 1b and 1c, the translations like the NAB and the NRSV ("the Word was God") are accurate so long as one does not thereby read into the passage a trinitarian theology that did not develop as such until the fourth century.

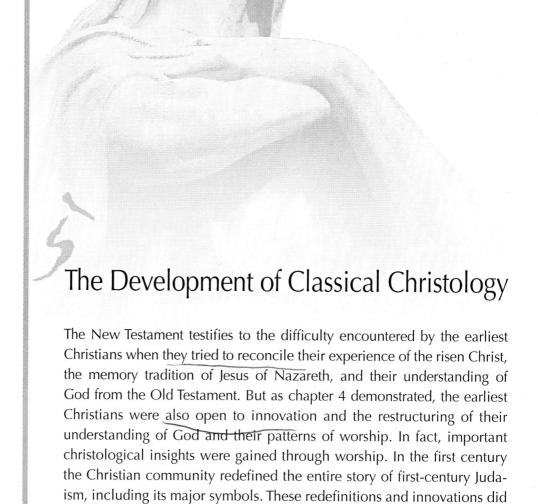

The Development of Classical Christology

The New Testament testifies to the difficulty encountered by the earliest Christians when they tried to reconcile their experience of the risen Christ, the memory tradition of Jesus of Nazareth, and their understanding of God from the Old Testament. But as chapter 4 demonstrated, the earliest Christians were also open to innovation and the restructuring of their understanding of God and their patterns of worship. In fact, important christological insights were gained through worship. In the first century the Christian community redefined the entire story of first-century Judaism, including its major symbols. These redefinitions and innovations did not proceed without controversy.

Any description of the early christological controversies tends to stumble because the vocabulary and the cultural setting remain hopelessly opaque for most students. But these classical controversies make more sense when we begin by considering the importance of the issues these early conflicts were addressing. Two basic christological questions guide this chapter. First, what precisely is the relationship between the Logos, incarnate in Jesus, and God? In effect, when we say that Jesus is the incarnate Logos, do we mean he is closely related to God, or that he is divine in the same sense that God is divine? Second, was Jesus truly a human being like the rest of us? Although some groups like the **Gnostics** denied that Jesus was a material human being, the vast majority of Christians affirmed the humanity of Jesus. But just how human was he? What is the relationship between the human being Jesus and the Logos, or the Son?

These two christological questions, taken together, act as a catalyst for exploring what Christians have experienced in the life, death, and Resurrection of Jesus Christ. The novelty of the Resurrection demanded from the earliest Christians that they develop new ways of speaking about Jesus and new ways of speaking about God. In the context of this theological innovation, new language developed and clarified the Christian experience of salvation in Christ. In sum, christological orthodoxy is born from theological innovation, but these innovations, in turn, set up new boundaries, new limits, to guide Christian thought, worship, and practice. Classical christological doctrines emerge to affirm both the humanity and divinity of Christ, and it is to this complex project that we now turn.

The Way to Nicaea (100–300)

At the close of the New Testament, we saw an important move toward Logos Christology, with its focus on the Jewish and Greek ideas of the divine Word (Logos) and its relationship to God and the world. This combination of early Jewish and Greek thought helped to set up the controversies and the doctrinal developments that took place in the two and a half centuries following the close of the New Testament and culminating in the theological battles at Nicaea and afterward. For many centuries, students of Christology have been tempted to see Greek thought as an intrusion into early Christian theology. But as scholarship in the twentieth and twenty-first centuries has demonstrated, even in the world of Jesus (first-century Palestinian Judaism), one cannot easily separate "Jewish," "Christian," and "Greek" thought. Greek ideas influenced and were affected by all of the cultures and religions in the Mediterranean basin. The labels "Greek" and "Jewish" are not meaningless, but we should be cautious about how rigidly we draw the lines between these groups. Additionally, the development of christological orthodoxy involves more than just the confluence of culture, or even politics; it involves the capacity to affirm judgments beyond narrative and symbolic discourse.

Developments Before the Fourth Century

By end of the first century CE, Christianity had become increasingly Gentile (mostly Greek) and began to orient itself and its mission to the urban centers of the Roman Empire. Around 160 CE, Justin (remembered as Justin Martyr because he was eventually killed for his faith) emerged to articulate a powerful argument on behalf of Christian faith. The task was not easy: he needed to explain how a man who was crucified by the Romans as a Jewish nationalist and revolutionary could be religiously meaningful for the diverse and cultured peoples of the Roman Empire. Jesus may have been the Jewish Messiah, but the Messiah was obviously no friend of Rome. What significance could Jesus have for Romans?

Justin, a convert to Christianity, made explicit use of Logos Christology as an apologetic or defensive strategy against those who thought a Jewish Messiah had no relevance beyond Palestine. He engaged in spirited arguments with Jewish interlocutors like Trypho, and addressed the question of Jesus' relevance for the Roman people—and for the emperor himself—in his *First Apology* (**apology** comes from *apologia*, Greek for "defense"). There Justin made the notion of the divine Logos and the ***logos spermatikos*** central to his exposition and defense of the Christian faith. The *logos spermatikos*, or "seminal word," was the idea that the divine Word was present in the world through a rationality that permeated everything. The ordering of the sun, moon, and stars, the order of nature, and especially the rationality of the human mind signified the connectedness of the created order with the realm of the divine. Justin reasoned that all philosophies and religions before Christ were simply human attempts to respond to the seminal word. But these philosophies and religions were really pointing to and preparing for the definitive moment when the divine Word would arrive in the world. For Justin, Jesus was the fulfillment not just of Israel's hopes but also the hopes of the entire world, thus making Logos Christology an important point of intersection between the world of Greek thought and early Christian theology.

While Justin Martyr was arguing for the universal religious significance of Jesus, other theologians began to entertain more pressing questions regarding the relationship between God and the Word, or the Son. For many second- and third-century theologians, the problem of how the one God could share his divine power or **monarchia** with the Son helped to focus this issue.

Adoptionists, or "Dynamic Monarchians," asserted that the Son is given a share in the divine power or authority because of his virtue. That is, the human being Jesus practiced virtue to such a heroic extent that God bestowed on him a share in his monarchia. Proponents of this position did not see the Son as inherently divine, but understood that the Son shared in the authority of God through God's gracious will. While this move helped to safeguard the oneness of God (recall the importance of this from our discussion of the Shema in the last chapter), it did not adequately distinguish the Son from other charismatic leaders from Israel's past (e.g., Jeremiah).

In contrast, **Modalists**, or "Modal Monarchians," asserted that the Son was a mere "mode," or operation, of God. For them, the words "Father" and "Son" do not signify anything about God's nature or being. Rather, these words simply name our particular experience of God—the Father is the Son, and the Son is the Father. The Modalists were able to safeguard the oneness of God but failed to grasp the distinctions between Father and Son so central in the Gospels.

In an effort to set forth a correct interpretation of Christian faith that would eschew these two problematic positions, the great African theologian Tertullian (ca. 160–220) argued that the Father is God from all eternity, and he is the origin of the divine power, or monarchia, because he is *spiritus* (spirit). For Tertullian, *spiritus* was divinity's material (a fine grade of matter, like ether). When the Father decided to create the universe, he "extruded" the Son, and the Son thus was also *spiritus*. The Son was really distinct from the Father, but this did not divide or diminish the divine *monarchia* any more than the emperor divides his authority when he commands an agent to do his bidding. While Tertullian successfully argued against the positions of the Adoptionists and the Modalists, he did so by making two important mistakes. First, Tertullian radically subordinated the Son to the Father. In fact, he made the Son less divine than the Father. Second, Tertullian articulated the relationship between the Father and the Son in materialistic terms: they are both divine because they are made of the same stuff (*spiritus*).[1]

Tertullian's materialistic subordination of the Son was rectified, to some extent, by Origen (ca. 185–ca. 255), the great Alexandrian theologian and biblical exegete. As the successor to Clement of Alexandria, the leader of the catechetical school of Alexandria, Origen was naturally a thoroughgoing Platonist, and therefore very suspicious of materialistic thought. You will recall that for Platonists ultimate reality is found beyond the material, which is only a shadow of the real world of forms or ideas. While Origen's thought is more complex than simple dualism of matter versus ideas, against Tertullian's materialistic understanding of the relationship between the Father and Son, Origen's Platonic idealism signifies an important insight.

For Origen, God fully transcends the created order and is beyond any material form. The properties of God are unknowable, but the Son, or the divine Word, is the expression of God—not extruded as a material substance, but immaterially and eternally. While Origen corrected Tertullian's materialism and emphasized the eternity of the Son's participation in the Father, he nonetheless subordinated the Son to the Father. For Origen, the Son was still a step down from God because the Son is divine through participation (*methexis*) while the Father is divine in himself. Origen made this explicit when he differentiated the Father from the Son using "the God" (*ho theos*) for the former and "God" (*theos*) for the latter.[2] This subordination of the Son and the theological tension it created would become an important factor in the fourth century as the Christian church moved from the status of a persecuted community to that of an institution sponsored by imperial power.

The Council of Nicaea (325 CE)

Legend has it that in 312, on the eve of a great military campaign, the young emperor Constantine had a vision of the *chi rho* (*X* and *P*, the first letters of the Greek word *christos*) and heard a voice saying "in this sign you shall conquer."[3] Constantine went on to defeat his rival, and subsequently became a defender and sponsor of the Christian church and its politics. Constantine believed that as the sponsor of the church he had an obligation to preserve good order, so when controversies arose in the church or the empire and threatened that good order, it was his responsibility to bring about resolution. When a controversy broke out in the city of Alexandria between its bishop, a man named Alexander, and a priest named Arius, Constantine inserted himself into the debate to bring about an end to the conflict.[4]

Arius (ca. 260–336) is often regarded as the greatest heretic (founder of a false theological teaching) of the early church. Many contemporary scholars rightly point out that most of our information about Arius and his position comes to us from his opponents (Arius's own works were destroyed after he was condemned) and should, therefore, be viewed as suspect. Nevertheless, the basic contours of his thought are fairly clear and undisputed. His lost work, the *Thalia* (pieces of it are preserved in the works of Arius's opponents), demonstrates continuity with the philosophical and theological tone of Alexandrian theology, especially as exemplified in the works of Philo and Origen. Like his predecessors, Arius wanted to preserve an essentially Greek understanding of God as removed from the material world. He therefore constructed an account of the world where the divine Word was an intermediary between the one God and creation. Such an understanding of the Word had the effect of distinguishing the divinity of the Father from that of the Son by means of a radical **subordinationism,** definitively separating the Father and Son. Two important Arian slogans demonstrate this: "There was a time when [the Son] was not," and, "Before [the Son] was begotten he was not." For Arius, God alone is unchanging and unbegotten (without beginning or origin), but the Son was created out of nothing by the will of the Father. Additionally, Arius asserted that only God knows himself and all things perfectly; the Son's knowledge of God and himself is imperfect, and thus he can only reveal God imperfectly.

Caesar and the Church

Constantine's patronage of the Christian Church was a mixed blessing by all accounts; some would even call it an unmitigated disaster for the church. The Edict of Toleration he issued jointly with his co-emperor Licinius in 313 gave Christianity legal standing and ended the horrible persecution that had broken out periodically in the empire. Yet with the emperor's favor came the emperor's influence and imperial politics. Since religion was a public and civil matter in the empire, Christians naturally began to appeal to him with their disputes and disagreements. For example, in a controversy in North Africa, he lent imperial weight to the condemnation of a group known as the Donatists. Constantine inclined toward Arianism, and in the Arian controversy was influenced by a variety of bishop-advisers to make life difficult for supporters of Nicaea, like Athanasius. In the East a model that many call "Caesaro-papism" began to emerge as the dominant ideal for church-state relations. In Caesaro-papism, the supreme ruler of the church was the emperor, who had the responsibility to protect and safeguard the church. In the West, however, with no strong imperial figure, the Bishop of Rome began to emerge as the most important political figure, and he sought to subordinate secular officials to the power of the church with varying degrees of success. With the rise of nationalism following the Reformation, pressure was increasingly brought to bear on the Roman Catholic Church to cede power to national leaders and subject the church to civil authority, but such attempts were usually rebuffed, and the Catholic Church often lost its standing and governmental support.

The Arian position gained considerable popularity because of Arius's effective use of Scripture and notable theologians like Origen. Nevertheless, Arius's bishop, Alexander, was unconvinced and called on Arius to recant his position. When Arius refused to submit to his bishop, the emperor eventually stepped in.

Constantine's initial intervention took the form of a letter to both Arius and Alexander in which he instructed the two parties to be reconciled to one another, "For as long as you continue to contend about these small and very insignificant questions, I believe it indeed to be not merely unbecoming, but positively evil, that so large a portion of God's people which belong to your jurisdiction should be thus divided."[5] The letter demonstrates that the motivation behind the emperor's intervention had more to do with his concern for order than theology. The theological issues at stake, however, were not lost in the drama; in fact, the debate provoked by Arius helped to crystallize the importance of the Incarnation for understanding Christian worship and the Christian experience of salvation.

When the emperor's attempts to impose a solution failed, he assembled a council of bishops to judge the case. Legend has it that three hundred and eighteen bishops attended the council, which was convened in the late spring of 325 in the small village of **Nicaea** at the emperor's summer palace. Thus the council is known as the Council of Nicaea, or Nicaea I. The bishops were quick to condemn Arius and his theology, but that was not enough for the emperor, who sought a summary statement of faith, a **creed,** which could be regarded as the standard for the church.

Although creedal statements were commonly used for catechumens (people preparing to be baptized), they were not applied to bishops, so the emperor's request that the bishops formulate and bind themselves to a creed was unusual. But the bishops yielded and used as their template a largely scriptural creed as the basic statement of faith. That creed was open to a wide range of interpretations since, as we have seen in the previous chapter, scriptural language is complex and highly symbolic. Because of this, the Fathers at Nicaea could not construct a definitive statement by using biblical images alone; the highly symbolic nature of scriptural language left any use of such language open to a variety of

Person of Interest

Helena, the Mother of Constantine

Helena (255–330) had humble origins but grew up to marry the emperor Constantine Chlorus, by whom she had a son, Constantine. When political circumstances required, her husband left her and married the stepdaughter of the emperor Maximian. When Helena's son became emperor in 306, she was given a prominent place in the imperial household and became a strong defender of Christianity and a promoter of archaeology in the Holy Land. She traveled there in 326 and erected large basilicas in Bethlehem, at the Mount of Olives, and the Church of the Resurrection at the tomb of Jesus. She is also reported to have found the true cross on which Jesus died. She was venerated as a saint almost immediately following her death, and she shares a feast day in the Greek Orthodox Church with her son, St. Constantine.

interpretations, Arian included. So the council added several phrases to the creed to make it impossible for Arians to assent to the creed by simply giving it their own spin.

The decisive Greek phrase was *homoousion tē patri*, which is translated as "[the Son is] one in being with the Father" in the creed that many modern Christians still use in the **liturgy** (often called The Nicene Creed or The Nicene Constantinopolitan Creed). The word **homoousios** was highly controversial at the time. It had been condemned by a local church council (a gathering of local bishops to address regional issues) held in the third century, when it was associated with the teachings of the Gnostics. Yet before the Council of Nicaea, Constantine's theological advisor, Ossius, the bishop of ancient Cordova, had adopted the term as a translation of the Latin word *consubstantialis*, which had become accepted in the Latin-speaking West (the western half of the Roman Empire, including Italy, Gaul, Spain, and North Africa). When the emperor adopted the term at Ossius's urging, its acceptance at the council was assured, even though some objected strongly to making a nonscriptural word normative for Christian faith. While the condemnation of Arius was the result of general consensus, the adoption of *homoousios* was more controversial; many bishops subsequently had doubts about the Nicaean formulation.

In the heated battles that followed the Council of Nicaea, the foremost proponent of Nicaea's statement of faith against those who sought compromise was Athanasius (ca. 295–373). Although he was only a deacon at Nicaea, Athanasius eventually succeeded Alexander as bishop of Alexandria. He became the staunchest defender of Nicene orthodoxy in the theological and political battles that took place in the decades following the council, and was the person most responsible for the eventual victory of Nicaea in the East. His work *On the Incarnation*, though written before the Arian controversy, offers an explanation and defense of the faith of Nicaea and reasons for Arius's condemnation. In this work Athanasius sums up the purpose of the Incarnation by stating, "God became human in order that humans might become God."[6] This startling statement of divinization (*theōsis*) is at the heart of Nicaea's condemnation of Arius and helps to put into bold relief the issues at stake.

Christians claim that in Christ we have experienced salvation— a transformative union with God, a participation in God's existence.

Christians experience this salvation through faith in Christ, through baptism into Christ's death and Resurrection, by eating the body and drinking the blood of Christ, and through adhering to the teaching of Christ. Christ, therefore, gives us salvation and mediates the presence of God, and through Christ we participate in God's own existence. Now if the Son was merely a creature and not truly divine, how could we participate in God's existence, or how could we have salvation? It was this line of reasoning that carried the day for the Nicaean party in the following decades, despite political developments that threatened to reverse the council's decision. Athanasius tenaciously fought for this theology and was successful to the point that he and the "symbol" (creed) of Nicaea became the standard of orthodoxy for centuries.

The Language of Nicaea: What Difference Does It Make?

The importance of Nicaea for the development of the Christian tradition can hardly be overestimated. One theologian, in particular, has helped to clarify this: the late Canadian Jesuit Bernard Lonergan.[7]

According to Lonergan's reading of second- and third-century theology, the church was struggling to express a judgment about the precise relationship between the Father and the Son. Tertullian attempted to set forth an adequate understanding of this relationship but did so by envisioning that relationship materially: the Father and Son are made of the same stuff. Origen corrected Tertullian by going beyond his materialistic explanation, but Origen's Platonic idealism confined his attempt to a world of gradations. For Origen there was only one origin of the divine— the Father—and the Son is divine only by participation. Neither Tertullian nor Origen could adequately express what had been experienced in Christ. The triumph of Nicaea was its ability to express the relationship between the Father and Son in a way that goes beyond "picture thinking" and idealist explanation. For Lonergan, a similar triumph can be seen in the journey through **Chalcedon** as the church wrestled with the second of the great christological questions: what is the relationship between the divine Son and the human being Jesus?

In the work of Lonergan, the christological controversies in the early church become the means for exploring human understanding and the power of language to shape that understanding. Affirmations of what is true, what is real, force us to transcend "picture thinking" and materialism to affirm what is so. The truth of any claim transcends its capacity to be presented in terms of materiality. While our culture is preoccupied with common sense and the material, an account of the development of the christological tradition may serve to provide a lesson in human cognition and the relationship between different types of discourse, or what Lonergan calls realms of meaning.

Political and Theological Conflict as Engines for Doctrinal Development: Constantinople I (381)

Following the decades-long battles over Nicaea, an emphasis on the second christological question began to emerge. Surprisingly, the controversy over how to understand the relationship between the divine Son and the human being Jesus began with one of the most ardent supporters of Nicene orthodoxy, the bishop of Laodicea in Syria, Apollinaris (in some texts spelled Apollinarius).

Apollinaris (310–390) was a vigorous opponent of Arius and a consummate Alexandrian theologian. Apollinaris's Alexandrian roots are no trivial matter, for the theological tendencies of this ancient center of Christian theology were pronounced. The **Alexandrian school,** particularly following the defeat of Arius, increasingly emphasized the full divinity of the Son and the unity of the divine Son with the human being Jesus. In fact, the starting point for Alexandrian Christology was Nicaea's affirmation of the divine Son as *homoousios* with the Father; only then did it ask how the divine Son was related to the flesh of humanity. While the Alexandrian approach is perfectly orthodox (right belief), it could be developed in a way that was less than orthodox, as was the case with Apollinaris.

Apollinaris's formulation of the relationship between the divine Son and the human being Jesus undermined the humanity of Christ. He understood the human person to be composed of two parts: the body or flesh (*sarx*, in Greek), and the rational soul or mind. If the divine Son was to be united to the human being Jesus, where could the Son fit in, so to speak? If you remove the rational soul, or the mind, from the human being Jesus, then the Son would be united to the flesh of the man Jesus but not to his rational soul, since he had none. For Apollinaris, the conscious subject of Jesus (his ego, or "I") is the divine Son and no other. This move seemed to answer the question of the relationship between the Son and Jesus, but compromised the humanity of Christ by reducing it to mere flesh. To grasp what Apollinaris is saying, imagine that you had a brain transplant; would it be appropriately called a "brain transplant" or a "body transplant"? Where should we locate "you" in this transplant process? Apollinaris essentially removed the mind and the will from Jesus so that the divine Son could take its place. But in that case, what is human about Jesus? His hands and feet, his nerve endings, his bones? You may ask, what difference does this make for understanding and receiving the salvation Christians claim has been made available in Christ? It makes a great deal of difference, as the theologians of the fourth century recognized.

The First Council of **Constantinople** (381) condemned the teaching of Apollinaris. The council emphasized the significance of Jesus' complete humanity for understanding Christian salvation. Gregory Nazianzen, the short-lived bishop of Constantinople, put it most pointedly: "What was not assumed [in Christ] was not redeemed; whatever is united to God is saved."[8] This is actually a corollary of Athanasius's famous maxim mentioned previously: "God became human in order that humans might become God." The union between God and humanity involves reciprocity: God solves the problem of sin in Christ by uniting all that God is with everything that human beings are. If we were to leave out some aspect of our humanity from this union, then we would not participate in God's own life, and thus be unredeemed, for sin does not originate in the flesh but in the operations of the mind, the will. When Matthew 5:29–30 instructs us to cut off the limbs that cause us to sin, the passage implies that sin rests not in a limb or some organ; rather, it rests in our mind, or will. The Gospel summons us to repent, to undergo conversion (*metanoia*, literally "change of mind").

The condemnation of Apollinaris at Constantinople I set Alexandrian theology on its heels. Alexandrians were in conflict with clerics in the Syrian city of Antioch where another approach to Christology had developed. The **Antiochene school** began with the human being Jesus, then asked how he is united to the divine Son. This christological approach

Alexandria and Antioch

By the end of the fourth century, around the time of Constantinople I (381), a theological and political rivalry developed between the cities of Alexandria and Antioch. These two cities had distinctive theological outlooks.

School	Alexandria	Antioch
Christology	This school adopted a Logos-sarx approach to Christology, which emphasizes the unity of the subject, Christ. This unity is achieved by having the divine Word (Logos) take over the higher functions of the human person Jesus, while the lower functions, are controlled by the flesh (*sarx*, in Greek).	This school adopted a Logos-anthropos approach to Christology, which emphasized the distinction between the human being Jesus and the divine Word (Logos). The two realities are conjoined yet maintain their respective properties, and the human being (*anthrōpos* in Greek) Jesus maintains his integrity as a human being.
Scripture	The Alexandrian approach to Scripture was allegorical. Every passage had a literal sense and a spiritual sense. The literal sense is what anyone who can read or understand the language can understand, but the spiritual sense of Scripture—its real meaning—was available only through the eyes of faith. What appears to be the obvious meaning of a passage (literal sense) is often not its real significance.	The Antiochene approach to Scripture was historical and literary. Every passage had a history behind it, and every passage was subject to literary convention. The Antiochene approach was, therefore, much closer to contemporary approaches to Scripture.
Some Chief Representatives	Athanasius, Apollinaris, Cyril of Alexandria, Dioscorus, Eutyches	Theodore of Mopsuestia, John of Antioch, John Chrysostom, Nestorius

is commonly called Logos-anthropos Christology (*anthropos* means "human being"). The condemnation of Apollinaris vindicated the Antiochene emphasis on the full humanity of Jesus, but it left unanswered how one was to speak of the humanity and divinity of Christ. This left open the door for a heated controversy that began in the early fifth century in the imperial city of Constantinople.

Political and Theological Conflict as Engines for Doctrinal Development: Ephesus (431)

Like some modern capitals (e.g., Washington, DC and Brasilia), Constantinople was a new city in a strategic location. It was built by Constantine as his new capital, intending to unite the culture of the eastern part of the Roman Empire with the western part. Though it was built on the remains of a small fishing village named Byzantium, it had no real history that would privilege one people over another or one theology over the other. But the unifying force of such a capital could never be fully realized. In fact, in the third canon, or law, of Constantinople I, it was declared that the church of Constantinople should rank above all other churches in the east and second only to Rome.[9] As such, the city and the church of Constantinople became a cause of division. Both Antiochene and Alexandrian bishops resented the prestige granted to the young city and tried to control its bishop and, perhaps, the emperor.

When an Antiochene was made bishop of Constantinople in the early fifth century, the scene was set for a major battle among these power centers. The new bishop's name was Nestorius (†ca. 451). There were a large number of Alexandrian monks living in the imperial city at the time, and it was their custom to honor Mary, the mother of Jesus, with the title **Theotokos** ("God bearer," or "mother of God"). Nestorius and his supporters regarded this as a theological misstatement. Mary was the mother of Christ (Christotokos) because she bore the God-man Jesus, but to call her Theotokos was inaccurate since the divine is eternal, while Mary was obviously not. Nestorius made the unwise choice of making his case in a series of sermons around Christmas in 428. These sermons aroused the anger of the Alexandrians living in the imperial city and also alienated most of the other residents of Constantinople. Nestorius was going to need allies for the fight he had picked, but none were close enough to protect him when the storm broke. Notice that, although the controversy sounds like it revolves around Mary, it actually centers on Christ. One should remember when discussing Marian doctrines that these doctrines are primarily about Christ.

Cyril (ca. 376–444), Bishop of Alexandria, hearing of these developments in Constantinople, was legitimately concerned over the theological

Marian Doctrines

The role of the Blessed Virgin Mary (BVM) has been a source of contention and misunderstanding between Protestant Christians and their Catholic and Orthodox neighbors. All Christians agree about the importance of the BVM in the story of Jesus and as a model of Christian faith. Yet the use of the Theotokos (Mother of God) and such Roman Catholic doctrines as the Immaculate Conception and Assumption are viewed by many Protestant Christians with alarm since they seem to place an emphasis on the BVM and not on Christ, in whom we have our salvation. The Roman Catholic Church, however, clearly emphasizes that doctrines about the BVM are "based on what it believes about Christ, and what it teaches about Mary illumines in turn its faith in Christ" (*The Catechism of the Catholic Church*, 487).

Eccentric devotion to the BVM has been a problem in Catholic circles for a long time — many readers may recall some relative who mumbled through the rosary on Sunday morning rather than participating in the Liturgy. In the earliest depictions of the BVM, and throughout most of history, the BVM never appears alone, but always with her Son or with the angel Gabriel as she receives the news that she is to become the mother of her Savior. Sometimes she is a throne, presenting the child to the devotee, leading them to a deeper faith. In Michelangelo's famous pietà, she holds the corpse of her dead Son, the divine Word, like a book and studies the body with intense devotion and sadness.

Marian doctrines, like Theotokos, are not about the importance of Mary per se, but about what God has done in Christ. Mary, the first to believe in the gospel, the first Christian, has experienced the redemption brought by Christ, and she prefigures that for which all Christians hope. She is the mother of Christians because she has experienced the unmerited grace of God working in Christ.

attack on the title Theotokos and the Christology behind it. But he also recognized an opportunity to seize the upper hand for Alexandria in the imperial city. Cyril urged the emperor to convene a council in 431 at the city of Ephesus on the Aegean coast of Asia Minor. Cyril brought with him a large contingent of bishops and monks from Egypt who supported him, while Nestorius waited for his supporters, including John of Antioch and others, to travel from as far away as Persia. Before Nestorius's supporters arrived, Cyril convened the council and had Nestorius condemned. For his part, Nestorius refused to attend the council without his supporters— some suspect that their tardiness was a deliberate attempt to disrupt the council since they knew that they did not have enough votes to prevail. When they arrived in the city four days later, they held their own meeting and had Cyril condemned. Appeals to the emperor followed; Cyril was upheld and Nestorius was condemned and removed as bishop. His supporters were furious.

The theological reasons for Nestorius's condemnation are complex but important for understanding subsequent christological discussions. Nestorius, along with virtually all Christians at the time, insisted that the Son's nature *(**physis**)* was divine and had its own concrete existence *(**hypostasis**)*. This was the orthodox teaching against the Modalists and others. This teaching was laid out first at Nicaea and then in the debates about the Holy Spirit at Constantinople I. Both councils defended the unity of God first by declaring that the Father and Son were "one in being" (Nicaea) and by declaring that there were three coequal *hypostases* in God (Constantinople I). Nestorius, as a good Antiochene theologian, also insisted that Jesus was a human being with a human nature *(physis)*. This human nature had its own concrete existence, or person *(**prosōpon**)*, which carried with it the meaning of "observable manifestation" and was occasionally used interchangeably with *hypostasis*. For Nestorius, the Incarnation involved the conjoining *(synapheia)* of these two natures so that each retained its own properties. Thus Nestorius was put in the position of positing a *prosōpon* of the union, a single object of perception, which he calls Christ. While Nestorius tried to articulate a Christology that defended the full humanity and the full divinity of Christ against what he saw as another version of Apollinarianism, he fell into a position that did not adequately express the full union of the divine Son with the human being Jesus. For Nestorius, the conjunction between the divine Son and the man Jesus was voluntary, that is, the conjunction came about because of God's gracious will, which united with the man Jesus. In subsequent letters defending his position, Nestorius argued that he really was concerned to articulate a substantial (i.e., real) coming together of the divine and human in Christ, but the formal maneuvers he used to articulate his position left his attempts suspect in the eyes of his contemporaries.

When Cyril heard Nestorius's explanation, it sounded to him like Paul of Samosata (whose teachings foreshadowed adoptionism) had come back from the grave. Nestorius's ideas seemed like a form of adoptionism and, therefore, a denial of the Incarnation. Cyril insisted upon the union of the two natures in Christ. Thus one could predicate of Jesus things that were proper to divinity and things proper to human nature, as had been customary for centuries—this is called the *communicatio idiomatum* (the communication of attributes). But as Cyril vigorously attacked the unpopular Nestorius, he adopted some important and controversial formulations himself. One formula stated, "Out of two natures (i.e., the divine and human natures) one incarnate nature of the Logos." Cyril thought that this phrase was completely orthodox, believing it came from Athanasius, but it actually came from the condemned heretic Apollinaris! Athanasius was such a popular figure after his death that he became synonymous with orthodox Christian faith. When Apollinaris was condemned, many of his supporters sought to preserve his works by attributing them to Athanasius, who indeed had inspired Apollinaris on some points. These writings, which we now call pseudo-Athanasian, were taken unknowingly by Cyril as genuine works of Athanasius and, therefore, completely orthodox. Subsequent insistence on this "one incarnate nature" formula, so robustly presented by Cyril, would become the basis for the next round in the christological and political battles between Antioch and Alexandria.

Schism and Compromise: Between Ephesus and Chalcedon (433 – 448)

Following the **Council of Ephesus** in 431 and its condemnation of Nestorius, a major split, or schism, occurred in the church. The Antiochene bishops, many of whom were not entirely in support of Nestorius's theology, nonetheless felt that they had been treated unfairly by Cyril and his supporters. Cyril, on the other hand, felt that truth had triumphed and was not terribly concerned about the animosity of the Antiochene bishops. The schism, however, attracted the attention of the emperor Theodosius II. Amid a fragmented and beleaguered empire (recall that the Germanic invasions were ravaging the western empire at this time), the emperor desired unity and a measure of uniformity to protect the common good. Theodosius put great pressure on Cyril and John of Antioch to work out their differences and find common ground. In 433, John and Cyril, under imperial pressure, hammered out a formula of faith to bring an end to the schism. This **Formula of Reunion**, as it is known, includes both characteristically Antiochene and Alexandrian positions. The main section of the formula reads as follows:

We confess then our Lord Jesus Christ, the only begotten Son of God, perfect God and perfect man, consisting of a rational soul and body, begotten of the Father before the ages as to his Godhead, and in the last days the Same, for us and for our salvation, of Mary the Virgin as to his manhood; the Same homoousios with the Father as to his Godhead, and homoousios with us as to his manhood. For there has been a union of two natures; wherefore we confess one Christ, one Son, one Lord.

In accordance with this thought of the unconfused union, we confess the holy Virgin to be *Theotokos*, because the divine Logos was incarnate and made man, and from the very conception united to himself the temple that was taken of her.[10]

As you can see, the formula contains several passages characteristic of either an Alexandrian or an Antiochene Christology. Notice the Alexandrian emphasis on identification of the divine Son as the subject of Jesus ("the Same"), the union *(henōsis)* of the divine and human rather than Nestorius's conjunction *(synapheia)* of the two natures, and the identification of Mary as Theotokos. The formula also contains several Antiochene elements: Christ is *homoousios* with both God and with humanity, and there is full affirmation of the human nature in Christ such that it is not diminished in any way. The Formula of Reunion testifies that although Alexandria and Antioch had very different approaches to Christology, their positions were not irreconcilable, provided each side demonstrated flexibility. Yet the politics of the day and the pettiness of many figures in these disputes made compromise difficult. In fact, compromise seemed to require that the civil authorities apply pressure.

More Politics and More Doctrine: The Council of Chalcedon (451)

Shortly after the tenuous reunion between Alexandria and Antioch, both Cyril and John passed away, and the union that had been forged between them proved to be somewhat unstable. Their successors carried on the theological and political battles their predecessors had heated up in the decades prior, and Constantinople remained in the crosshairs of the Alexandrians.

In 434, Proclus became bishop of Constantinople. He was a great supporter of Alexandrian theology. However, he was moderate enough to show respect to his great Antiochene predecessor in the see of Constantinople, John Chrysostom, by bringing his body back from exile and burying him with high honors in the Basilica of the Apostles in the newest part of the city. Proclus had written a letter to the church of Armenia (called the *Tome of Proclus*) setting out for them the orthodox doctrine of the Incarnation. It stated that "there is only one Son, for the natures are not divided into two hypostases, rather the awesome economy of salvation has united the two natures into one *hypostasis*."[11] Here we find an example of a crucial distinction made neither by Nestorius nor Cyril: the distinction between nature and *hyspostasis*, or "person."

When Flavian became the bishop of Constantinople in 446, the Alexandrian desire for a fight reached a climax. During a meeting of all the bishops in the region of Constantinople in 448 (called the Synod of Constantinople), an elderly bishop named Eusebius of Dorylaeum interrupted the proceedings by bringing an indictment against the monk Eutyches, who was a powerful figure and very close to the imperial family. Eusebius charged that Eutyches had repudiated the Formula of Reunion signed by John and Cyril in 433. Eutyches had been insisting that "out of two natures" there was only "one incarnate nature of the *Logos*." This last phrase, used years earlier by Cyril, became a battle cry for those Alexandrians who felt that too much had been given away to the Antiochenes in the Formula of Reunion. Eutyches was convinced that he should make a stand. The indictment of Eutyches for insisting that there was "one incarnate nature of the Logos" (this is often called **Monophysiticism**) forced the bishop of Constantinople, Flavian, to put Eutyches on trial for heresy. Now such a trial is a combination of what we would think of as both a criminal and a civil procedure. The defendant stood to lose property, job, freedom (a conviction often meant exile), and perhaps even his life. Meanwhile, keeping abreast of these developments was the new bishop of Alexandria, Dioscorus, for whom the condemnation of Eutyches represented an opportunity to undo the Formula of Reunion and gain a definitive victory for Alexandria.

The indictment and conviction of Eutyches centered on his denial of the Formula of Reunion, and this represented a serious problem for Flavian in his attempts to stabilize Constantinople. Years earlier, at Ephesus in 431, the bishops were hesitant about adding to or changing the basic statement of Christian faith that had been articulated at Nicaea. The bishops therefore declared that no one was to add to that statement of faith, and that there was no standard of orthodoxy other than Nicaea. Eusebius and Flavian, unfortunately, had used the Formula of Reunion as the standard of orthodoxy when they condemned Eutyches; this was in violation of the rule set forth at Ephesus. The enemies of Flavian and Eusebius now had a powerful weapon.

Dioscorus, the bishop of Alexandria, was able to persuade Emperor Theodosius II to convene a council at Ephesus again. The council was held in 449 with Dioscorus presiding and Flavian as the defendant. Leo, the bishop of Rome (pope) at the time, supported Flavian in an important letter (Leo's Tome) and sent two legates, or representatives, to the council, but it soon became evident that the deliberations at Ephesus were even less fair and transparent than Cyril's council had been. Through intimidation and threat Dioscorus engineered the exoneration of Eutyches and the condemnation of Flavian, who died on his way into exile at the hands of his captors. The papal legates (the pope's representatives at the council) were forced to flee the scene and stow away on a ship to report to Leo the disastrous events that had taken place. In a letter to the empress Pulcheria, Leo characterized the meeting at Ephesus as a *latrocinium*, a **"Robber Council."**

The death of Theodosius II, however, began to reverse the fortunes of Dioscorus, and at the behest of Leo, the new emperor, Marcian, called for another council, this time at Chalcedon. In 451 the council met and reversed the findings of the Robber Council. Eutyches's position was condemned, and Dioscorus was deposed and even taunted in the council chamber as the "murderer of Flavian." The bishops then set forth a formula—not a creed—to articulate the orthodox belief of the Christian church regarding the divine and human natures in Christ. The formula combined the best aspects of Cyril's theology (from his second letter to Nestorius), Flavian's statement of faith against Eutyches, and Leo's Tome.

The Emergence of Rome in the Christological Controversies

What is so special about the Bishop of Rome, whom Catholics call the pope (a title derived from the affectionate Latin term for father, *papa*)? That question can be tricky! Let's begin by talking about Peter and the Twelve. As you may recall from chapter 2, many scholars agree that the Twelve were a feature of Jesus' ministry. He selected this group as a sign of the reconstitution of Israel and its twelve tribes. Many of these figures are just names to us, and perhaps to the evangelists as well, since many of them apparently were not remembered by the early church, except as names on a list. But several of these figures are prominent in the early church, and among these Peter seems to have a special place. He appears frequently in stories about Jesus, is depicted as interacting with Jesus in meaningful ways, and is prominent in Luke's narrative of the early church in Acts. Matthew's Gospel (particularly Matthew 16:13–20), along with John 21:15–19, was especially important in establishing notions of Peter's pastoral role and place in the church.

The second part of the question connects Peter to Rome. As early as the first century, Christian writers have narrated the story of Peter's death in Rome during Nero's persecution in the mid-60s CE (1 Clement 5) and writers in the second century confirmed this (e.g., Ignatius, *Epistle to the Romans* 4.2; Irenaeus, *Against Heresies*, 3.1.2, 3.3.1). Apparently by the second century, and perhaps even earlier, Christians had erected a shrine over the grave of Peter; over this shrine Constantine eventually built the Basilica of St. Peter in the fourth century. Constantine's basilica was replaced in the sixteenth and seventeenth centuries with a new basilica, but the shrine at the tomb of Peter remains under the high altar. You may have seen it in the television broadcasts of the burial of Pope John Paul II in 2005.

The association of Peter with Rome is long-standing, though he is associated with Antioch as well (cf. Galatians 2:11–21). Movement from an account of Peter's place in the early church and to his presence and martyrdom in Rome is a long way from demonstrating the basis for papal power and authority. In fact, in the first three centuries of the Christian era, the authority of the bishop of Rome was not neatly defined. He certainly exercised total authority over the churches in Italy, and substantial authority over the churches in North Africa, France, and Spain. In the East, the bishop of Rome was highly respected and often sought out in times of crisis or indecision, but it is not clear that eastern bishops viewed themselves as under his authority. In fact, the emperor seemed to exert the most influence and was often viewed as an arbitrator in disputes, though the precise role of emperor in the East is complex and fluid. But amid the christological controversies, several bishops of Rome began to assert their authority over the churches in the East. In particular, Damasus I (304–384) in the battle against Arianism, and Leo I (†461) against Eutyches and Monophysitism, used their position to enhance the power and prestige of the papacy. In fact, reports say that when Leo's Tome was read at Chalcedon (451) the bishops responded, "Peter has spoken!"

Universal papal power (*plenitudo potestatis* in Latin) was actively and robustly defined and defended by Gregory I (540–604) and then Gregory VII (1021–1085). The latter, following a century of papal impotence, boldly declared the universal power of the papacy in his *Dictatus Papae*. In this document, Gregory lays out twenty-one points of papal power, including the power to legislate universally, the power to appoint and depose bishops and clergy,

The Emergence of Rome in the Christological Controversies *(continued)*

and the power to release citizens from their obligations to their rulers. In short, the pope may judge anyone, but no one may judge the pope.

While some of this might at first appear outrageous, one should recall that Gregory claimed these powers during a period when the church was subject to gross abuse at the hands of secular political authorities. The church had become an arm of the local ruler, and he appointed his own clergy and often made his own rules along the way. Gregory vigorously asserted the independence of the church from secular powers by placing it above those powers. He was followed by others equally vigorous in their defense of the papal authority, most notably Innocent III (1160–1216). Many of these moves, however, became problematic when less than virtuous men were elected pope. Such was the case in the late Middle Ages and at the eve of the Reformation, and papal authority soon gave way to local autonomy and eventually to nationalism in many corners of the Christian world.

In more recent times, the office of pope has become both a source of strength and a cause of division. An important example of the former is Communist Poland, where the forces of oppression were engaged by the Catholic Church; the power of the papacy to confront tyranny was evident in the visits of John Paul II to Poland in 1979 and 1983. With the demise of Communism in Poland, the Catholic Church has become embroiled in political controversies, which have eroded its influence and credibility.

The personal charisma and spiritual vision of John Paul II cannot overshadow a main dividing factor for many Protestant and Orthodox Christians from Catholic Christians: the doctrine of papal infallibility. Defined at the First Vatican Council (1869–1870), the doctrine declares that the pope, when speaking as supreme teacher and pastor of the universal Church (in Latin this is often referred to as speaking *ex cathedra*, or "from the [teacher's] chair"), defines a teaching on faith or morals to be held and believed by all, he is preserved from error by grace and the power of the Holy Spirit. In Catholic circles, this is understood as an extension of the presence of Christ and the power of the Spirit in the life of the Church, the Body of Christ. Yet many Protestant and Orthodox Christians—including many who like and respect the pope as a pastor and advocate for the gospel—find such claims of authority and infallibility dangerous and disturbing. The ministry of the Bishop of Rome is to serve as a principle of unity in the church, yet it is often an obstacle to unity with other Christians. In light of this fact, the late John Paul II issued a document titled *Ut Unum Sint* ("That They May Be One," 1995), in which he encouraged theologians to discuss ways of understanding and exercising the Petrine ministry, as it is called. Protestant and Orthodox Christians found this helpful and appropriate.

The Formula (or Definition) of Chalcedon thus provides a synthesis of christological insights in the fourth and fifth centuries.

Therefore, following the holy Fathers [the bishops at Nicaea], we all teach with one accord all to acknowledge one and the same Son, our Lord Jesus Christ at once complete in Godhead and complete in

The First Five Ecumenical Councils: A Timeline

The study of the early councils can be confusing. The following timeline does not include all of the relevant names and dates, but offers a simplified schematic for study purposes. At the top, the names of the figures whose positions were condemned at a council are given in *italics*. The next row contains the names of theologians whose positions were vindicated at each council; these names are underlined. The names of each of the councils are given in CAPS below that. Finally, the names of the emperors are given below the dates in the timeline. Below you will find a table for understanding the dynamics of the councils in the context of Alexandrian and Antiochene theological battles.

	Arius	*Apollinaris*	*Nestorius*	*Eutyches and Dioscorus*	*Theodore of Mopsuestia*
	<u>Athanasius</u>	<u>Gregory Nazianzen</u>	<u>Cyril</u>	<u>Leo and Flavian</u>	<u>Leontius</u>
Irenaeus	NICAEA (325)	CONSTANTINOPLE I (381)	EPHESUS (431)	CHALCEDON (451)	CONSTANTINOPLE II (553)
200 CE	300 CE	400 CE	500 CE	600 CE	
Constantine	Theodosius I	Theodosius II	Marcian	Justinian	

Alexandria ←→ **Antioch**

Nicaea

Nicaea's affirmation of the full divinity of the Son became a central piece in Alexandrian theology; the defense of Nicaea became a concern of those who succeeded Athanasius as bishop.

Ephesus

Nestorius's caution about too closely identifying the divine nature with the human being Jesus seemed, in the ears of Alexandrian theologians, tantamount to denying the Incarnation. The condemnation of Nestorius was a great victory for Alexandria, and in the subsequent battles, the Alexandrians were ever watchful for the reemergence of Nestorianism.

Constantinople I

The condemnation of Apollinarianism and the assertion that Christ was fully human, including a rational soul, was an important victory for Antiochene Christology.

Chalcedon

Chalcedon's affirmation of the full humanity of Jesus, without confusion or mixture with the divine, was precisely what Antiochenes felt Nestorius had tried to express, albeit poorly. The Alexandrians had difficulty accepting Chalcedon, and many of them did not. Subsequent attempts to put an Alexandrian "spin" on Chalcedon (i.e., Leontius) made little difference to the Alexandrians.

humanness truly God and truly human consisting of a rational soul and body; of one substance of the Father as regards to his Godhead, and at the same time of one substance with us as regards His humanness; like us in all things except sin; as regards His Godhead, begotten of the Father before all the ages but yet as regards his humanity begotten for us and for our salvation of Mary the Virgin the God bearer; one and the same Christ, Son, Lord, Only-begotten, recognized in two natures, without confusion without change without division without separation; the distinction in the natures being in no way annulled by the union, but rather the characteristics of each nature being preserved and coming together to form one person (*prosōpon*) and one subsistence (*hypsotasin*) not parted or separated into two persons but one and the same Son and Only-begotten God the Word, Lord Jesus Christ even as the prophets from earliest times spoke of Him and our Lord Jesus Christ Himself taught us, and the creed of the Fathers has handed down to us.

The essential clarification made at Chalcedon was the distinction between nature (*physis*) and person (*prosōpon*, or hypostasis), a distinction Cyril himself and many others had failed to make, but which Proclus had begun to articulate. Like Nicaea's *homoousios*, the Formula of Chalcedon does not provide the reader with a picture of the union of natures in Christ; rather, the formula provides us with theological-grammatical rules for talking about this union: "without confusion without change without division without separation; the distinction in the natures being in no way annulled by the union." Chalcedon therefore provides an answer to the second christological question (the relationship between the human being Jesus and the divine Son) that is much like the first christological question (the relationship between God and the Son). Like Nicaea, Chalcedon also self-consciously sets out its formula as a definitive guide for "acknowledging" Christ, that is, how to think and talk about Christ.

Ancient and Modern Christianity Beyond the Western Comfort Zone

Most modern Christians assume that Christianity is a western religion, uniquely at home in the world of Greece and Rome. Yet Christianity had taken root in a number of Asian and African cultures long before many northern European nations accepted the gospel. Still to be found in most of these nations are unique forms of Christianity unrelated to that brought by European missionaries.

Armenia is the oldest officially Christian nation. In the late third or early fourth century, the Armenian king Tiridates III converted and received baptism from St. Gregory "the Illuminator." The sons of Gregory succeeded him as bishops and leaders of the church in Armenia. In fact, a son of Gregory attended the Council of Nicaea (325). For various political reasons, the Armenians did not accept the Council of Chalcedon and are thus regarded as Monophysites by Roman Catholics. In many respects the Armenian Church reflects both Eastern Orthodox and Roman Catholic sensibilities (the latter due to the influence of the crusaders), though with distinctive elements. The disintegration of the nation of Armenia under Persian, Arab, and especially Turkish influence has been disastrous. In the early twentieth century, the modern Turkish state acted against the Armenians, brutally murdering countless people and forbidding the Armenian language and customs. A small percentage of Armenians have entered into communion with Rome, but most Armenians remain part of the autonomous Armenian Orthodox Church.

Egypt has enjoyed a sizable Christian population since the second century. Tradition says that it was evangelized by Mark the evangelist, but the origins of Christianity in the area are complex. In the disputes following Chalcedon, Christians in Egypt refused to accept the doctrine of two natures, and insisted that Cyril's formula was correct ("out of two natures one

incarnate nature of the Logos"), though they would reject the label "Monophysite" that Roman Catholics give them. Egyptian Christians (called "Copts," the ancient name for Egypt) developed their own identity, even though they were severely persecuted by the imperial government in Constantinople for their refusal to accept Chalcedon. The arrival of Muslim Arabs in Egypt brought relief from imperial persecution, but also brought second-class citizenship. Generally Copts were given latitude to practice their religion, but periodic and often ferocious persecutions destroyed churches and compelled many people to abandon the faith, an egregious example being the persecution of Caliph el Hakim in the eleventh century. By the Middle Ages, Egypt had become a majority Muslim nation, though with a sizeable Christian minority. Coptic Christians today play a vital role in the life of Egypt, though Muslim extremists have launched periodic and vicious persecutions against them, particularly in the countryside. The vast majority of Copts belong to the autonomous Coptic Orthodox Church, but a few are in communion with Rome.

Ethiopia had close contacts with Coptic Christianity, from which it adopted a Monophysite Christology. Over the centuries, however, the Ethiopian church developed its own voice. Christianity came to Abyssinia (Ethiopia) in the fourth century, and its popularity ebbed and flowed in response to a variety of circumstances, especially the influence of Islam in the region and pressures applied by Rome and various European political powers through missionaries. The Ethiopian Orthodox Tewahido Church, the only pre-colonial form of Christianity in sub-Saharan Africa, has an elaborate culture and history. Ge'ez, a Semitic language related to Hebrew and Arabic, is the liturgical language. Ethiopian Christians preserve an elaborate narrative in which they identify

Ancient and Modern Christianity Beyond the Western Comfort Zone *(continued)*

themselves as part of the lost tribes of Israel. Their sacred city is Axum, where they claim the Ark of the Covenant is housed. In keeping with their close identification with Israel, they have adopted many aspects of Jewish dietary law and insist on modest dress for women (hair covering). Over half of the population of Ethiopia and Eritrea are Christian.

India is home to a great variety of religions, but when Portuguese missionaries arrived in the fifteenth century, they were stunned to find a long-practicing, autonomous Christian community (Malabar Christians). These Christians, located in the southwest portion of the subcontinent, trace their heritage to Thomas, one of the Twelve, whose purported grave near Mylapur was an important place of pilgrimage. Apparently, Malabar Christianity was connected to the Nestorian churches of Syria and Persia, though the Malabar Christians seemed to the Roman Catholic Portuguese to be completely orthodox and were quickly received into communion with Rome. Subsequent struggles with Roman control of the church alienated some, and a minority have variously aligned themselves with other Orthodox, Oriental (i.e., Nestorian), and Anglican churches.

Iraq and **Iran** are known today as hot spots of fervent Islam, but for centuries Christianity has had a place in the story of these nations, and still does. Christianity spread to Mesopotamia and Persia very early in the Christian era. Many of Nestorius's supporters were from these regions. With the disaster at Ephesus and the subsequent battles over Chalcedon, the Christians of the East simply went their own way and flourished for centuries, even through part of the Islamic period.

China was introduced to Christianity before Russia, Norway, and even Sweden. In fact, Nestorian missionaries from Persia and Syria brought the gospel to China in the seventh century. Archaeologists have found numerous crosses throughout central and western China, but most important, the discovery of the monument at Singan-fu, an ancient capital of China, has served to verify Nestorian missionary success. The monument was discovered during roadwork in 1625. It was erected in 781 and contains script in both Chinese and Syriac (the language of the Nestorian churches) recounting the arrival in China of Nestorian missionaries in 636. The Christian presence in China eventually faded by the late Middle Ages due to changes in imperial power and competition from Buddhism and Confucianism. Western Christianity was introduced in the Middle Ages and again in the sixteenth century.

The Aftermath of Chalcedon (451–553)

While on the surface it may seem as though Chalcedon resolved the story of classical Christology with a general consensus uniting the church, nothing could be further from the truth. Dioscorus and many of his supporters remained defiant and used the politics of the empire to separate themselves from the other churches, despite the efforts of several emperors and bishops to counter such moves. To this day, the vast majority of Egypt's ten million Christians (Coptic Christians) do not subscribe to Chalcedon.

Additionally, the Christians of Armenia and the thirty million Christians of Ethiopia are Cyrillian-Monophysite and do not accept Chalcedon.[12] For them the impasse was stated clearly by the great champion of Cyrillian-Monophysitism, Philoxenus of Mabbugh (440–523). Philoxenus insisted that every nature *(physis)* has a person *(prosōpon)*; if there are two natures in Christ, then there are two Christs. This sounds inescapably Nestorian to the ears of those who do not affirm a distinction between "person" and "nature." Philoxenus repeatedly affirms, however, that the Son became a perfect human being, and this perfection necessarily included a human soul and human intelligence. Thus a close examination of the seemingly Monophysite position of Philoxenus shows him to be orthodox.

While the Latin West was largely content with Chalcedon, the conflict continued in the churches of the East. The failure of Chalcedon to solve the ecclesiastical divisions of the fifth century immediately should not be surprising; many western churches continued to profess an Arian faith for centuries following Nicaea. But attempts to reconcile the Christians of Egypt fostered a somewhat problematic interpretation of Chalcedon. A notable sixth-century supporter of Chalcedon was Leontius of Byzantium. In an effort to win over the Cyrillian-Monophysites, Leontius tried to explain the orthodoxy of Chalcedon in a way that would allow the opponents of Chalcedon to hear something other than Nestorianism in the language of two natures. Leontius stated that the human nature of Christ is neither an acted *hypostasis* nor without *hypostasis*; rather, the human nature of Christ was *enhypostasia*.[13] That is, the human nature of Christ does not have its own separate concrete existence *(hypostasis)*; rather, the human nature of Christ has its concrete existence "in" the *hypostasis* of the divine Word. This is what has often been described as the **hypostatic union**. Leontius's formulation does not say that the human nature of Christ is thus diminished in any way—it retains all of its properties, including a rational soul. What Leontius wants to clarify is that the human nature of Christ does not exist alongside the divine; rather, these two are united. The human nature of Christ is *in the hypostasis* of the divine nature.

Leontius's Christology is completely orthodox, and was vindicated at **Constantinople II** in 553. Yet the circumstances in which it was articulated, when the state was looking for ways to heal the schism that had

Person of Interest

Theodore of Mopsuestia

Theodore of Mopsuestia (350–428) was one of the greatest and most articulate of the Antiochene theologians. As the bishop of Mopsuestia, he was a close friend of another Antiochene theologian, St. John Chrysostom, the bishop of Constantinople. While his account of the Incarnation was used by Nestorians to support their doctrines, he had developed his doctrine to combat the threat of Apollinaris. Nestorius and his supporters began using Theodore's Christology after he died. This Christology supplied Nestorius with some of his salient points: a hard distinction between the eternal Word and its shrine, the human being Jesus, and the notion of a single *prosōpon* resulting from the conjunction (not union) of the two natures. The posthumous condemnations of Theodore and other Antiochene theologians at Constantinople II (553) were viewed by many bishops at the time as excessive and inappropriate. Many scholars today take a much more sympathetic view of his Christology. Theodore was also a great exegete (interpreter of Scripture) who advanced a less allegorical and more historical approach to Scripture. Many contemporary exegetes find his biblical commentaries highly instructive for this reason.

divided the church between Monophysitism and Chalcedon, conspired to distort its contribution over time. At Constantinople II, Emperor Justinian and others issued posthumous condemnations of the great Antiochene theologians of the fourth and fifth centuries, including Theodore of Mopsuestia. Many contemporary scholars feel that the unintended effect of these condemnations, along with approval of Leontius's theology, was a diminishment of Christ's humanity in christological reflection. Such a move, though not formally intended, has caused many contemporary theologians to revisit the teaching of Chalcedon and "recover" the full humanity of Jesus. In so doing they are also revisiting the theology of Theodore of Mopsuestia and even Nestorius. Such developments have raised important and controversial questions about the value and applicability of classical Christology for contemporary theology.

Conclusion

The classical christological controversies discussed in this chapter are difficult to grasp, and many students question the extent to which this material is relevant. The dismissal of classical Christology, though tempting in many ways, is not an option that is consistent with Christianity as an historical faith. These controversies remain important for several reasons, whatever one's judgment may be about the contemporary viability of the doctrines that emerged from them. First, these controversies illustrate the importance of theological clarity and right judgment. This sentiment may sound a bit dogmatic, and it may belie the complexities of propositional statements ("God is . . ."), but the realm of **theory** plays an important role in religious faith and its expression (and an important role in personal relationships as well). Second, the story of the christological controversies provide apt illustration that theological orthodoxy, rather than the mere repetition of received formulae, is really the product of innovative and creative thinking. Because this thinking always reflects the particular cultural and historical circumstances in which that thinking takes place, orthodoxy must always remain an open rather than closed system. It always requires a measure of innovation. In addition, the story of the classical christological controversies helps set the stage for understanding and assessing the issues confronted in contemporary Christology.

Questions for Understanding

1. How did the Modalists understand the relationship between God (the Father) and the Son? Why might this position be problematic?

2. Describe Origen's views on the relationship between God (the Father) and the Son. How is his position different from Tertullian's?

3. Explain Arius's position on the relationship between the Logos and God. What Scripture passages helped Arius to make his case?

4. Who was Apollinaris, and what did he say about Jesus? Why was his Christology condemned at Constantinople I?

5. What role did politics play in the Council of Nicaea and its aftermath?

6. Why did Nestorius object to honoring Mary with the title Theotokos?

7. Why did the Alexandrians object to the statement of faith made at the Council of Chalcedon?

8. Some have described Nicaea and Chalcedon as bookends to classical Christological questions. In what way can these two councils be understood to encapsulate or enclose the debate?

Questions for Reflection

1. Do you think most Christians could articulate the importance of the Nicene faith? As an experiment, talk to three friends, family members, or acquaintances who self-identify as Christians, and ask them to explain the relationship between "Jesus" and "God." Do they make explicit reference to the Nicene Creed? Do they express a heretical position (subordinationism, adoptionism, modalism)?

2. In contemporary iconography, Jesus is depicted in a variety of ways. Perhaps you recall how he was depicted in a children's Bible from your youth. Our iconography of Jesus often says as much about ourselves as it does about Jesus. For example, in a Vietnamese church, one may encounter an image of Christ with Asian features and dressed in traditional Confucian style. In Ethiopian iconography, Jesus and his disciples are depicted as Africans. These images reflect our conviction that in Jesus everything that it means to be human, including our ethnicities, has been taken up into God and redeemed through the Incarnation. This is reflected in Gregory Nazianzen's famous statement, "What was not assumed is not redeemed." With this in mind, are these ethnocentric depictions of Jesus appropriate? Are there any limits in such iconography? Could Jesus be depicted as a woman? Explain.

3. In this chapter we encountered many important philosophical terms (e.g., *homoousios, prosōpon*). These terms are either not found in Scripture, or they do not play any important role in New Testament Christology, but they are decisive in normative statements of faith (i.e., creeds, the *Catechism*). Is it appropriate to move beyond Scripture in this way in order to standardize Christology? Should the church move beyond these terms and categories, or are they essential for understanding what the church believes about Jesus? Explain.

4. Politics and rivalry seem to play important roles in the unfolding of christological doctrine. This is also a factor in modern times (note the history of Vatican II). Are politics and rivalries antithetical to real religious dialogue? Explain.

Endnotes

1   See Tertullian, *Against Praxeas*, 7.
2   See Origen, *Commentary on John*, 2.2.
3   Lactantius, *On the Deaths of the Persecutors*, 44. Eusebius, *Life of Constantine*, 1.28, offers the Greek version: *toutō nika*)
4   The bishops of Rome, Alexandria, Antioch, and eventually Jerusalem and Constantinople were regarded with great reverence in the early church. They had enormous power and influence over other churches in their areas. Starting in the sixth century, these bishops were called "patriarchs," but during the period in question the leaders of these churches were given only the title "bishop."
5   Constantine's "Letter to Alexander and Arius," quoted in Leo Davis, S J, *The First Seven Ecumenical Councils 325–787: Their History and Theology* (Collegeville, MN: Liturgical, 1983), 55.
6   *On the Incarnation*, 54.11.
7   Bernard Lonergan, *The Way to Nicaea: The Dialectical Development of Trinitarian Theology* (Philadelphia: Westminster, 1976).
8   *Letter 101 to Cledonius.*
9   The canon actually states, "The bishop of Constantinople shall have primacy of honor after (*meta*) the bishop of Rome because Constantinople is the new Rome." Many Orthodox Christians would argue that the word "after" (*meta*) in the canon does not make Constantiople inferior to Rome but should be read in a temporal sense: Constantinople is chronologically "after" Rome.
10   See Robert V. Sellers, *The Council of Chalcedon: A Historical and Doctrinal Survey* (London: SPCK, 1953), 17–18.
11   Migne, *Patrologia Grecae*, 65.651, quoted in Davis, 164.
12   While the acceptance of Chalcedon has proven problematic for these churches, many Christian churches still reject the Council of Ephesus and support Nestorius. These churches, mostly in modern-day Syria, Iraq, and Iran, sent missionaries as far as western China in the fifth and sixth centuries. The reading of the christological councils here is done from a Roman Catholic perspective, though I hope Coptic, Assyrian (so-called Nestorian), and other Christians do not take offense. Many aspects of these early theological debates reflected conceptual and linguistic concerns as well as political and cultural issues.
13   For an excellent discussion of the issues involved and the implications of misreading Leontius's Christology, see LeRon Shults, "A Dubious Christological Formula: From Leontius of Byzantium to Karl Barth," *Theological Studies* 57 (1996): 431–46.

The Work of Christ

Imagine the infant Jesus, wrapped in swaddling clothes and lying in Mary's arms in Bethlehem. Now imagine that a menacing silhouette suddenly appears in the doorway. It is one of Herod's soldiers, who has been sent to Bethlehem on orders from the king to destroy all male children less than two years old (Matthew 2:16–18). His mother clutches the babe desperately in a futile attempt to stop the insanity, but the soldier prevails and takes the child out to the town center, where he unceremoniously slaughters the baby along with the other children. Mary, another victim of the outrageous political violence of her era, finds the corpse of her dead son among the carnage. Weeping and mourning, she commits the body to an appropriate burial place. In this imaginary scenario, would the death of the child Jesus still have religious significance, or would it simply be a horrific crime? Would the murdered infant still be our savior?

This exercise helps to illustrate the problems Christians face when they attempt to articulate Jesus' saving work solely in terms of his death. While no Christians have ever argued that a scenario like the one offered above would be redemptive, the example helps to draw attention to the Christian tradition's emphasis on the death of Jesus—often divorced from his life and ministry—and helps us to understand how this emphasis can be problematic. Christians claim, "Jesus died for our sins"; what does this mean?

With this question we enter a branch of theology traditionally called **soteriology**: discourse about how Christ saves us (the Greek word *sōtēr* means "savior"). Even the word *save* raises questions: from what are we saved, and why do we need saving? Since Christians affirm that Jesus saves us from sin, any account of Jesus as Savior requires an account of sin. As we shall see, one's understanding of sin will structure one's account of how Jesus saves. For example, if one conceives of sin as tantamount to a disruptive noise that wakes a sleeping god (as in the Babylonia creation story, *Enuma Elish*), then one might expect that salvation would entail placating, appeasing, putting to bed, or possibly even killing the irate god. If, on the other hand, sin is understood as a crime against the sovereign ruler of the kingdom, then perhaps a kind of punishment is in order, one that fits the crime. In this chapter we examine some of the most popular images of sin and the corresponding approaches to soteriology that have flourished in the Christian tradition.

Biblical Images of Salvation

The Prophets and Salvation History

The primary model for understanding God (YHWH) as Savior comes to us from the prophetic tradition. The prophetic model of salvation, as the name suggests, originates in the theology articulated by the Old Testament prophets and their disciples; in the New Testament it is developed further by the evangelist Luke.[1] Of course, at the time most of the Old Testament prophets were active, there was no consistent vision of afterlife.

Sacrifice in Ancient Israel

Human Sacrifice

Although not condoned in Scripture, one can see that the practice of human sacrifice is not far removed from the experience of ancient Israel. The command to engage in *cherem* (holy war), in which human beings and animals were dedicated to God through their destruction, is off-putting to the modern reader. The most chilling account of human sacrifice in the Bible is that of Jephthah, the judge who made a vow to sacrifice the first thing he met upon his victorious return from battle (Judges 11:29–40). His daughter rushed out to greet him upon his arrival, and Jephthah made good his promise to God. Then we have the *aqedah* or "the binding" of Isaac, in which God commands Abraham to sacrifice his son and, at the last minute, stops him with a prohibition against human sacrifice in Israel. The divine commandment was apparently unheeded at various points in Israel's history. We see in the prophets several references to the practice of child sacrifice for a deity named Molech (2 Kings 23:10; Jeremiah 32:35), though the practice was condemned in Scripture (e.g., Leviticus 18:21).

Animal Sacrifice

Various animals, both small and large, were regularly sacrificed in Israel. These sacrifices fell into different categories based on the purpose of the ritual involved and what was to be done with the animal.

Holocaust, or Burnt Offerings

The holocaust was an offering exclusively designated for YHWH and meant to acknowledge God's holiness. After the victim's throat was cut and the blood was drained from the body and offered to God, it was skinned, quartered, and burned. The burning of the animal, the fire and the smoke, rose toward heaven and delivered the sacrificial victim to God. Such a sacrifice was offered on solemn occasions.

Peace Offerings

In the peace offering the most prized portions of the animal (fat, kidneys, liver) are offered to God, while the remainder is split between the priest and the beneficiary of the sacrifice.

Expiatory Sacrifices

The Torah distinguishes between two types of expiatory offerings, "sin offerings" and "guilt offerings," but the precise limits of the distinction are unclear to modern scholars. While the words used to designate each of these sacrifices differ, the rituals outlined in the Torah and the reasons for them overlap considerably. In these offerings the priest ate the portions of the animal not offered to God.

Grain Sacrifice

The *minha* was the standard offering of grain and oil, either in raw form or baked. The priest would burn a portion of the offering to God and eat the rest. There was also a table on which two rows of six cakes (the "showbread") were placed every Sabbath. At the end of the week, the priest would eat the old cakes.

Thus "salvation" meant being preserved from death and destruction here and now. God was Savior by acting in history to secure justice. For the eighth-century prophets, God's saving action in history involved the use of human beings, entire nations, and historical events to correct injustices and mete out punishments. The process by which justice is restored and Israel saved from destruction unfolds over the centuries.

In the book of the prophet Isaiah, for example, salvation is worked out over the long haul of history. In the first part of Isaiah (chapters 1–39), the oracles and poetry most closely associated with the eighth-century Jerusalem prophet, human beings are called upon to suffer for the sins of the nation. The inability or unwillingness of various kings and their people to trust in YHWH and abide by the covenant makes this suffering appropriate. But in Second and Third Isaiah (Isaiah chapters 40–55 and 56–65, respectively) we find that YHWH eventually proves to be a loving redeemer and the restorer of Judah and Jerusalem, whose acts manifest his *chesed* (loving mercy). These chapters from Second and Third Isaiah emerged from the final decades of the Exile in Babylon and the return to Jerusalem at the end of the sixth century BCE, a century and a half after the lifetime of Isaiah. The canonical book, therefore, testifies that over the long course of history, God's purpose, God's faithfulness, unfolds and brings about the salvation of his people.

The Priestly or Cultic Approach to Salvation

While an historical approach to soteriology dominated the prophetic tradition, the priestly traditions of Second-Temple Judaism swung soteriology in a more cultic direction and exerted considerable influence on the soteriological language in the New Testament. There is perhaps no better summary of Hebrew sacrifice than the rituals surrounding Yom Kippur (the **Day of Atonement**) in Leviticus 16.

In this context the Hebrew word ***kapporet*** plays an important role. It is often translated as "mercy seat," or "propitiatory," and refers to the Ark of the Covenant's gold cover, over which YHWH was enthroned. This is where God "sits" (hence the notion of "mercy seat"). The ark was a major symbol in the history of Israel. At a literal level the ark was a box made of wood and clad in gold. It had a lid, or cover, on which stood the figures of two cherubim with wings folded over the ark. Two poles for carrying the ark ran parallel horizontally through two rings on each end of the ark. Inside the ark were the tablets of the Law, the commandments given to Moses on Sinai (see 1 Kings 8:9), but the Letter to the Hebrews (9:4) asserts that the ark also held a vessel containing manna (the bread that fed the Israelites when they wandered in the wilderness after their departure from Egypt) and the staff of Moses by which YHWH showed his power. The ark was the symbol of YHWH's presence with Israel, but YHWH was not to be identified with the ark; rather, YHWH sat "enthroned above the cherubim" (1 Samuel 4:4; 2 Samuel 6:2; Psalm 80:2). This throne (the *kapporet*) was the focal point of the rituals on the Day of Atonement.

Leviticus 16 tells us that on the day when the high priest made a sacrifice to take away the sin of the people of Israel, the high priest offered a bull and a goat before he entered the inner sanctuary of the temple (or, in Leviticus, the tabernacle), the Holy of Holies, where the ark was kept. This was the only day out of the year that anyone entered this holiest place. The high priest was to apply the blood of the sacrificed animals on the *kapporet* and then go outside to another goat—the **scapegoat**—dedicated to destruction with the name Azazel. Azazel was the name of the demon in the desert where the goat was taken, though some suggest that the name means "precipice," or "cliff," referring to the place where the goat would meet its end. The high priest pronounced the sins of the people and touched the goat, thereby transferring the sins of the people to the goat. The goat was then driven out of the community. Impurities were eradicated by the blood of the offering, but deliberate sins could not be eradicated, only carried to the wilderness where, it was hoped, they would never return.

The Yom Kippur ritual thus revolves around two important concepts.[2] First is the sacred substance, blood, which contains the life force, a power that properly belongs to God and not human beings. It is a dangerous and dynamic force that can destroy as well as cleanse. In this context, blood has the force to cleanse the sanctuary of impurities. Second is a transference and expulsion of sin from the community, so that through a combination of ritual actions Israel may be both purged of sin and cleansed. Some New Testament authors will play with, or perhaps conflate, these rituals as they explore the religious significance of Christ's death.

René Girard's Theory of Sacrifice

René Girard, an important and popular French literary critic, offers a sweeping and comprehensive account of the origins of violence and sacrifice that resonates with common experience. Girard understands the origins of human violence in terms of "mimetic desire" (from the Greek *mimesis*, "imitation"). Girard's theory states that human beings learn to desire what their peers and elders teach them to desire. It logically follows that if we all desire the same things (limited in number), the result is anxiety and violence. Such anxiety and violence are regulated by a society through the scapegoating mechanism: society transfers its guilt and anxiety onto an individual, who is then driven out and destroyed. The scapegoat thus restores balance within society and paradoxically becomes an object of worship, invested with supernatural or even divine power. From this, societies develop moral codes, rituals, and myths, all of which serve both to mask foundational violence and to perpetuate the "benefits" of that violence. Girard argues that Jesus is the perfect scapegoat, the one who lays bare all of the violence inherent in religious systems and throughout human culture.

The Saving Work of Jesus in the New Testament

The notions of sacrifice contained in Leviticus are not really shared by any of the New Testament authors, including Paul. Before the first century, the theology of Jerusalem's sacrificial system had been subjected to substantial **spiritualization**. The rituals were beginning to be interpreted metaphorically or analogously in a way that emphasized personal interaction with God. While all Jews—including Paul—saw religious value in the ongoing sacrifices of the temple, the meaning of these rituals had developed considerably. A good example appears in Paul's Letter to the Romans, particularly Romans 3:25, where Paul expresses the redemptive value of Christ's death with the Greek word **hilasterion**, a translation of the Hebrew word *kapporet* (the New American Bible translates *hilasterion* as "expiation"). In first-century Judaism, the mercy seat was the object of the Jewish people's religious imagination. Since the *kapporet* was central to the biblical instructions for the removal of impurity and sin, and since it had long been removed from the temple after the Babylonian destruction of Jerusalem in 586 BCE, it necessarily became invested with great symbolic and metaphorical power for Paul and other Jews of his time. Jewish readers of Paul would have instantly recognized this metaphorical power and disabused Gentile Christians of possible literal misinterpretations. For Paul, a sacrificial term like *hilasterion* allowed him to express an understanding of Jesus' death as the effective means for gaining reconciliation with God.

The Letter to the Hebrews, which is not from Paul, understands Christ's death as the culmination and end of the temple's sacrificial system. Hebrews stands in the tradition of Hellenistic popular philosophy with its propensity toward dualism (matter and form, old and new, perfect and imperfect). The understanding of the temple and priesthood in Hebrews reflects this dualism. The temple foreshadowed and prepared for the death of Christ. An elaborate **typology** (i.e., a discourse that reads the figures and events in the Old Testament as foreshadowing the saving work of Christ) spells this out in Hebrews, chapters 4–10. The literal, historical temple service is dismissed as ineffectual and banal. Christ is the true high priest—of the priestly order of Melchizedek, not Aaron or Zaddok. Christ offers himself as the perfect sacrifice. The death of Christ, the true sacrifice offered by the true high priest, is definitive and totally effective.

But the New Testament account of Christ's saving work is not limited to sacrificial metaphors. One of the images used by Paul is the idea of ransom (*apolutrōsis*), expressing a transaction that has set human beings free (from sin). Within a secular context, a ransom was the price paid to free, or "redeem," a slave from bondage. The notion of ransom was also used within the martyr tradition of the Maccabean period. The death of righteous Jews at the hands of their persecutors was understood as a ransom for the nation:

> These, then, who have been consecrated for the sake of God, are honored, not only with this honor, but also by the fact that because of them our enemies did not rule over our nation, the tyrant was punished, and the homeland purified—they having become, as it were, a ransom (*apolutrōsis*) for the sin of our nation. (4 *Maccabees* 17:21–22; RSV)

The author of Maccabees interprets the death of these righteous martyrs as the means by which the nation is released from its enslavement to foreign oppression. Their death was vicarious—that is, their death was said to be "for the nation," as Jesus' death is said to be "for us." Their death was thought to have brought about the liberation of the nation held in bondage by a foreign oppressor. In the case of Christ, the bondage is obviously metaphorical: we are enslaved to sin. While *apolutrōsis* and other metaphors used by Paul are not necessarily cultic, they still identify the death of Jesus as the decisive element for understanding how Christ saves.

Through these and other images, the New Testament attempts to convey the meaning of Christ's death. As with New Testament Christology, New Testament soteriology makes use of symbols and narratives at the heart of Jewish life. One should always keep in mind the metaphoric value of such language as sacrifice, ransom, and redemption. The fact that the New Testament uses and even combines a variety of cultural and social metaphors—including sacrifice and ransom—to express what has been achieved in Jesus should give one pause. One might understandably long for the soteriological equivalent of the Council of Nicaea to bring clarity to this maze of biblical images. Yet no such council ever took place. Theologians and preachers throughout the centuries have developed their soteriologies "without a net," but that does not imply a lack of concern for clarity and orthodoxy.

Soteriology through the Middle Ages

Soteriology in the Patristic Era (100 CE–700 CE)

In the Patristic Era, biblical imagery became the catalyst for imaginative approaches to soteriology. Some of those approaches were deeply rooted in Scripture, while others were more imaginative than biblical. Irenaeus (ca. 130–200), martyr and bishop of Lyons, forged a systematic approach to soteriology that was deeply rooted in the prophetic model we have seen in Isaiah and Luke. For Irenaeus, God saves us through history, by uniting God's self with the history of the world. Salvation thus unfolds in a drama of human and divine action as the divine plan (*oikonomia*) progresses through several interrelated stages. The Incarnation is the key event for Irenaeus, for Christ sums up the story of God and humanity. In this "recapitulation" (*anakephalaiōsis*), Christ reverses the disobedience of Adam (see Romans 5:12–21). Christ, the Incarnation of God, affects a union between God and humanity that destroys sin and brings about a transformation of human beings so that they become divine. Irenaeus, like so many who come after him, synthesizes the variety of images found in the New Testament to offer a systematic narrative account of Christ's saving work. But such an approach inevitably leaves questions unanswered as people seek out the intelligibility of Irenaeus's myth.

The mythic language of patristic theology is perhaps most apparent in the ransom theory. This is not really a theory, but a narrative. The sin of Adam enslaved human beings to sin; Christ, therefore, was offered as a ransom, a payment to the devil. Origen was perhaps the most famous proponent of this approach, though it was criticized by other theologians of the time, especially Gregory Nazianzen.[3] But the image of ransom, so prevalent in Scripture, admitted other narrative inventions in the patristic period. For example, Gregory of Nyssa, in chapters 22–24 of his *Catechetical Orations*, likens the Incarnation and Christ's death to a fisherman using a fish hook. The devil had held humanity as slaves since Adam had sold himself to the devil. The sinless Jesus was then offered as payment for the release of the devil's claim to humanity. But the bait (Jesus' humanity) masked the hook (the divinity of Christ) so that when the devil seized Jesus in death, the divine nature of Christ was revealed and, like a fish who swallows the hook along with the bait, the devil was caught in a trap from which he could not escape; he was forced to give up his claim on humanity and his claim on Christ. Other theologians of the period also included the notion that with the devil thus conquered, Christ, in the abode of the dead, was able to summon the souls of the dead that he had just won, and lead them out of death and into heaven. This last image is rooted in passages like 1 Peter 3:19, and 4:6, where Christ is described as penetrating the abode of the dead in order to preach the gospel, thus making all creation accountable to God's mercy.[4]

But patristic soteriology was not dominated by this story line, vivid as it was, nor was it exclusively wedded to biblical imagery. Theologians always sought to be faithful to biblical imagery, but this did not preclude theological innovation. Athanasius, the great champion of Nicaea, refused to focus on any one moment in the life of Christ as decisive for our salvation. Rather, for Athanasius, the entire life of Christ brings salvation.[5] The cross plays a special role, and sacrificial as well as redemptive language is used to describe its effectiveness, but coupled with such imagery is the emphasis on divinization *(theōsis* or *theopoiēsis)*. Recall from the previous chapter Athanasius's famous maxim: "God became human so that humans might become God." The Incarnation not only removes sin but also provides a model of the moral life. The divine image is restored through Christ (the original gift of creation that was lost through sin), and the power of his Resurrection is an exhortation to treat death without fear and even with disdain. Divinization describes the saving work of Christ in terms of participation (*methexis*): all that is human is taken up into God. God is not lowered, but human beings are elevated. The *Catechism of the Catholic Church* quotes Athanasius's "Letter to Seraphim": "[God] gave himself to us through his Spirit. By the participation of the Spirit, we become communicants in the divine nature. . . . For this reason, those in whom the Spirit dwells are divinized."[6]

The Patristic era was awash in narrative and symbolic soteriologies. Such approaches have the value of vividly portraying the saving power of Christ's death. Vivid narration is no small achievement, but it often raises as many problems as it solves. For a community to form and pronounce judgments of faith—doctrines—in a clear and systematic way it must cultivate theoretical language. Of course, such systematic presentations can never substitute for the religious experience that provides the basis for narrative and theory. The patristic accounts fall short of answering the difficult question, how does Jesus take away the sin of the world? Not until the Middle Ages would theologians begin to articulate more theoretical accounts of Christ's saving work.

Medieval Soteriology (1000 CE–1500 CE)

One of the greatest thinkers of the Middle Ages was Anselm (1033–1109), a Benedictine monk who became the Archbishop of Canterbury. He is credited with offering a definition of theology as "faith seeking understanding" (*fides quaerens intellectum*), and he used a sharp sense of reason to explore the truths he affirmed in faith. Perhaps his most famous—and misunderstood—contribution to theology is the work known by its Latin title *Cur Deus Homo?* ("Why Did God Become Human?"). In this work Anselm sets out to discover "the necessary reasons" why humanity had to be redeemed through the Incarnation, death, and Resurrection of Jesus. Like all theology, the answer Anselm constructs reflects his own location—it is medieval in its idiom and outlook—but that does not mean that it has nothing to offer us today.

Medieval society was governed by a series of reciprocal obligations between different classes of people. In our context, we rely on the rule of law—passed by a duly elected legislature, interpreted by competent and independent judges, and enforced by a conscientious and freely elected executive. However, our system has problems. Elections are sometimes marred by fraud, our legislature can be dominated by special interest groups and lobbyists, and the executive often lacks wisdom. Because of this we often feel as though an injustice has been done, and our laws have been corrupted. Not so in the medieval context. The lord of an estate had rights to his land by virtue of his birth, or by exercise of power, and he had ownership of the people on the land. This was not necessarily viewed as unjust, for the lord of the manor provided capital, means for people to make a living, and protection. This reciprocity between lord, knights, tradesmen, and serfs was often oppressive by our standards, but also provided for a certain amount of stability and security. There were no legislative bodies. Any courts were operated by the lord of the estate to settle disputes between equals, but there was no court in which one could sue the lord. The lord enjoyed rule by virtue of heredity and divine sanction, and one owed respect and honor to the lord. When those who were under the power and protection of a lord failed to be loyal, or if they somehow offended the honor of the lord, they were required to make "satisfaction." That is, they had to perform some act whereby the honor, the right relationship between servant and master, could be restored. Sometimes the offense was of such a kind or degree that the only fitting act of satisfaction was death.

We must be careful not to place God in the position of a medieval lord when reading Anselm; he explicitly excludes any such notion. But at the same time we cannot ignore the political and social situation that helps to structure Anselm's language about atonement. For Anselm, God is not a petty medieval landlord. Rather, God is "One than whom nothing greater can be conceived." God is the creator of existence, and human beings owe God complete obedience of intellect and will and complete love. But human beings have sinned and thereby violated God's honor—they have denied that their existence comes from God and that they owe God everything. They have thereby disrupted the order of the universe. Of course, God's honor is not the petty pride of some self-important nobleman. Rather, God's honor is really God's godliness, God's very divinity. Sin, in a sense, compromises, challenges, or threatens God's divinity because it separates creature from Creator. For Anselm, God is utterly justified in allowing creation to cease, to give humankind the destiny it has chosen: oblivion. This would be fitting for God's justice. But God's love will not permit it. The resulting tension between God's justice and God's love seems irreconcilable.

Anselm finds the solution to the problem of sin in the tension between God's love and God's justice in the Incarnation. Human beings, because they already owe God everything, cannot offer anything to God that would make satisfaction for their offense and restore the order of the universe. Even if they gave everything to God, they would only be giving God what is already and always required. What is necessary is a sinless human being who would not be required to die; the death of this person would be an offering to God because this person would not deserve death. A mere human being, however, could not really make satisfaction for the sins of humanity since that sin is an infinite offense against God. But if the perfect human offering described above were also divine (and therefore infinite), the death of that person would have infinite value. As perfectly human and perfectly divine, Jesus made satisfaction for human beings as a human being by offering God his death. This satisfaction has infinite value for others. It is a vicarious or "supererogatory" act (it benefits others rather than the one who acts). It restores balance and order in the universe; it restores God's honor.

Anselm's emphasis on the death of Christ as vicarious (supererogatory) satisfaction was supplemented in later years by the work of the great scholastic theologian Thomas Aquinas. For Aquinas, the theologian is not concerned with the "necessary reasons" for Christ's death as was Anselm; rather, the theologian's task is to ascertain how the saving work of Christ was the appropriate way God freely chose to redeem the world from sin (i.e., as a matter of **convenientia**).[7] Thomas determined that it was appropriate for many of the same reasons Anselm deemed it necessary, but with an important twist: for Aquinas, the death of Christ was not the primary offering to God. Rather, Christ's loving obedience even to the point of death was the offering that makes satisfaction for our sin. Christ offered to God not "what was required," but something God loved more than he hated the offense.[8] Human beings are thus reconciled to God through God's love and the love and obedience of Christ. Anselm's model is preserved by Aquinas, but its theme is subtly changed.

Peter Abailard (1079–1142; often spelled Abelard), the great theologian of Paris, challenged Anselm's approach more directly by stressing the idea that Christ was a model, an example of God's love for humanity. The crucified Christ thus acts as a summons to human beings to enkindle the love of God within humanity and thereby put away sin. In his commentary on Romans, he modifies the sacrificial language of Paul to create a different image of God and the work of Christ:

> Now it seems to us that we have been justified by the blood of Christ and reconciled to God in this way: through this unique act of grace manifested to us—in that his Son has taken upon himself our nature and persevered therein in teaching us by word and example even unto death—he has more fully bound us to himself by love; with the result that our hearts should be enkindled by such a gift of divine grace, and true charity [love] should not now shrink from enduring anything for him. . . . Our redemption through Christ's suffering is that deeper affection [dilectio] in us which not only frees us from slavery to

Person of Interest

Peter Abailard

Abailard (1079–1142) was a prodigy and a great annoyance to his superiors. A gifted student, he was able to poke holes in the arguments of his teachers, who were some of the most respected minds in France at the time. He began his teaching career in Paris at a young age and attracted enormous audiences. In the Middle Ages, students paid their professors directly, and enthusiasm for a professor meant wealth and security, sometimes to the detriment of other faculty. He eventually fell in love and had a torrid affair with Heloise, one of his pupils and the niece of an important church official. When the affair was discovered Abailard sent Heloise, whom he had secretly married, to a monastery in an effort to protect his reputation. In retaliation for the treatment of his niece, Heloise's uncle had Abailard castrated, and he left Paris in 1118 to enter a monastery. Heloise and Abailard kept up a correspondence over the years, and these letters attest to their mutual devotion. Controversy continued to hound him later in life: his doctrine on the Trinity was condemned at a French council and St. Bernard of Clairvaux, the great mystic, led a heresy trial against him.

sin, but also wins for us the true liberty of sons of God (Romans 8:21), so that we do all things out of love rather than fear. (*Exposition of the Epistle to the Romans*, 2.3)[9]

Abailard was not the only one to emphasize a "moral" or "subjective" approach to soteriology. Among the great theologians of the Middle Ages was the English mystic Julian of Norwich (1342–ca. 1414), a laywoman who took a vow as an anchoress (a recluse attached to a church). She received a series of revelations in 1373, which she published together with elaborated reflections some twenty years later under the title of *Shewings*. In this work Julian uses the term "oneing" to describe the union between the divine and the human through God's love. Julian's revelations are anchored in the conviction that God's very being is love. Even sin cannot challenge the loving nature of God. God's love is both intimate (homely) and respectful (courteous). God desires to be generous and faithful to his creatures, but in a way that demands a similar response. Her soteriology rejects the image of God as judge and offers, instead, the possibility of imaging God as a loving mother who refuses to allow us to be lost.

In *Shewings*, Julian describes the human self as suffering between reluctance and freedom. Freedom rests with God. The heart's deepest desire is to do God's will, but we are reluctant to accept that; we fear that by doing God's will, our desires will be lost. Freedom is thus compromised by choosing against what God wills. Yet God embraces human beings in an eternal bond of love, which enables the exercise of human freedom.

Julian describes the role of human beings in the economy of salvation as the imitation of Christ, a free response to God's love. Through the contemplation of Christ's life, death, and Resurrection, one begins to exhibit the loving obedience of Christ. Christ thus "wants us to be his helpers, giving all our intention to him, learning his laws, observing his teaching, desiring everything to be done which he does, truly trusting in him."[10] Through contemplation and imitation, our oneing with God is furthered. Julian thus provides us with a fine example of medieval moral soteriology that emphasizes the importance of prayer and the process of personal transformation.

Julian and Abailard's emphasis on the subjective dimension of Christ's saving work, as well as the patristic idea of divinization *(theōsis)*, have been obscured in the history of western theology, particularly through an overemphasis on the death of Christ and its role in Anselm's theology. His account of atonement as vicarious suffering and the restoration of divine order in the universe had great appeal in a world where order, especially hierarchical order, was paramount. Even today, many theologians dismiss subjectivist soteriologies because they make salvation contingent on human response, and neglect much of the cultic language found in Scripture. But Anselm's thought as well is often diminished by misinterpretation and misunderstanding. Unfortunately, the pluralism and rich ambiguity of the patristic and medieval accounts of Christ's saving work eventually succumbed to the pressures of modern societies and the polemics of the Reformation and Counter-Reformation and the corresponding demise of soteriology in Christian theology.

The Reformation and the Counter Reformation

The Reformation began as an effort to reform the Roman Catholic Church. Luther and many of the reformers were more interested in seeing the Church address the troublesome abuses and theological issues of the time than in forming new religious affiliations that would lead to the fragmentation of Christian Europe. However, the times and personalities were such that confrontation was the order of the day. The pope and the emperor both condemned Luther, and those in authority within the Church rejected the changes the reformers sought. The Reformation thus swept through Europe among those who were tired of the abuse and corruption and sought spiritual renewal.

The authorities in Rome eventually realized that they could not successfully impose their will; they had to undertake a systematic approach to the defense of the doctrines and practices they had previously upheld through coercion. It is telling in this regard that although Luther posted his "Ninety-Five Theses" in 1517, the Council of Trent did not meet to address the situation until 1545. Many of the most blatant abuses of ecclesiastical power and privilege were addressed with some success, but the council articulated most of the theological issues (especially justification, the sacraments, and the authority of the Church) in opposition to the position of the reformers in a harsh and polemical tone.

The Council of Trent met in many sessions through 1563 and established a counteroffensive against the reformers. The Counter Reformation, as it was called, defined the religious spirit of the Society of Jesus, the Carmelites, and many missionary orders in the following centuries. These orders brought the gospel to newly discovered lands in the sixteenth, seventeenth, and eighteenth centuries. The tenor and spirit of the Counter Reformation was often defensive and argumentative as well as triumphal. Only recently have the Catholic Church and Protestant churches emerged from their Reformation-Counter Reformation postures and adopted more positive attitudes toward each other. The Second Vatican Council (1962–1965) and the bilateral dialogues it spawned are indicative of such developments.

The Reformation and the Doctrine of Penal Substitution (1500–1600)

The Protestant Reformation of the sixteenth century was a complex religious, theological, cultural, and political event. Its causes and consequences are far beyond the scope of this book, but a few relevant points about the Reformation should be noted at the beginning of our discussion of the **penal substitution** theory of redemption.

In response to the outrageous excesses of late medieval theology and church practices, the great Reformer Martin Luther (1483–1546) sought to retrieve a more biblically oriented and simpler form of Christian faith. Late medieval scholasticism had introduced a range of ideas that Luther, and many others, thought moved away from the basics of Christian faith as it is expressed in the New Testament. But the reformers were not longing for the "good old days" of the first-century church. Many important theological innovations were offered by the reformers, and many of their criticisms of church practice reflected an early modern understanding of the human person and society, including the importance of the individual and democratic ideals. But a major point of emphasis in the sixteenth-century Reformation was the rejection of traditional ecclesiastical authority in favor of a less centralized and (comparatively) democratic form of church governance. At the theological level, Luther insisted on the autonomy of the believer in the interpretation of Scripture. But perhaps the most central aspect of Luther's theology was his insistence on the essentially gratuitous nature of our redemption. Salvation is a gift, pure and simple.

Luther's theology begins with a basic premise accepted by all Christians: human beings are redeemed through the work of Christ, and we receive these benefits through God's gift of grace in faith. In other words, we are made right with God—we are "justified"—through faith. This may seem quite obvious—one might rightly wonder what alternative understanding of the gospel was being promulgated at that time. Luther's Catholic opponents argued that while justification was the gift of faith and thus totally unmerited in the strict sense, Christians were required to respond to grace, in particular by engaging in acts of penance and charity (works of love, or *caritas*). There were complex arguments about how best to understand the response to grace that was required from human beings, yet it was acknowledged that the response of love was itself a grace freely given by God, so that any talk of "merit" (getting what one deserves or has earned) was really a matter of God crowning or rewarding God's own gifts—one does not earn one's salvation! However, due to widespread ignorance and poor pastoral practice, many ordinary Christians assumed that one does, in fact, earn one's salvation through penance and other good works. In the sixteenth century, a practice emerged that helped to push Luther over the edge and into public conflict with church and governmental authorities: the buying and selling of **indulgences**. The logic of indulgences was fairly straightforward: as part of one's penance—and not as a condition for the forgiveness of sin—Christians could donate funds to the work of the church. Such charitable acts helped to make satisfaction for sins, provided the acts were sanctioned by the church and thus united to Christ's act of satisfaction. In the early sixteenth century, one of the major charitable works for which the church sought funds was the rebuilding of St. Peter's Basilica in Rome. This massive project required massive funds, and the clergy who were tasked with fundraising easily succumbed to bad theology in order to meet their goals. A contribution to this work constituted the purchase of an "indulgence." That is, the church, through its power to bind and loose sin and through its treasury of merit, would accept this gift as penance. One could also transfer the indulgence to loved ones, living or dead, so that their penance would be shortened, either in this life or in the next (i.e., in **Purgatory**, the place of penance in the afterlife prominent in Catholic theology at the time).[11] Such practices provide us the background for Luther's understandable insistence on a theology more explicitly focused on the grace of God's saving work.

Luther's commentaries on Scripture laid the basis for his soteriology and the ground rules for the debate that would follow: he insisted that only data from Scripture could be admitted to the discussion. For the most part the positions of the church fathers and scholastic theologians were judged inadmissible, since they often wander far from Scripture and draw upon philosophical speculation. Luther writes of Paul's letters that he "guarded his words carefully and spoke precisely," thus reinforcing his focus on the meaning of the biblical author in the text at hand.

Luther's insistence on the literal sense of the text exercised an important control on the speculative theology of the scholastic period. The literal sense is not to be equated with literalism or naïve fundamentalism; rather, the literal sense could be historical, proverbial, or parabolic provided that is the evident intent of the passage in question. Scholastic theology tended to regard the literal sense of the text as the least important and argued that the real or spiritual meaning of Scripture could be unlocked only through allegory or other complex forms of interpretation. Such interpretations usually required an appeal to authorities like church fathers in order to be legitimate. But modern theologians sometimes misinterpret Luther's soteriology as simply a return to biblical imagery, particularly its narrative dimensions.[12] Luther's restoration of biblical imagery was never unadulterated. Rather, his own dogmatic concern to emphasize the utter gratuity of salvation as well as the social setting of early modern Europe played important roles in Luther's reading of Scripture and in his soteriology.

Luther's soteriology, while borrowing many biblical images, finds its coherence as a novel theological move, a move that has become the default soteriology for many Christians today. Luther emphasizes Jesus' role as a representative of all humanity. As such, Jesus is the individual who endures the suffering and death human beings merit because of their sins. The result is a "happy exchange": Christ takes on our punishment while we share in Christ's righteousness. This soteriology is termed "penal substitution." Luther's *Commentary on St. Paul's Epistle to the Galatians* summarizes this approach:

> All the prophets of old said that Christ should be the greatest transgressor, murderer, adulterer, thief, blasphemer that ever was or ever could be on earth. When He took the sins of the whole world upon Himself, Christ was no longer an innocent person. He was a sinner burdened with the sins of a Paul who was a blasphemer; burdened with the sins of a Peter who denied Christ; burdened with the sins of a David who committed adultery and murder, and gave the heathen occasion to laugh at the Lord. In short, Christ was charged with the sins of all men, that He should pay for them with His own blood. The curse struck Him. The Law found Him among sinners. He was not only in the company of sinners. He had gone so far as to invest

Himself with the flesh and blood of sinners. So the Law judged and hanged Him for a sinner.[13]

This position is quite clear. Sin incurs the penalty of death, but Christ takes on this penalty, substituting himself in our place and bearing our punishment. Since Christ suffered the penalty for sin, we do not need to suffer the penalty, provided we are united to Christ in faith. Similarly, John Calvin (1509–1564), another prominent reformer, presented another version of penal substitution. Calvin used the idea of criminal

Person of Interest

John Calvin

John Calvin (1509–1564) was one of the most influential reformers of the sixteenth century, arguably second only to Luther. He was born in France and seemed from an early age to be headed for a life of ministry. He studied theology in Paris, but abandoned an ecclesiastical career in favor of the law. After a few years living a scholar's life and gaining a reputation as a sharp mind, Calvin was invited to Geneva to help solidify the Reformation there. His career in Geneva eventually helped change the course of Protestant theology, as well as life throughout Europe and North America. At Geneva, Calvin implemented a strict moral code, which was enforced through the city government. He envisioned a city governed entirely on biblical principles. Calvin's tactics were resented by the people, and he was eventually expelled from the city. While in exile in the city of Strasbourg, Calvin began work on one of the most important theological works in the Christian tradition, *The Institutes of the Christian Religion*, in which he articulated his vision of Protestant theology.

In 1540 a new crop of city officials in Geneva invited Calvin back to the city. As soon as he arrived, he set about constructing a synthesis between church and state. He went so far as to erect a city government in which the clergy were intimately involved in matters of policy, law, and especially punishment of wrongdoers. He also set about reforming the city's moral code, making it the most uncompromising in Europe. By the middle of the sixteenth century, Geneva was in Calvin's complete control. It eventually became an important center for Protestant Christians from all over Europe, who were forced to flee their homelands because of wars or persecutions. Protestant Christians from as far away as the Netherlands and Scotland came to Geneva to find refuge and fell under the influence of Calvin's doctrines and practices. When they left Geneva, they took Calvinism with them, eventually transforming the face of Europe and America.

law to understand the saving significance of Christ's death. For Calvin, Christ "was made a substitute and a surety in the place of transgressors and even submitted as a criminal to sustain and suffer all the punishment which would have been inflicted on them."[14] The analogy of criminal law is stronger in the writing of Calvin, the ruler of Geneva, and therefore his articulation of penal substitution is also more boldly articulated.

For many Christians today, penal substitution is the doctrine that fully and clearly accounts for the salvation that has been accomplished in Christ. But many scholars, including many Protestants, are beginning to recognize tensions between penal substitution and a fuller, more complex, and biblically founded account of soteriology.[15] For one thing, in the penal substitution model the understanding of sin is problematic. Sin seems to be a violation of God's law, and the relationship between sin and death is not organic. Death is simply willed by God's justice. Moreover, penal substitution offers an utterly objectified account of redemption: the problem of sin is "taken care of" independently of Jesus' call to conversion. In other words, "Jesus died so I don't have to." Finally, in penal substitution God wills and inflicts the violent death experienced by Jesus. God decrees that sin merits death, and God is the enforcer of this punishment. "The wrath of God" toward sin is visited upon Jesus so that the suffering of Jesus is at the hands of the Father. Some critics of this view rather flippantly allege that this makes God a "divine child abuser."

While Protestant soteriology focused upon penal substitution, Catholic Counter-Reformation piety began to place a strong emphasis on the suffering of Christ; in the pastoral theology and practice of many churches, meditation on the suffering of Christ became central. In some versions of the Catholic devotional called the stations of the cross we are encouraged to consider that the pain Christ endured was caused by our sin—the more we sin, the more suffering Christ endures. We can help share the suffering of Christ, "filling up what is lacking in the afflictions of Christ" (Colossians 1:24) by uniting our suffering to that of Christ. Such devotional language is powerful and not to be casually dismissed—it has tremendous value when understood properly. But at the same time, such language envisions a world in which pain and suffering are punishments for sin that can be divided or borne away provided we are disciplined enough.

Soteriologies: A Simplified Comparative Chart

Name of Model	Major Figures	Understanding of Sin	Summary	Some Strengths and Shortcomings
Prophetic	Isaiah Luke	Sin is failure to exercise mercy toward the oppressed and marginalized, thus forgetting God's covenant. The effects of sin are oppression and violence.	God acts in history, through concrete events and people, to rescue the righteous and judge the wicked.	This model emphasizes the concrete realities of sin and death, but it can also ignore the moral significance of the individual in favor of a long-term communal approach to sin and salvation.
Sacrificial	Paul and the author of Hebrews	Sin compromises God's holiness, God's justice, and the mercy God has shown Israel.	The sacrifices of the temple were designed to foreshadow the work of Christ, whose blood, like that of the bulls and the goats, unleashes the power of divine forgiveness and reconciliation.	This model integrates Israelite temple theology with the story of Jesus, thus providing for continuity between the covenants, but it fails to incorporate the significance of Jesus' life and ministry for his saving work.
Ransom (Patristic)	Origen, Augustine	Sin is offering one's allegiance to the devil rather than to God. Sin results in the subjugation of humanity to the devil.	The devil has dominion over human beings. Christ, in the disguise of human flesh, gives himself over to death so as to take the place of human beings in death. As the devil seizes Jesus, he discovers that Jesus is without sin and cannot be touched by death. The devil, having overplayed his hand, must sacrifice his dominion over all human beings.	The playful and vivid imagery of this model is wonderful, but the logic of such a theology of deception hardly seems worthy of the God of Israel.
Divinization	Athanasius	Sin is turning away from God, our Creator. The result of this turning away includes the loss of the divine image with which human beings were created.	God became human in Christ. This union restores the divine image and raises human beings to participate in God's own life, a life beyond the fear and ignorance in which sin thrives.	This approach incorporates the entire life of Christ in an account of redemption, but it also employs a range of images and metaphors that lack theoretical rigor—how does divinization happen?

Soteriologies: A Simplified Comparative Chart (continued)

Name of Model	Major Figures	Understanding of Sin	Summary	Some Strengths and Shortcomings
Vicarious Satisfaction	Anselm	Sin violates God. Anselm uses the notion of honor to convey this. Sin has the effect of disordering the universe God has created.	The death of a sinless human being is an offering to God, but the infinite offense that humanity has committed requires an act of infinite value, so Jesus, as the God-man, makes satisfaction for our sins.	Anslem introduces a "theoretical" approach to soteriology, but both his search for the necessity of the Incarnation and his focus on the death of Jesus limit its value. Also, the social setting for his theory raises questions, as does the minimal role played by conversion.
Moral Exemplar	Abailard, Julian of Norwich	Sin is a failure to love God above all. It results from and also causes us to forget God's love for us.	The cross is a sign of God's love for us. It calls us to remember God's love and turn away from sin.	Abailard and Julian focus on the love of God, the teachings of Jesus, and the importance of conversion, but they do not adequately differentiate Jesus from other martyrs.
Penal Substitution	Luther, Calvin	Sin is a violation of divine law. The sanction for such violation is death.	Christ takes our place. Christ dies so human beings do not have to die.	This approach emphasizes the complete gratuity of God's salvation, but also makes God the origin of Jesus' suffering. Also, it is not clear what role conversion has in this approach.

Conclusion

In 1 Corinthians, Paul describes the cross of Christ as a scandal or stumbling block (*skandalon*). In contrast, many Christians today use the cross as a fashion accessory or a talisman, its meaning, its power to provoke, seemingly lost. The cross troubles no one (except civil libertarians when they see it on public land). When asked to explain the salvific work of Christ, Christians typically respond, "Christ died for our sins." When pressed for further elaboration, they often slide into some form of penal substitution or ransom theory. Such approaches, while intelligible and appropriate to some degree, no longer make sense; they strain the credulity of those who hear such explanations. What is required is an account of the work of Christ that incorporates three elements: (1) an appropriate understanding of Jesus' call to conversion, (2) an account of the importance and limitations of the practice Jesus modeled, and (3) a responsible interpretation of Christ's death and Resurrection. A contemporary soteriology needs to move beyond traditional language without abandoning the tradition, expressing orthodoxy through innovation.

Questions for Understanding

1. Describe the prophetic model of salvation. Do you find any features of this approach troubling or appealing?

2. Describe the liturgical, or sacrificial, model of salvation. Why do you think so many Christians still spontaneously identify Christ's saving work with sacrifice? What makes this view attractive?

3. Describe Anselm's theory of the atonement. Is it dependent on a medieval social structure? Explain.

4. How do Abailard and Julian of Norwich challenge Anselm's approach to soteriology?

5. Describe the doctrine of penal substitution. How does it differ from Anselm's theory?

Questions for Reflection

1. Ask a self-identified Christian acquaintance, "How does Jesus save us from sin?" How does the person respond? Does his answer reflect one of the soteriologies mentioned in this chapter?

2. Mel Gibson's film *The Passion of the Christ* stirred a great deal of controversy when it was released. What are some of the reasons for this controversy? Were these reasons theological? From what you know about the film, do you think these concerns were well founded?

3. When Anselm explored the necessary reasons for the Incarnation, he located that necessity in an understanding of sin. John Duns Scotus (1264–1308), another prominent theologian, saw the Incarnation as part of the divine plan from the beginning—God's plan for creation and furthering the communion between God and humanity. The atoning work of Christ was secondary to this plan, almost an afterthought. Examine the position of Scotus (see *The New Catholic Encyclopedia* [New York: Gale, 2002]) and support the approach that seems best to you.

Endnotes

1   Some of the material in this section comes from the first section of Richard Clifford and Khaled Anatolios, "Christian Salvation: Biblical and Theological Perspectives," *Theological Studies* 66 (2005): 739–69.

2   See Stephen Finlan, *Problems with Atonement* (Collegeville, MN: Liturgical, 2005), 11–38.

3   See his *Orations*, 45.22.

4   Cyril of Jerusalem, *Catechetical Lectures*, 14.18–19.

5   George Bebawi, "St. Athanasios: The Dynamics of Salvation." *Sobornost* 8 (1986): 24–41; Christopher Smith, "The Life of Christ Structure of Athanasius' *De Incarnatione Verbi*," *Patristic and Byzantine Review* 10 (1991): 7–24.

6   *CCC*, 1988.

7   Thomas uses *convenientia* frequently in the following articles on Christology: *Summa Theologica*, 3.Q.1; Q.46; Q.50.

8   *Summa Theologica*, 3.Q.49; A.4.

9   Peter Abailard, *Exposition of the Epistle to the Romans*, 2.3, quoted from *A Scholastic Miscellany: Anslem to Ockam*, trans. and ed. Eugene R. Fairweather (New York: Macmillan, 1970), 283–84.

10   *Julian of Norwich: Showings*, trans. Edmund Colledge and James Walsh, Classics of Western Spirituality 57 (New York: Paulist, 1978), 292.

11   The Church still affirms the doctrine of Purgatory, but connects it to the necessity of penance or purification that leads to fullness of intimacy with God (the Beatific Vision). Interestingly, many Protestant Christians will affirm the idea of purification upon one's death, but would not espouse the idea that living Christians could assist the dead through such purification. See *CCC*, 1031.

12   Cf. Gustav Aulén, *Christus Victor* (New York: Macmillan, 1961). Aulén's account of soteriology wrongly characterizes the soteriologies of both Anselm and Luther.

13   *Commentary on the Epistle to the Galatians*, translated by Theodore Graebner; (Grand Rapids, MI: Zondervan, 1949).

14   *Institutes of the Christian Religion*, 2.16.10.

15   For an excellent critique of penal substitution from an Evangelical perspective, see Joel Green and Mark Baker, *Recovering the Scandal of the Cross: Atonement in New Testament and Contemporary Contexts* (Downers Grove, IL: InterVarsity, 2000).

Christology and Social Transformation

It is difficult to be a Christian today due to such factors as the pornogrification of our culture, rampant materialism, and the thoughtless celebration of wealth. But perhaps the main difficulty rests at a far more fundamental level, namely the credibility of the Christian claim that through Christ sin has been conquered. Scenes of violence, suffering, and desolation abound in our neighborhoods. Our homes are saturated with electronic images of these evils beaming through the television and Internet. Yet in church, on television, and on the net we find images of shiny, earnest, and beautiful faces proclaiming, "Jesus loves you," or triumphal processions winding through St. Peter's Square. Pontifical ceremonies can be deeply moving experiences, and heartfelt reminders of Jesus' love for us can be tremendously uplifting, but they contrast sharply with images of ongoing violence and despair, straining the sensibilities of many modern people. How can we affirm that "Jesus saves" when sin and evil are all around us?

Forty years ago, a young Joseph Ratzinger (now Pope Benedict XVI), began his celebrated book *Introduction to Christianity* with Søren Kierkegaard's familiar parable about a clown who, after seeing a major fire in the village, tried to warn the villagers of the danger.[1] The villagers, knowing what clowns do for a living and thinking it was part of his clown act, laughed and ignored his warning. To save the village, the clown needed to do more than just remove his makeup and don more respectable clothes. According to Ratzinger, Christianity requires more than a change of costume or updated language to win a hearing from "the villagers."

The current situation requires recognition of the fundamental commonality between the nonbeliever and the believer. We cannot, as Christians, fool ourselves into thinking that we possess sure knowledge of God and that the secular world is ignorant or bereft of that knowledge. We must not segregate religious knowledge from the world of science and politics. Rather, believers and nonbelievers must cooperate and challenge one another, finding a synthesis between faith and science, reason and revelation, as we address the problem of suffering and broader questions of human existence. Recognition of this commonality, however, could dilute the Christian faith into a bland humanism. In other words, the recognition that "we are all in the same boat" as human beings and that we all struggle in the darkness of ignorance could lead us to marginalize or otherwise neglect the experience of God's revelation in Christ, or lead us to downplay the claims of Christian faith.

Such fears, however, are not the inevitable outcome of the accord between believers and nonbelievers—if such a dichotomy is even appropriate. Rather, Christians are equipped with resources that nonbelievers do not recognize, but the task, questions, and concerns of nonreligious humanists are not altogether dissimilar from those of Christians, even though their methodologies might diverge. Ratzinger is convinced that the credibility of Christian faith, and the nature of Christian faith itself, demands that Christians recognize that they are not in possession of all

Person of Interest

Søren Kierkegaard

Søren Kierkegaard (1813–1855) is the founder of modern existentialism and one of the most important theologians of the nineteenth century. He was annoyed and dismayed at the kind of Christianity that had taken root in his native Denmark and throughout Europe at the time. Kierkegaard saw orthodox Christianity as a puppet of the state and believed it affirmed the world's petty morality. Christianity had become bourgeois and superficial. As an ardent individualist, Kierkegaard insisted that human reason and reflection on God can only lead to frustration since God is beyond our reason: any reflection on God can only yield paradoxes. Since human beings are egoists (self-absorbed), they need to experience despair to make a leap of faith and emerge on the other side of the despair, the vertigo that constitutes human existence. While his account of faith and reason does not easily conform to the Roman Catholic tradition, his thought has been highly influential in German and Scandinavian Protestant thought and increasingly in the English-speaking world. Some of his most important works are *Fear and Trembling*, *The Concept of Anxiety*, and *Either Or*.

the answers, but are on a journey of faith, which may often be fraught with uncertainty. The journey is made possible by the assurance of faith, and this assurance is not of our making: it is the product of God's outreach and self-communication. Perhaps modern culture, even a **post-Christian** culture that seems hostile to Christian faith, may supply resources for the Christian community to find its voice in a world of outrageous violence.

In this world, evil and suffering abound; the media wallpaper our lives with disturbing images. How do Christians respond to the pervasive experience of evil? Many Christians have chosen to emphasize "personal salvation" in a way that makes it "individual salvation." Such approaches are often escapist, depicting this world as simply a test, a valley of tears that is passing away. Such individualism and escapism do not address the suffering of the world or its causes, and thus make Christianity appear incredible and irrelevant. Although complete and static answers to the great questions that plague the human condition are unattainable, we must not succumb to the temptation to use the word *mystery* as an escape mechanism, allowing us to opt out of our responsibility to bear witness to salvation in the world. If Christian faith proclaims that God has redeemed the world in Christ, such salvation must be demonstrable, not simply a mystery in the most evasive sense of the term. This chapter discusses the contributions of several theologians who have made a case for the credibility of Christian claims about salvation.

Can We Still Talk about Sin?

The last chapter addressed the history of soteriology, or the way earlier Christians have understood how Christ saves. In this chapter we consider contemporary reappraisals of the soteriological tradition, particularly as offered in the work of two authors we have already introduced: Bernard Lonergan and William Loewe.[2] Loewe has made the recovery of Lonergan's thought central to the renewal of the soteriological tradition, particularly by articulating a more adequate understanding of sin.

Accounts of sin often fail to address the dynamic, real-world power of sin. Sin is often characterized as a spiritual problem for the individual: I lie to avoid looking bad in public; I have lustful thoughts about coworkers; I grow angry when stuck in traffic. The reality of sin and hope for salvation would seem to be the strengths of the Christian tradition, but such is not the case. Both Lonergan and Loewe recognize that Christians need a new account of sin, one that moves beyond the notion of "breaking God's law"—as if God were a schoolteacher with classroom rules posted on the wall. Certainly the notion of divine law is still valuable, but a more adequate understanding of sin will reveal its relationship to suffering and dehumanization.

In an effort to give an account of Christian faith and its power to overcome sin, Loewe argues that the modern historically conscious world necessarily moves us away from the mythological view of the world, something that Paul Ricoeur calls our first naïveté. For Ricoeur, a French philosopher of language, our modern religious understanding begins with a first naïveté that emphasizes the importance of myth and symbol. We recognize these elements as essential in an account of our religious worldview. For example, we read the story of Adam and

Ricoeur and Fowler on Faith Development

The French philosopher and theologian Paul Ricoeur outlined a process by which religious people pass from childish understandings of religious language to more developed and critical approaches—from an initial naiveté, through a critical awakening, to a recovery of religious symbol and language (a second naiveté). James Fowler, one of the preeminent experts on religious development today, offers a more psychologically elaborate account of this phenomenon in his book *Stages of Faith* (Harper & Row, 1981). For Fowler, faith (Christian or otherwise) is a holistic orientation to that which is universal. This orientation goes through six stages, listed below. The first three could be grouped under Ricoeur's "first naiveté," while the conjunctive stage (and possibly the universalizing stage) may correspond to his "second naiveté." Some have criticized the use of Fowler's stages as normative accounts of faith development, but others have found his approach helpful for providing non-normative descriptions of the intersection between cognitive, moral, and spiritual development.

Intuitive-Projective (3–7 yrs)

Imagination runs wild in this stage. Children absorb social mores at this time, but can also be victimized by images of terror and threats of punishment.

Mythic-Literal (school-aged children)

At this stage, symbol and ritual begin to be integrated into a coherent but literal view of the universe. The imagination of the previous stage gets controlled, and the universe begins to make sense and have rules that both punish and reward.

Synthetic-Conventional (adolescence–adulthood)

This stage is called "conventional" because it is the stage in which most people remain. This stage demands a complex pattern of socialization and integration, and faith is an inseparable factor in the ordering of the world. But the stage also emphasizes conformity to accepted notions and prevailing values.

Individuative-Reflective

This is the stage of doubt, anxiety, and struggle where one begins to question long-held assumptions and beliefs. Most people who progress to this stage do so in their thirties and forties as they gradually begin to move away from the group to which they have belonged and which supplied them with identity.

Conjunctive

This stage acknowledges the paradox of faith and doubt. One begins to encounter and understand the reality behind religious symbols and even begins to connect that reality to the symbols used in other traditions. In the individuative-reflective stage, faith came under fire; now it is rehabilitated, but in a different way. Persons in this stage, however, still struggle with identity and therefore maintain identification with their own groups.

Universalizing

In Fowler's ultimate stage of faith development, there are none of the apprehensions about group identification and loyalty that were expressed in the previous stage. People at this stage become obviously abnormal—the drive to self-transcendence stands out. They challenge parochial approaches to morality and authority and become leaders in the search for a universal faith.

Eve as a straightforward account of the first two human beings and their confrontation with a talking snake. But when we expose that faith to a series of critical questions that arise from our experience of the modern world, that initial trust in the myth and symbol is broken. At this point many become skeptical and irreligious. But Ricoeur holds out the possibility that faith can persevere and integrate critical questioning with the myth and symbol of the first naïveté. What Ricoeur calls a second naïveté emerges on the other side of this process. Here one freely engages myth and symbol while recognizing their true power as well as their limitations. For Loewe, when we realize that human history is mostly a product of our choosing and doing and is therefore our responsibility, we are then forced to recognize our responsibility for the tragic direction of history (though not all tragedy is the product of human action). Christians can no longer blithely dismiss evil as the work of unseen demonic forces, or blame disasters on God by identifying them as punishments for sin. An adequate contemporary approach to sin must address the paradox of history: history is a product of human achievements, but at the same time it eludes our understanding and control and leaves us helpless in the face of suffering and evil.

A Contemporary Account of Sin

A contemporary understanding of sin must move away from the symbolic narratives in Scripture toward a formal account of sin that acknowledges the massive scale of alienation and dehumanization in the modern world. In our globalized society, economic systems reinforce the exploitation of resources and people for the sake of a small segment of the population; consider the rate at which the United States consumes oil. These systems find legitimation from a wide range of ideologies, including religious ideologies, resulting in a subtle but profound transformation of our moral discourse. We now reduce questions of meaning and value (what is truly good?) to the merely pragmatic (what works?). Pragmatism is not bad, but we find ourselves unable to ask one another to suffer for what is truly good. Current political and economic debates in the United States and around the world reflect this unwillingness to suffer. Take, for example, the decision of the Internet search company Google. Under pressure from the Chinese government, the company agreed to curtail the ability of its search engine to locate and provide access to sites the government has outlawed or deemed subversive (e.g., Web Sites that advocate democracy). Google's decision was pragmatic: if you want to have access to the fastest growing market in the world, you need to play by the government's rules, even if that means cooperating in the suppression of basic human rights. Such pragmatism leads to a general resignation to and acceptance of current conditions. "Sure people are suffering," we say, "but what can we do?" Such acceptance legitimates current conditions and structures a limited field of moral vision. It is attributable to what William Loewe calls "bias" (a concept he takes over from Lonergan).

Loewe describes three different forms of bias: individual, group, and general bias. Each of these biases impedes real progress in history, resulting in decline, destruction, and alienation. Individual bias takes the form of egoism, a pervasive form of selfishness. Egoism is not the spontaneous, instinctual acts of the human animal for self-preservation. Rather, egoism sabotages intellectual operations to serve self-interest: our thinking and valuing are skewed in favor of our own selfish desires. Similarly, group bias is self-interest at the level of a particular group, such as a religious sect, a nation, a class, or an ethnicity. Since the criteria for satisfaction have shifted from the individual to the group, it is easy for one to become deluded and mistake group bias for "good order." What is truly good, and what might require a particular group to suffer for the benefit of others, is ignored in favor of decisions that promote "our" interests. A nation's foreign policy is often phrased in an explicitly biased manner: we will act to protect our interests. These interests coincide with trading and energy concerns rather than concern for justice or human rights.

A third form of bias, the general bias of common sense, is a deeper, more pervasive force that in some ways underwrites the other forms of bias. Common sense, in this instance, refers to the universal or common concern for the concrete and the practical. Common sense is, therefore, essential for the day-to-day business of human living. Grocery shopping, cooking, and building a house or shelter are all expressions of common sense—hunger needs to be satisfied with food, and shelter provides safety from the weather. The general bias of common sense extends "its legitimate concern for the concrete and the immediately practical into

Lonergan and the Notion of Bias

Individual Bias

Individual bias makes people focus on themselves. They fail to ask, what is true? and, what is good? Instead, they are stuck in the rut of asking, what is good for me? and, what is true for me?

Group Bias

Group bias is similar to individual bias, but enacted on the level of a group. The questions of value (what is good?) and fact (what is true?) are asked and answered from the perspective of the group. Nationalism is one of the most obvious examples of group bias: what benefits us determines national policy, and "truth" consists of that which affirms our values and our self-identity.

General Bias

The general bias of common sense sounds like a good thing—wouldn't it be great if everyone used common sense? But Lonergan sees that human beings are often given over to the tyranny of "what works" and "what I can see." Common sense is not a bad thing, but when it is celebrated as a pervasive assumption about reality, it wreaks havoc in history. When people subscribe to the general bias of common sense (usually unconsciously, as with all the biases), they ignore the human vocation to transcend themselves, their group, and what can be sensed. What is really real and really good in the universe is beyond me and my interests.

Overcoming Bias in Conversion

In Lonergan's writings, *conversion* is the process by which bias is overcome, a dramatic leap beyond the horizon of meaning and value that defines us and the world in which we locate ourselves. Our intellect may undergo conversion (intellectual conversion) so that we move from seeing reality as simply a matter of senses to recognizing that it is much more. Our valuing can undergo conversion (moral conversion) so that we no longer think that what is good for us individually is really good, but that what is really good may work against our personal interests in the short run. Finally, we can understand that we are loved by God beyond all reason, and that we are called to complete self-transcendence and union with God in love through religious conversion. These conversions can happen in any order, but they tend to have an impact on one another.

disregard of larger issues and indifference to long-term results."[3] Humanity turns to common sense to deliver it from individual and group biases motivated by self-interest. Common sense, however, is unable to meet this challenge; common sense must be led, at a deeper level, by something more. General bias prevents common sense from acknowledging and embracing ideas that consider a higher viewpoint in history. It is unable to address questions concerning long-range consequences of particular actions or values. Its pervasiveness and insidiousness generates "the longer cycle of decline." General bias fuels the other biases and results in both social and personal decline and decay. Suffering and evil are thus attributed to our inability to move beyond our **horizon** (i.e., the limit of our field of moral vision) of common sense, to surpass self-interest or the interests of our tribe, and embrace real value, that which is truly good.

Such an account of sin does not seem explicitly religious; one may wonder what difference Jesus makes in all of this. The Christian proclamation of salvation in Christ must be made intelligible and credible in light of an account of sin as bias, and this is accomplished by Loewe through an interpretation of the Law of the Cross.

Conversion and the Law of the Cross

The Law of the Cross is a principle of transformation presented to us in the story of the life, death, and Resurrection of Jesus. The principle unfolds through three distinct moments. First, sin is death. Sin brings death. Sin kills. The discussion of bias clearly illustrates this: when one's horizon of meaning and value is skewed, truncated, or myopic, one acts out of bias. What is good simply means what is good for me or for us. Moreover, what is good is defined in pragmatic terms. Such a field of moral vision brings about violence and suffering. However, while sin is death, if the death and suffering caused by sin is accepted out of love, it can be transformed, and this is the second movement in the Law of the Cross. In other words, when we are injured by the thoughtlessness, the bias, or the sin of others, we can respond out of love. Though we experience pain and suffering, the death of sin, we have the capacity to see sin as the product of disvalue and can embrace the suffering that has been inflicted upon us, not passively, but proactively.

The Law of the Cross formulates a principle of transformation that makes it possible for human beings, living in a world dominated by sin, to achieve **authenticity** and become fully what God has created us to be. It is described by Lonergan variously as "being in love in an unrestricted fashion," or as "a state of unreserved openness to value." It is this "being in love" that makes living the Law of the Cross possible, but it is also the Law of the Cross, this principle of transformation, that structures our "being in love." Authenticity is, therefore, not a personal achievement gained through self-help books and seminars, however helpful they might be on any given occasion. Rather, it is the result of God's self-gift in grace experienced and received in community. This self-gift is uniquely mediated to the world in the person of Jesus and perpetuated by the witness of the church, particularly through its stories, symbols, and uniquely in its liturgy, all of which inform the life and practice of the church.

Loewe thus brings the soteriological tradition to a fuller theoretical statement and integrates biblical language and experience of conversion with the centrality of the cross in Christian theology. Loewe's interpretation of the Law of the Cross thus stands out as a remarkable example of the drive within contemporary Christian theology to articulate a socially responsible soteriology centered on the transformation of human interiority—how we think and value—not simply on an individual level but as a community. This has implications for the entire planet. This is the recovery of Christian credibility in the face of massive suffering, and the desire to actualize the redemptive love Christians claim they have experienced in Christ.

The Importance of Christian Doctrine for Social Change

The horrific cry of those millions who senselessly suffered and died as the result of Nazi atrocities and Allied indifference has profoundly shaped twentieth-century theology and made it come to terms with its own role in the concrete suffering of millions. There is probably no better example of the impact of the Holocaust on Christian theology than the work of Jürgen Moltmann. Like many theologians in the twentieth century, Moltmann has worked to connect God with human history, particularly through his conviction concerning the nature of God, the revelation of that nature, and the process of history.

Revelation is not to be understood as a supernatural incursion into the natural world; rather, revelation is a promise about the future experienced and anticipated in the here and now. God becomes known, indeed becomes God, within history. In his book *The Crucified God*, Moltmann begins with the bold truism that the concept of God is determinative for a given culture, society, and individual. If we are cruel and vindictive, our "god" tends to be cruel and vindictive.

The Holocaust and Christian Theology

The Holocaust is the name often given to the systematic attempt to exterminate European Jews under Nazi occupation during World War II (1939–1945). The word *holocaust* is the Greek translation of the Hebrew *shoah*, an offering to God burned on an altar. Many Jews (as well as homosexuals, handicapped, Poles, Czechs, gypsies, and others deemed inferior) were cremated in the ovens at death camps like Auschwitz, and the burning of these victims is made sacred by the term *holocaust*, or *shoah*. The Holocaust has had a major impact on Christian theology, particularly in the way it has necessitated a radical reassessment of Judaism by the Christian church.

The Christian church has a long history of directly or indirectly promoting the marginalization of the Jewish people. Of particular concern is the theological marginalization of Judaism in Christian preaching since the early centuries of the Common Era. Major figures and saints were noted for their homilies against the Jews (e.g., John Chrysostom, *Adversus Iudaeos*) in which Jews were called "dogs" and pitiable for rejecting God. Martin Luther wrote several disturbing pieces against the Jews (e.g., "The Jews and Their Lies"), even calling for their expulsion from Germany. The history of this language sowed the seeds of anti-Semitism deep within the soil of Christian Europe, and these seeds came to horrible fruition in the Nazi atrocities.

After the war, Christians began to take stock of anti-Semitism and the role Christian theology and preaching had played in the Holocaust. At the Second Vatican Council (1962–1965), the declaration *Nostra aetate* contained a revolutionary paragraph (no. 4) in which the church affirmed that "God holds the Jews most dear for the sake of their Fathers; He does not repent of the gifts He makes or of the calls He issues" and that "the Jews should not be presented as rejected or accursed by God." Indeed, during the pontificate of Pope John Paul II, the irrevocability of the Jewish covenant was regularly affirmed (e.g., "Address to the Jewish community of West Germany at Mainz," November 17, 1980: "The Old Covenant . . . has never been revoked").

Without a revolution in the concept of God . . . there can be no revolutionary faith. Without God's liberation from idolatrous images produced by anxiety and hubris, there will be no liberating theology. Man always unfolds his humanity in relation to the divinity of his God, and experiences himself in relation to what appears to him as the highest being.[4]

The modern God is thus a God of apathy (*apatheia*), and the modern human being is the apathetic person of success. "Faith in the apathetic God leads to the ethics of man's liberation from need and drive, and to dominion over body and nature." The result of this apathy is carelessness about our actions, as these create suffering and oppression, poignantly reflected in the scene from Elie Wiesel's *Night* in which three prisoners are hanged in retaliation for an escape attempt. One of the condemned prisoners, a small boy, dies slowly as the other prisoners are forced to watch. As the prisoners file past, someone asks, "Where is God?" Moltmann's response to Wiesel's story is that we can only talk about God's presence in the person of the youth hanging from the gallows. In other words, God is present as the suffering one. Such a notion deeply disturbs the western concept of the *apatheia* (impassibility) of God, which western theology traditionally sees as essential for God's love to be truly free. The Christian tradition has adopted a concept of love that demands absolute freedom. "True love arises out of freedom from self-seeking and anxiety, and because it loves *sine ira et studio* [without passion or prejudice], one understood apathy as the presupposition for *agape* [love]."[5] Yet, as Moltmann demonstrates, the classical idea of God's *apatheia* cannot be fully reconciled with the Jewish and Christian experience of God. In the prophets and in the story of Jesus, both the Jewish and Christian traditions insist that God suffers with and does not stand apart from the oppressed. The doctrine of God's *apatheia* has superseded these experiences of God over the centuries, but post-Holocaust theologies like that of Moltmann serve to recall such powerful traditions.

The Christian experience builds on the message and promise of the prophets and its continuity with the covenant of Israel, but Christians also find themselves in a new "God situation" as a result of their experience of Christ. In the cross of Christ we find our own inescapable suffering as it exists in God. So if human beings form themselves and their societies based on their image of God, a revised image of God then creates a different kind of society, one built not on progress, success, and action, but on fellow suffering, sympathy, and radical patience. In such a theology God cannot be the God of the establishment (church, government, dominant social class) but must be identified with what and who is marginal. The suffering of the marginal must be recognized as the suffering of God, and must be embraced. In the end, what emerges is something like the Law of the Cross.

> Where [human beings] suffer because they love, God suffers in them and they suffer in God. Where this God suffers the death of Jesus and thereby demonstrates the power of his love, there men also find the power to remain in love despite pain and death, becoming neither

bitter nor superficial. They gain the power of affliction and can hold fast to the dead . . . and despite [this] remain in love.[6]

Moltmann transforms Christian doctrine through an appeal to the historical specificity of our encounter with God, and this appeal enshrines the virtue of hope rather than so-called progress. It is the hopeless world that is condemned to progress (as defined by the canonization of general bias), condemned to rely on its own devices, which are unequal to the "good intentions" of human beings. Such a world ignores suffering and cannot embrace the God who suffers and yet promises liberation. For Jews and Christians, God is the one who suffers with us amid the promise that suffering is not the last word; rather, God calls us to faithfulness, to live beyond the desire to control that lies at the heart of progress. Jesus is the sure sign to Christians of God's suffering with us as well as the hope that history will unfold God's lordship over time.

Revolutionary Christology

Much of contemporary theology has been heavily influenced by what has come to be called liberation theology. Like the theologies discussed above, liberation theology seeks to address the concrete conditions of the marginalized and their suffering. Liberation theology emerged as a discernable movement in the middle of the twentieth century in response to the suffering of the marginalized in Latin America. There the Catholic Church had long been allied with the colonial powers and the ruling class, but liberation theologians sought to transform the Church so that it identified with the poor over and against the powers of oppression. Gustavo Gutierrez, often regarded as the father of liberation theology, was educated within the European system, as were many others who followed his thought. In European universities, liberation theologians appropriated the philosophical and political thought that dominated the region, a form of Marxist humanism. That political philosophy, along with the theological revolution precipitated by the Second Vatican Council (especially its emphasis on the laity and its call to action on behalf of justice), contributed to the formation of liberation theology as a distinct religious and theological movement.

Elizabeth Cady Stanton

Elizabeth Cady Stanton (1815–1902) was one of the most important pioneers in the women's movement in the United States. She is most closely associated with the cause of women's suffrage, although she also worked to abolish slavery and abortion. Along with her friend Lucretia Mott, she helped to organize the first women's rights convention at Seneca Falls, New York, in 1848. Stanton and Mott joined with Susan B. Anthony to form the National Woman Suffrage Association in 1868, believing that denying women the right to vote was a primary injustice that perpetuated the suffering of women. Although Stanton had been raised as a Presbyterian, she began to regard traditional Christianity as patriarchal and the Bible as an important instrument in the oppression of women. Biblical texts (especially 1 Corinthians 14:34–35 and 1 Timothy 2:11–14) were regularly used to subordinate women. To address this situation, she undertook a new Bible commentary that would serve to liberate women from oppression; the project, called *The Woman's Bible*, appeared in the late nineteenth century. There Stanton anticipates developments that would come to dominate contemporary feminist biblical interpretation by giving prominence to neglected passages that present women in a favorable light and marginalizing texts that legitimate the oppression of women.

Contemporary feminist theology is a form of liberation theology, even though the roots of feminist theology reach back into the nineteenth century and beyond (see, for example, Elizabeth Cady Stanton). Both theologies share a common methodological approach that runs through several distinct moments, or steps.[7]

1. The suffering of the marginalized provides theology with its primary data, and a lived commitment to addressing this suffering is the starting point for theology.

2. The starting point for theological reflection is not philosophy, but the social sciences, which help to explain in concrete terms how and why the marginalized are oppressed while also providing for ways to address that oppression.

3. The Christian tradition is to be read with a **hermeneutics of suspicion** (hermeneutics are principles of interpretation). A hermeneutics of

suspicion helps to uncover the way the Christian tradition itself has contributed to the oppression and marginalization of people.

4. A **hermeneutics of retrieval** recovers some elements of the tradition that have been omitted, lost, or suppressed in the history of the tradition; voices that have been silenced must be given recognition, and new symbols need to be created and offered as the tradition is re-symbolized to promote liberation of the oppressed.

5. **Praxis**, or critically informed action on behalf of the marginalized, is the unique criterion for theology: the value of a theology may be judged by how well it remedies injustice and oppression. Praxis thus leads back to point 1, immersion and commitment to the oppressed. Theology must also maintain continuity with the church's proclamation of the gospel. The use of the term *praxis* affirms that liberation theologies seek a liberation that is religious, social, political, economic, and personal.

We will not examine the oppression of women here; such an account would be beyond the scope of the present chapter. Rather, we will consider the two areas that deal directly with the christological tradition as such: the hermeneutics of suspicion and the retrieval of subjugated knowledge in feminist theologies.

Karl Marx, Liberation Theologies, and the Magisterium

The movement of European economies from an agrarian to an industrial base was coupled with political transformations, including a shift from monarchies to representative forms of government. Neither of these transitions occurred without great suffering and tumult. Amid these transformations Karl Marx (1818–1883) offered a provocative analysis of social structures, economies, and governments that would change the world. Marx's materialistic analysis of history included the following points:

- Social development is based on the development of productive forces, which are material.

- The forces of production and the corresponding social relationships they produce progress independently of the will of human beings.
- Ideologies and supporting institutions provide a superstructure for society, i.e., society at every level is organized and stratified for production.
- The state is an instrument of repression used by the ruling class.
- When social relationships, determined by the forces of production, become a hindrance to further progress of production there is revolution.

Marx also discussed the nature of a commodity as "fetish." For Marx, a commodity is an object that

Karl Marx, Liberation Theologies, and the Magisterium *(continued)*

is the product of human labor put in relation to other objects of human labor as it is circulated. This second aspect of the commodity creates its quality as fetish. Marx's point is that commodities, particularly within industrial economies, take on a life of their own apart from the production of the item. Consumers in the bicycle store do not see the labor and craftsmanship that went into the bicycle, only the commodity. They desire it. They must have it. Advertising reinforces the fetish nature of the commodity. The desire becomes increasingly problematic to the extent that the human being who creates a product is invisible to the consumer—we ignore the conditions in the garment worker's sweatshop when we hit the mall. It is easy to see how industrial workers can be exploited and increasingly dehumanized in such a system. But the psychology of desire and production go unchecked and unquestioned, and the economy and its forces become almost an object of worship.

Marxist analysis of economic suffering and dehumanization at the hands of governments and economic interests has become an effective tool for many theologians. In Latin America, the birthplace of liberation theology, the Roman Catholic Church has frequently expressed itself through a Marxist analysis of economic forces. The materialism of such an analysis has caused concern in Rome and created a firestorm of controversy. The rise of liberation theology in Latin America in the 1960s

and 1970s resonated with many Latin American bishops. The conference of Latin American bishops (CELAM) began to express its concerns about poverty and the church's silence on the suffering of the poor. In several conferences, CELAM echoed the themes of liberation theology, particularly at Medellin, Colombia (1968), and at Puebla, Mexico (1979). These conferences spoke of the Church "listening to the cry of the poor and becoming the interpreter of their anguish," and articulated the theme of liberation in Catholic theology. But during the pontificate of John Paul II, the Congregation for the Doctrine of the Faith (CDF) issued two documents on liberation theology in which suspicions about the use of Marxist tools of analysis were expressed. The first document ("Instruction on Some Aspects of Liberation Theology," dated August 6, 1984, and published September 3, 1984) praised the purpose of liberation theology but warned against an uncritical acceptance of atheistic Marxism as a dominant principle. The fear was that the gospel would be reduced to materialism and its call to transcendent value would be ignored. Negative reaction to the fairly harsh tone of the first document was heard in Rome and throughout the Church, and the subsequent CDF document ("Instruction on Christian Freedom and Liberation," 1986) was much more positive in tone, affirming the need of the Church to be in the service of the marginalized.

Strategies of Suspicion and the Importance of Symbolic Discourse in Feminist Christology

While Marxists have been particularly adept at performing economic and political analyses of western culture, the need arises for an analysis of language and communication that subverts the exploitative dimension of communication. Many contemporary philosophers have performed just such an analysis.[8] Within this philosophical focus on language and society, philosophers have noted that any effort to create an ideal speech situation must be preceded by an examination of the prevailing patterns of discourse within a given community. Such an examination will focus on the tendency of the community to marginalize or exclude certain voices in its discourse and the corresponding **canonization** of terms and symbols that become normative for any given culture or community.

To illustrate this concept, think about the pressure you felt to dress and act a certain way in junior high school, and how those who did not conform were marginalized until they conformed. Maybe conformity was identified simply by the kind of backpack you had or the clothes you wore, but such things were part of the language of school, and that language set up some brutal boundaries between who or what was accepted and who or what was not. If you do not think this was the case at your school, chances are you were one of those who fit in, one who found it natural to conform. But if you talk to someone who felt marginalized at your school, you will discover an entirely different experience. Language and symbols have the power to exclude and brutalize, as was eloquently portrayed in the teen angst film *The Breakfast Club.*

As dominant forms of discourse are established in society, some forms of speech and symbols are privileged over others on the basis of a set of preconceived notions of what is normative. Acceptable linguistic expression comes to be viewed as "natural," a given. It achieves objective status so that any challenge to the hegemony of a cultural symbol system is understood as a challenge to the larger social order. The result of this privileging is the linguistic oppression of minority voices and their identification as dangerous or subversive.

Feminist hermeneutics attempts to unmask the ideology inherent in contemporary theological discourse. First, feminist theologians address the nature of theological language to mitigate its univocal interpretation. In other words, they recognize that theological language is necessarily imprecise and cannot capture the experience and reality of God literally, but only by analogy. Such a move brings to the fore the work of Thomas Aquinas on the **analogia entis,** or the analogy of being. For Thomas, all statements about God must first be negated (*via negativa*). To say that God is Father means first of all that God is not a father. God does not contribute genetic material to create a new life; God does not, strictly speaking, have a spouse. Rather, our experience of fathers provides the basis for saying that God is like a father: God is faithful, strong, dependable, and loving. But every positive statement of this sort (*via positiva*), must be rounded off by the conviction that whatever qualities are possessed by even the most idealized father, God's fatherly qualities (love, faithfulness, etc.) are infinitely greater *(via eminentiae)*. Such is the teaching of the Catholic Church in the *Catechism*:

> Admittedly, in speaking about God like this, our language is using human modes of expression; nevertheless it really does attain to God himself, though unable to express him in his infinite simplicity. Likewise, we must recall that "between Creator and creature no similitude can be expressed without implying an even greater dissimilitude" (Lateran Council IV: DS 806); and that "concerning God, we cannot grasp what he is, but only what he is not, and how other beings stand in relation to him." (St. Thomas Aquinas, *Summa Contra Gentiles* I, 30, in *CCC*, 43)

The reaffirmation of Church teaching on the analogical nature of "God-talk" relativizes propositional claims about God as "Father" and "Son" and leaves room for creativity and the recovery of alternate language, including images of God as "mother" (e.g., Isaiah 42:14, 46:3–4, 66:13; Psalm 131:2; see also *CCC*, 239). The recovery of analogy also focuses attention on the power of the symbol in theological discourse.

Central to feminist hermeneutics, both in the hermeneutics of suspicion and in the retrieval of the tradition, is the analysis of symbolic language, a common concern across the spectrum of contemporary philosophy and theology. Paul Ricoeur, for example, emphasizes a "surplus of meaning" within symbolic discourse. The symbol goes beyond itself and pushes the mind of those who encounter the symbol. It provokes new ways of thinking. This recovery and exploration of the symbolic and analogical nature of theological discourse helps to ground feminist hermeneutics as enriching the tradition by offering a wider range of language while also acting as a remedy to the stagnant and distorting language of a male-dominated church. Paul Tillich's account of the six characteristics of **symbols** adds further dimensions to a feminist account of symbol in theology:

1. The symbol directs us to that reality which is beyond our grasp.

2. The symbol participates in that reality.

3. The symbol opens up levels of reality that would otherwise be inaccessible.

4. The symbol emerges from a region beyond reason.

5. The symbol is dynamic, not static.

6. The symbol points to that which transcends the world.[9]

This account relativizes the symbolic discourse of the past and makes androcentric (male-centered) language open to change and improvement. The limits of such change, however, have become a source of controversy.

The Hermeneutics of Retrieval

Several different trajectories have emerged within feminist theology, and only a brief sketch is possible here. One of the most important issues involves the divide between radicals and reformists. Many feminist theologians, employing a hermeneutics of suspicion, conclude that the entire Christian tradition is so saturated with patriarchal bias that it cannot be redeemed. These so-called radical theologians insist on the creation of an entirely new religious system centered on the experience of women; only then can the misogyny of the Christian tradition be eradicated. These theologians may have identified themselves as Christians formerly, but are among those who now describe themselves as post-Christian. The vast majority of feminist theologians do not go so far. Rather, having subjected the Christian tradition to a hermeneutics of suspicion, they insist that the tradition has not always been misogynistic. The tradition does indeed provide women with the resources to re-symbolize Christianity in a way that is in keeping with the concerns of women but also preserves the integrity of the tradition. One important exemplar of reformist feminist theology is Elizabeth Johnson.[10]

Elizabeth Johnson does not soft-peddle the problems of the tradition: "At root the difficulty lies in the fact that Christology in its story, symbol, and doctrine has been assimilated to the patriarchal world view, with the result that its liberating dynamic has been twisted into justification for domination."[11] Johnson notes that the maleness of Jesus reinforces a patriarchal image of God, and the maleness of God marginalizes women. In support she quotes a passage from Augustine.

> Woman does not possess the image of God in herself, but only when taken together with the male who is her head, so that the whole substance is one image. But when she is assigned the role of helpmate, a function that pertains to her alone, then she is not the image of God.[12]

Johnson also notes that the maleness of Jesus and the patriarchal image of God serve to reinforce an androcentric (male-centered) anthropology in which the male sex is made normative. For example, the Catholic tradition has argued that women cannot represent or symbolize Christ appropriately because Christ was male.[13] Since the priest acts *in persona Christi* (in the person of Christ) in the celebration of the sacraments, the ecclesiastical participation of women is limited.

> It is indeed evident that in human beings the difference of sex exercises an important influence, much deeper than, for example, ethnic differences: the latter do not affect the human person as intimately as the difference of sex, which is directly ordained both for the communion of persons and for the generation of human beings. In Biblical Revelation this difference is the effect of God's will from the beginning: "male and female he created them" (Gen 1:27). (*Inter Insigniores*, no. 5)

For Johnson and others, a normative, male-centered anthropology puts the salvation of women in jeopardy, in view of the principle articulated by Gregory Nazianzen: "What was not assumed was not redeemed" Christians must therefore reject a dualistic anthropology that envisions male and female as unique and essentializing aspects of human existence and adopt a "single-nature" anthropology. Such an anthropology does not identify an abstract "humanness" and relegate sexual difference to mere biological function (specifically, the sexual differences that allow humans to procreate). Rather, Johnson argues that human nature exists in "an interdependence of multiple differences," or a "multipolar" anthropology.[14] In other words, there are all kinds of ways in which individual humans differ (height, class, religion, age, etc.), sex being only one difference among many. Johnson asks why human beings must be differentiated and defined by sex rather than any other factor. It is precisely within the recognition of our differences that individual human persons are recognized. If one changes any single element within the complex of differences that constitute a specific human person, one in fact changes the person. Human nature requires us to celebrate diversity to celebrate humanity and live authentically.

In light of Johnson's critique of the Christian tradition and its privileging of certain texts and symbols, feminist theologians turn their attention to the hermeneutics of retrieval. They seek to uncover those forgotten voices within history and move them to the center. One of the more important examples of subjugated knowledge involves Wisdom, or **Sophia Christology**. The wisdom tradition of Israel provides the appropriate resource for reconstructing, or "re-symbolizing," Christology.

While many contemporary Christians, particularly those from more conservative traditions, feel uncomfortable or threatened by feminism in general and feminist theology in particular, most are quite familiar with wisdom literature (Songs of Solomon, Proverbs, Ecclesiastes, and Sirach) and accept it as uncontroversial. Yet when wisdom literature is used as part of a feminist hermeneutics of retrieval, many conservative Christians start to feel ill at ease because they have never considered that the Wisdom of YHWH in this literary tradition is figured as female in both Greek (*sophia*) and Hebrew (*hokmah*). As such, the Wisdom Tradition provides an excellent countermeasure to the exclusive use of the masculine to refer to God. Johnson envisions several benefits to Wisdom Christology: (1) A relation to the whole cosmos is built into the wisdom tradition so that Christology is not simply centered on human beings, but includes all of creation. (2) Wisdom Christology is able to respond favorably and inclusively to other religious traditions. (3) Wisdom is connected to the poor and the oppressed. (4) Through Wisdom Christology, the significance of women within the ministry of Jesus and the early church is also emphasized. Johnson's retrieval and cultivation of Wisdom Christology and her movement away from Logos Christology reflects her concern to ground Christology, and indeed all theology, in the effective use of analogy and symbol.

As with many feminist Christologies, the retrieval of Jesus' own attitude toward women is central to Johnson's Christology. Johnson and other

Some Additional Forms of Contemporary Feminist Theologies

Naming or labeling is a powerful and precarious enterprise; the following chart needs to be read with this in mind. Listed below are some major forms of feminist theology that have not been discussed in this chapter. They are, in some ways, species of the more general field of feminist theology.

Name	Basic Concerns	Some Major Representatives
Eco-feminist	• Concern for the connection between patriarchy and the exploitation and violence done to the natural order • Views technological progress and globalization with great suspicion and concern, particularly for its impact on the environment	Carol Adams Mary C. Grey Sallie McFague
Mujerista	• Emphasizes the experience of Latinas, particularly Hispanic American women, taking their stories as primary material for constructing a theology of empowerment	Ada María Isasi-Díaz
Womanist	• The experience of Black women, viewed as being significantly different from that of European women around whom modern feminism revolves, defines the concerns of this liberationist theology	Katie Cannon Alice Walker Delores Williams

reformist theologians contend that the egalitarian nature of the community of disciples was gradually lost and replaced with an imperial model of discipleship in the early centuries of the Christian era. Ideas of lordship and submission became normative, and the role of women became more and more marginal to the community. Johnson and others insist that the egalitarian and liberating character of Christian discipleship must be recovered in light of the crucified Jesus, for "the crucified Christ embodies the exact opposite of the patriarchal ideal of the powerful man, and shows the steep price paid in the struggle for liberation." This interpretation of Jesus has been received with less than open arms in some quarters, especially in Rome where such egalitarianism is viewed as an attack on the hierarchical structure of the church, often viewed as divine in its origin.

In her assessment of Elizabeth Johnson's Christology, Shannon Schrein concludes that Johnson, unlike many of her fellow theologians, remains

Christ-centered and robustly within the Christian tradition as she labors to "braid a footbridge" between Christian theology and the concerns of feminist theology. Her commitment to the principles of analogical language and the control of analogy in theology, as well as her recovery of Wisdom Christology and the egalitarian practices of Jesus and the earliest disciples, all ground her commitment to the Christian tradition. At the same time, the concerns within her Christology provide a footbridge to other religious traditions and create the possibility of transforming dialogue with religious "others."[15]

Postcolonial Christology

Colonialism had a devastating effect on the way Christianity was spread around the world in the modern era. The remnants of this impact can be observed in the pages of various editions of children's Bibles found in almost every Christian home. I can remember the children's Bible my grandmother gave me for my First Communion. I loved the pictures and the abbreviated stories. I remember, in particular, the pictures of Jesus; he had reddish hair, blue eyes, and looked very much like Barry Gibb from the 1970s pop group the Bee Gee's. For me, this was an affirming and friendly image. But what about my schoolmates? How did they react to these pictures? For me, the children's Bible was a reaffirmation of my own position of privilege and power, but surely a reminder of the marginalization of the African identity and culture of some of my schoolmates, and I was utterly oblivious to these concerns.

The experience of cultural marginalization is more acutely felt throughout the regions of the world where a European Jesus and a European church have been identified with colonial powers and colonial violence. With the political emancipation of so many colonized nations over the past half century, a cultural and religious emancipation has followed. The Eurocentric assumptions of Christianity, that is, the assumption that Christianity is *essentially* expressed within Western culture, have been called into question among indigenous peoples in South America, in the Philippines, in Africa, and especially in Asia. What has emerged is often called **postcolonial Christology**, since it addresses the violence and structural marginalization of indigenous or native peoples throughout history, but especially in connection with the colonialism of European nations in the past several centuries. Such an approach to Christology has rendered pictures of Christ that are a far cry from those in the pages of my children's Bible.

Postcolonial Christology in Asia

While postcolonial Christology is most often associated with Latin America and the practice of liberation theology, Asia is another region where colonialism has wreaked havoc and where Christians are now articulating postcolonial theologies. Peter Phan has offered some important reflections on the legacy of colonialism in Asia and its impact on the church there.[16] "Imagine that the earliest disciples of Jesus had turned to the East rather than to the Greco-Roman world to carry out the Lord's 'great commission' [to preach the gospel to every nation]."[17] You may recall the presentation of classical Christology in a previous chapter and the decisive role played by Greco-Roman culture in the emergence of that Christology. What would have happened if the questions or issues were different? In recent decades, many Asian theologians have begun to explore how a postcolonial perspective on Christology can serve the christological tradition by re-imaging Christ for people who are no longer subjugated by a colonial Christianity. They seek to make the claim that "Jesus saves" credible once again in a world of sin, violence, and exploitation.

Phan's overview of postcolonial Christology takes account of the unique factors that comprise the Asian context: poverty, totalitarianism, and religious pluralism. In Asia the overwhelming majority of the people suffer in horrific poverty brought about by the exploitation of a few, Japan being the only major exception. The political response to the problem of poverty has taken the form of totalitarianism, usually some form of dictatorship often sponsored by foreign (i.e., western) powers. Often these systems, whether socialist or capitalist, fail to address the system of oppression and even make matters worse through the neglect of indigenous sensibilities reflected in folklore and religion. Phan expands upon this last factor by listing five neglected features of Asian religious life that might help address the violence and suffering of most Asians: (1) introspection, (2) the religiousness of the poor and the poverty of the religious, (3) the practices of Asian religion, (4) monasticism, and (5) Asian culture in general.

C. S. Song and the Crucified People

One of the most influential postcolonial Asian Christologies is offered by the Taiwanese-born theologian Choan-Seng Song. Although Song spends much of his time teaching in the United States, he still derives much of his inspiration from the stories, real and mythological, of Asian people oppressed by both church authorities and sociopolitical powers. His theology and particularly his Christology are essentially narrative. For Song, these stories serve as the vehicle for theological insight, or ***satori*** (a Japanese Zen term expressing sudden insight or enlightenment). Since the stories of the Asian people are those of poor, suffering, and powerless people, an authentic Asian theology, in Song's view, is necessarily a liberation theology. Such a theology does not begin with abstract doctrines, but with the particular sociopolitical and cultural situations of the people among whom God's love and suffering are manifested in the work of liberation.

Song makes use of traditional Asian narratives to unpack his theology. In *The Tears of Lady Meng: A Parable of People's Political Theology*,[18] Song retells a famous Chinese legend (there are many different versions of the story) about a woman whose husband was conscripted to build the Great Wall. After a year of waiting in vain for his return or news of his well-being, Meng decides to journey to the Great Wall. After much hardship, she finally finds a group of workers who have been taken from her village and forced to work on the Wall. She asks them about her husband, but they tell her that he has died and is buried under a portion of the Wall. At this news, she begins to wail and mourn; her tears are so abundant that they bring down the section of the Wall where her husband has been buried. The workers are ordered to rebuild that section of the Wall, but each time they do it collapses. Eventually, the emperor becomes infatuated with Lady Meng and seeks to marry her. She agrees on the condition that the emperor build a large funeral pyre (a large ceremonial fire, often placed on a river barge, upon which the body of the deceased is burned) for her late husband. When the emperor arranges for the pyre, Lady Meng throws herself on the fire. As her body is consumed by the flames, the ash falls into the river and turns into silver fish. Song uses the story to illustrate both the power of the people's suffering, symbolized by Lady Meng's tears, and the political power of self-sacrifice, symbolized in Lady Meng's act of defiance against the emperor. For Song, Meng's self-sacrifice illustrates the political power of Christ's Crucifixion, the power to resist and subvert the forces of oppression and tyranny and promote liberation.

It is on the basis of the liberation theology concealed in the people's stories, folklore, mythologies, art, dance, and music that Song develops his christological trilogy (*Jesus, the Crucified People; Jesus and the Reign of God; Jesus in the Power of the Spirit*).[19] Underlying his Christology is the attempt to discover how the event of the Word-becoming-flesh (John 1:14) continues today in the life of Asian peoples. To achieve this goal, Song suggests that the christological hermeneutic has to be a "people hermeneutic." In other words, we discover who Jesus is by connecting to the lives of the poor, the outcasts, and the socially marginalized. For Song, God is the story of Jesus, and Jesus is the story of the people who suffer.

For Song, the cross of Jesus brings together the suffering of the people with the love of God expressed in Christ. The cross tells the story of human rejection and unmasks that suffering as the work of social and political powers defending their privilege and control. Song argues against Moltmann's notion that the cross represents an event in the life of God. Rather, the cross is the quintessential example of human violence against other humans.[20] The life and ministry of Jesus stands out in sharp contrast to such violence. In Song's meditation on Jesus' temptations, Jesus stands against manipulative human relationships, rejecting the powerful and coercive tactics offered to him by satanic powers. At the end of the day, Jesus stands with humanity, sharing a meal at a round (Asian) banquet table, where all have an equal place and an equal share. For Song, the question regarding the identity of Jesus and his religious significance can only be answered through negation. The question is not, who is Jesus? Rather, it is, where is Jesus? Song's response identifies Jesus with the marginalized and suffering.

Chung Hyun Kyung and *Minjung Christology*

Through a variety of works—especially *The Struggle to Be Sun Again*—Chung Hyun Kyung has offered a comprehensive presentation of Asian women's theology as a plea to God in search of justice and healing. Her theology, an embodied and critical reflection on Asian women's experiences, begins with those experiences and not with such elements of the Christian tradition as Scripture, doctrines, or liturgy. Chung presents these experiences as stories of Asian women she identifies as ***minjung*** (Korean for "the popular mass"). She emphasizes that she is a "second-generation liberationist," with a theology distinct from that of previous liberationists. The previous generation primarily undertook the task of dealing with colonialism and its impact on Asian peoples. As a second generation liberationist, Chung and her colleagues have moved on; they now do theology from their own feelings and experiences. She argues that if Asian women theologians do not permit themselves "to fully experience who [they] are, [they] will not have the power to fight back and create [their] own space."[21]

Chung contends that as Asian women live through the hardship and suffering of obedience to family and society, they need a language that can give voice to that suffering as well as to their poverty and oppression by colonial forces. The most popular image of Jesus in this context is that of liberator and revolutionary, but these images are tempered with feminine images of Jesus as mother. As mother, Jesus is confrontational in the

Cosmic and Metacosmic Religiousness

The Sri Lankan Jesuit Aloysius (Alois) Pieris, in his book *An Asian Theology of Liberation* (Maryknoll, NY: Orbis Books, 1988), distinguishes between "cosmic" religiousness and "metacosmic" religiousness. For Pieris, cosmic religion, or more generally cosmic religiousness, is a religious disposition oriented toward the management of our natural environment (e.g., making the crops grow, protecting the clan or the family from enemies, and ensuring procreation). Cosmic religiousness is ultimately oriented toward metacosmic religiousness, in which the practical concerns of day-to-day living are subordinated to more transcendent concerns. Within metacosmic religiousness there is greater systematization and a concern for reality beyond the practical.

Metacosmic religiousness is able to accommodate the questions and concerns of cosmic religiousness so that many of the rituals and theologies endure within the framework supplied by the metacosmic religion. Buddhism as it is practiced throughout Asia exemplifies the interplay of shamanistic (cosmic) religions and the metacosmic concerns of Buddhist teaching: one can go without contradiction to the shaman in the morning and then visit the Buddhist monastery in the afternoon for instruction from the monks.

Many theologians today ask, to what extent can the Christian (metacosmic) system accommodate cosmic religiousness? Historically, elements of the pre-Christian religions of northern Europe endured and influenced people long after they began to embrace Christianity. Could the same hold true today?

face of oppression while also compassionately suffering with those who suffer. Such images, Chung argues, help to give strength to Asian women in their struggle for justice and freedom.

In addition to traditional symbols and images, Chung and other Asian women theologians create images and symbols out of their own experiences and resources. One such image is of Jesus as a shaman (a priestess of indigenous religious tradition who primarily offers healing and protection). Jesus is a Korean shaman who helps Asian women release the **han**, that is, the unresolved resentment, indignation, and sense of helplessness and total abandonment in the face of injustice that have accumulated over centuries of oppression suffered by the *minjung*. In the context of Korean folk religion, *han*-ridden ghosts often wander the country looking for justice and revenge. Chung sees in such lore the politics of memory and the need to address the countless thousands who have died unjustly, crying out for justice. The identification of Christ with the shaman who rids people of *han* thus signals the importance of memory and exorcism through resistance, suffering, and witness.

In the context of Asian women's Christology, Chung points to the problem of a high-descending approach to Christology for the *minjung*. In an Asian context, with its blend of folk religion and forms of Buddhism, such a Christology makes little sense. Chung cites Lee Oo Chung and her account of how traditional Korean gods achieved their status after death.[22] For these figures, divinity came about through a series of trials and suffering. With persistence and through suffering, these figures successfully negotiated a variety of challenges to achieve divine status. Chung Hyun Kyung argues that such is the approach of an Asian women's Christology. Not by looking for "rescue" but through faithful witness, through suffering, and even through bloodshed, Asian women can find union with God.

Conclusion

Are the doctrines affirmed in previous centuries no longer held to be true? Are modern Christians completely free to innovate in the name of orthodoxy? Are there any limits? In this chapter we have seen that contemporary concerns regarding the credibility of the Christian faith are a motivating factor in the reappropriation of the tradition. Such reappropriation can collide with traditional doctrines. Attempts to limit innovative interpretations of traditional Christianity can raise troubling theological and ecclesiological issues. The work of Asian postcolonial theologians further complicates matters by reappropriating the tradition while also engaging non-Christian religious traditions as primary sources for doing theology. In chapter 8, the limits of a Christian commitment to Jesus are pointedly explored as we raise the question of Jesus' unique offer of salvation against the background of other religions and savior figures.

Questions for Understanding

1. What is bias? Distinguish between individual, group, and general bias.

2. What are the three steps, or moments, in Lonergan's Law of the Cross?

3. What is *convenientia*, and how does it free Lonergan and Loewe to articulate a soteriology that differs from Anselm and the reformers?

4. Why is an appreciation of the analogical nature of theology central to feminist theology?

5. Describe Johnson's "multipolar" anthropology. Why is this important for her Christology?

6. What factors make doing theology in an Asian context unique?

Questions for Reflection

1. Do christological doctrines help to transform lives, or are they an obstacle to such transformation? What doctrines do you think most effectively promote transformation? What doctrines are most problematic in this regard?

2. Loewe and Moltmann have leveled a robust critique of modern accounts of history as progress and the way the Christian church has been co-opted in such accounts. Stanley Hauerwas, a prominent Methodist theologian and admirer of Moltmann's theology, has argued that Christians must live "out of control" to challenge the prevailing notions of progress and success. Can you think of people—famous or

otherwise—whose "out of control" lives helped to subvert prevailing assumptions about progress?

3. In chapter 5 we considered Gregory Nazianzen's famous maxim, "What was not assumed is not redeemed." At the end of that chapter, one of the review questions asked if the depiction of Christ as a woman was problematic. Given what Elizabeth Johnson has written, has your opinion changed? Explain. Do such re-symbolizations of Christianity pose dangers? Are there any limits to the ways the Christian faith may be legitimately re-symbolized?

4. How do the christological proposals offered by Song and Chung challenge classical Christology?

Endnotes

1   Joseph Ratzinger, *Introduction to Christianity*, trans. J. R. Foster (New York: Herder, 1969), 15–17.

2   See William P. Loewe, "Towards a Responsible Contemporary Soteriology," in *Creativity and Method*, ed. Matthew Lamb (Milwaukee: Marquette, 1981), 213–27.

3   Bernard Lonergan, *Insight: A Study in Human Understanding* (London: Dartman and Todd, 1956), 226.

4   Jürgen Moltmann, "The Crucified God," *Theology Today* 31 (1974): 16–18,16.

5   Ibid., 11.

6   Ibid., 17.

7   See Francis Schüssler-Fiorenza, "Systematic Theology: Tasks and Methods," in *Systematic Theology: Roman Catholic Perspectives*, ed. Francis Schüssler-Fiorenza and John Galvin (Minneapolis: Fortress, 1991), 63–65.

8   Elisabeth Schüssler-Fiorenza, *Bread Not Stone: The Power of Feminist Biblical Interpretation* (Boston: Beacon, 1984); Rebecca Chopp, *The Power to Speak: Feminism, Language, God* (New York: Crossroad, 1992).

9   Elizabeth Johnson, "The Symbolic Character of Theological Statements about Mary," *Journal of Ecumenical Studies* 22 (1985): 312–35, 321; see Shannon Schrein, *Quilting and Braiding: The Feminist Christologies of Sallie McFague and Elizabeth A. Johnson in Conversation* (Collegeville, MN: Liturgical, 1998), 28–29.

10 Some of Johnson's popular works on feminist theology and Christology include *She Who Is* (New York: Crossroad, 1992) and *Consider Jesus: Waves of Renewal in Christology* (New York: Crossroad, 1992).

11 Johnson, *She Who Is*, 151.

12 Augustine, *On the Trinity*, 12.10. Quoted without citation in Johnson, *Consider Jesus*, 101.

13 See the document from the Congregation for the Doctrine of the Faith, *Inter Insigniores* (October 15, 1976).

14 Johnson, *She Who Is*, 154–56.

15 Shannon Schrein, *Quilting and Braiding: The Feminist Christologies of Sallie McFague and Elizabeth A. Johnson in Conversation* (Collegeville, MN: Liturgical, 1998), 105–6.

16 Peter C. Phan, "The Asian Face of Jesus," *Theological Studies* 57 (1996): 399–430.

17 Ibid., 399.

18 C. S. Song, *The Tears of Lady Meng: A Parable of People's Political Theology* (New York: Orbis, 1981).

19 C. S. Song, *Jesus, the Crucified People* (Minneapolis: Fortress, 1990); *Jesus and the Reign of God* (Minneapolis: Fortress, 1993); *Jesus in the Power of the Spirit* (Minneapolis: Fortress, 1994).

20 Ibid., 98–99.

21 Chung Hyun Kyung, "'Han-pu-ri': Doing Theology from Korean Woman's Perspective," in *Frontiers in Asian Christian Theology*, ed. R. S. Sugirtharajah (Maryknoll, NY: Orbis, 1994), 52–62, 53.

22 Lee Oo Chung, "Korean Cultural and Feminist Theology," *In God's Image* (1987): 34, cited in Chung Hyun Kyung, "Who Is Jesus for Asian Women?" in *Asian Faces of Jesus*, ed. R. S. Sugirtharajah (Maryknoll, NY: Orbis, 1993), 230–31.

Jesus and Other Religions

"I am the way and the truth and the life. No one comes to the Father except through me" (John 14:6). Passages such as this are found throughout the New Testament. They provide powerful testimony to the earliest church's faith in the decisive place of Jesus in God's offer of salvation. We saw in the previous chapter's discussion of the Law of the Cross that this offer of salvation is made real and effective in the lives of people through transformation, or conversion. Since this transformation is mediated by the story of Jesus, can someone experience conversion without explicit faith in Jesus?[1] If so, is Jesus thereby rendered irrelevant? Does he become merely pragmatic (if his story helps you to be converted, great; if not, find something else)?

Christian interpretations of Biblical passages such as John 14:28 have undergone a major shift in recent decades given the increasing sense that Christians are not alone. The vast majority of people in the world do not hold explicit faith in Jesus. We no longer have to imagine non-Christians in a distant land and theorize about how they might be saved; the non-Christian is now our neighbor, classmate, best friend, spouse, or child. Our recognition of religious pluralism has become much more concrete and intimate than in previous eras. Two factors in particular have contributed to this development. One is the collapse of an exclusively Christian culture in the wake of the Enlightenment. This led to the privatization of religious commitments and freed people from social pressures to self-identify as Christian. The other factor is technology, which has increased the overall mobility of the world's population. We can travel easily and communicate instantaneously with other parts of the world. These changes have put western Christians increasingly in direct contact with non-Christians so that it is no longer a question of sending missionaries abroad to remote and exotic lands to discover the non-Christian: the non-Christian is right here. In the face of this experience, how does one affirm the passage from John's Gospel quoted above? Should we evangelize our neighbors and convert them to Christianity?

The significance of **religious pluralism** can be grasped most appropriately when considered in light of the suffering of our world. Suffering in the world seems to be expanding. Christians believe that this suffering is directly related to sin, and that salvation—the solution to the problem of sin—is accomplished in Christ. Yet as we discussed in the previous chapter, Christians must recognize that the contemporary experience of suffering, and Christian silence in the face of that suffering, represents one of the greatest obstacles to the credibility of Christian faith and an obstacle to the intelligibility of the claim that we have been saved through the blood of Jesus. Are Christians not called to address the problem of suffering? Does this task not require Christians to cooperate with non-Christians? If we are to be credible as Christians, we must reach out across confessional and religious boundaries. What can we say about those who, out of their own religious convictions, join us in addressing suffering in our world? We will begin to explore this question by considering proposed theologies of religious pluralism and the controversies surrounding them.

Christian Response to Religious Pluralism

The second-century bishop Cyprian of Carthage famously wrote, *"Extra ecclesiam nulla salus est"* ("Outside the church there is no salvation").[2] Cyprian's statement was directed at Christians who tried to leave the church community to practice the faith independently. Cyprian derided such attempts by boldly declaring that such a move placed one outside the church. Employing a favorite image of Paul and the early church, Cyprian asserted that one is thereby separated from the Body of Christ. Cyprian's maxim was picked up by Origen and often repeated in other contexts. It has come to signify a position called **exclusivism**: without explicit faith in Christ and participation in the life of the church one cannot find salvation. Christ is God's definitive offer of salvation. If there is salvation through some other means, then Christ is simply one option among many.

An exclusivist position may be articulated in terms of the church (the **ecclesiocentric position**). That is, "You must belong to this church in order to be saved." But many conservative Evangelical Christians articulate an exclusivist position without reference to the institutional church. For them, salvation comes exclusively through explicit faith in Jesus, often expressed through the "sinner's prayer," acceptance of Jesus as Lord, and the experience of being born again in faith (John 3:3).[3] Apart from explicit faith one cannot be saved, though in the case of those who have had no possibility of knowing Christ (for example, those who die in infancy), pastoral practice has usually affirmed God's leniency.

The exclusivist position might sound like something from the distant past, a vestige of the intolerance more characteristic of the Inquisition than of modern times. Yet it is a position still widely held today. Its clarity and simplicity help to reinforce the importance of faith in Christ. It also underwrites missionary efforts as directed in the pages of the New Testament (e.g., Matthew 28:18–20). For many people it seems like the obvious Christian position on religious pluralism. In the twentieth century, however, a new position began to be articulated, though many would argue that the position itself wasn't new, merely its formulation.

At many points throughout the long history of Christianity, as Christians have reflected on both the fact of religious pluralism and the theological principle of God's unbounded mercy and desire that all would be saved, they began to articulate notions of faith and grace that included those outside the visible church. Early on we find the notion that God was present in other religions "preparing" people for the advent of the gospel (e.g., Justin Martyr). Others, like Nicholas of Cusa (1401–1461), went even further. Upon learning of the fall of Constantinople to Islamic armies in 1453 and reflecting on the centuries of violence between Christian and

Religion, Tolerance, and Armed Conflict: Islam and Christianity

Within Islam, Christians and Jews are called "people of the book" and are regarded as having heard the revelation of God, albeit imperfectly. While both the Muslim and the Christian faiths decree tolerance and love, the history of both religious traditions is marred by religious violence.

Since the time of the Roman emperor Theodosius I (around 381 CE), Christians inaugurated various forms of persecution against those who opposed them. Christianity spread in the early centuries of the first millennium CE largely through the efforts of the peaceful missionary work of Celtic monks. But after key figures had accepted the Christian faith, those who opposed the faith within these tribes or nations were persecuted, often violently. In the second millennium CE, Christian armies increasingly embraced the notion of holy war, war as a religious duty. When the first crusade was called by Pope Urban II in 1095, the rhetoric he employed was that of holy war: it was an obligation for Christian knights to secure the Holy Land from the Saracens (the common name among Christians at that time for those who followed Islam). Throughout the Middle Ages and well into the modern period, European Christians regularly legitimated violence against non-Christians (the crusades, the colonization of Africa and the Americas) and even against

other Christians (the Thirty-Years War). Perhaps the most obvious example of Christian violence against Muslims and Jews is what happened in Spain in the early sixteenth century. Following the conquest of Granada, the last Muslim outpost in Spain, the victorious Christians expelled those Jews and Muslims who would not convert to Christianity and persecuted with great vigor those whose conversions were deemed insincere.

The expulsion of Jews and Muslims from Christian Spain stands in sharp contrast to the relative peace and religious diversity that Spain had enjoyed in some areas under Muslim control. Places like Toledo, an ancient center of Christianity prior to the Muslim invasion in the eighth century, were diverse and thriving cities, with Muslim rulers and Jewish and Christian merchants and officials living in relative harmony. In fact, many scholars point to a religious toleration in the Muslim world in contrast with the extremism many laypeople today assume to be characteristic of Islamic peoples. While Christians and Jews have at times been persecuted violently in Islamic history and today, the historical situation is complex, and these persecutions should be read in light of Christian attitudes to Muslims and Jews in medieval and early modern Europe.

Islamic forces, Nicholas offered a visionary treatise where Christ (along with Saints Peter and Paul) affirmed truth in the various religions and summoned them to unity and peace.[4] Official Roman Catholic teaching, though not always the champion of tolerance toward non-Christian religions, moved to the forefront of developing a theology of religions in the twentieth century, particularly with two documents issued by the Second Vatican Council (1962–1965).[5]

The Christian Response to Religious Pluralism at Vatican II

One of the most highly anticipated documents to come out of the Second Vatican Council was the *Dogmatic Constitution on the Church*, known by its Latin title *Lumen gentium*. This document laid out an understanding of the church that represented a significant departure from the language used in ecclesiology throughout the nineteenth and early twentieth centuries. Instead of defining the church through legal and structural models, *Lumen gentium* used a far more relational model. Rather than defining the boundaries of the church or the offices of ministry within the church, *Lumen gentium* emphasized the living presence of the Triune God in the life of the church. In so doing, *Lumen gentium* was able to offer a more expansive account of the church that included those who did not hold explicit faith in Jesus. Section 16 of the document provides an important example of this.

> Nor is God remote from those who in shadows and images seek the unknown God, since he gives to all [people] life and breath and all things (Acts 17:25–28), and since the Savior wills all [people] to be saved (1 Timothy 2:4). Those who, through no fault of their own, do not know the Gospel of Christ or his Church, but who nevertheless seek God with a sincere heart, and, moved by grace, try in their actions to do his will as best they know it through the dictates of their own conscience—those too may achieve eternal salvation (cf. DS 3869–72). Nor shall divine providence deny the assistance necessary for salvation to those who, without any fault of theirs, have not arrived at an explicit knowledge of God, and who, not without grace, strive to lead a good life. Whatever good or truth is found amongst them is

considered by the church to be preparation for the Gospel and given by him who enlightens all [people] that they may at length have life.

A related document, *The Declaration on the Relation of the Church to Non-Christian Religions* (*Nostra aetate*), strikes a similar chord.

> The Catholic Church rejects nothing of what is true and holy in these [non-Christian] religions. She has a high regard for the manner of life and conduct, the precepts and doctrines which, although differing in many ways from her own teaching, nevertheless often reflect a ray of that truth which enlightens all men [and women]. Yet she proclaims and is duty bound to proclaim without fail, Christ who is the way, the truth and the life (John 14:6). In him, in whom God reconciled all things to himself (2 Corinthians 5:18–19), men [and women] find the fullness of their religious life.
>
> The Church, therefore, urges her sons [and daughters] to enter with prudence and charity into discussion and collaboration with members of other religions. Let Christians, while witnessing to their own faith and way of life, acknowledge, preserve and encourage the spiritual and moral truths found among non-Christians, also their social life and culture. (no. 2)

Vatican II articulated what has generally come to be termed **inclusivism**. Like the exclusivist position, the inclusivist model posits the universal salvific significance of Christ—Christ is the universal savior and the only means of salvation. But unlike the exclusivist model, the inclusivist approach affirms that the saving mystery of Christ, available to Christians in and through the church, also reaches beyond the visible boundaries of the church to reach followers of other religious traditions. For the inclusivist, Christ is the unique mediator between God and humanity, but the saving action of God in Christ is realized through the Spirit, which brings those inside the church together with those outside. The church is not superfluous in this case; rather, the church is the visible sign of Christ's saving work in the world, but it is not the exclusive vehicle of that work. Those who are outside the visible confines of the church find the salvation that only comes through Christ, but they find it in the religious traditions to which they belong. These traditions inspire faith in God and offer the means to respond to God. The inclusivist model tries to demonstrate that Christ is present in these traditions, albeit anonymously. The inclusivist position has been criticized on several points, but Karl Rahner's notion of the **anonymous Christian** perhaps most clearly crystallizes the issues at stake.

Karl Rahner and the Anonymous Christian

The phrase "anonymous Christian" was used by Karl Rahner (1904–1984) in the context of his ambitious and revolutionary theological project. One of the main goals of Rahner's work was to overcome the extrinsicism of popular Catholic imagination and prominent Protestant theologians like Karl Barth, who held an extrinsic view of revelation and grace and emphasized God's intervention in the created order. Rahner wanted to give an account of God's saving work that did not depict God as "coming down from heaven" to visit our world. Building upon the work of Joseph Maréchal and others who were seeking to integrate the work of Kant and Aquinas, Rahner developed a theology in which the human person was the focal point of God's revelation and the foundation of theology. This anthropological orientation focused on the act of knowing or understanding at the heart of human existence and emphasized the human capacity to know and love God. Rahner believed that every act of knowing contains within it an orientation toward infinite Being as the a priori— "the condition for the possibility"—of knowing or understanding.

An analogy will illustrate Rahner's thought. When reading this book you focus on various clusters of letters and read them as words, words that have meaning to you. But have you considered the paper? The paper behind the letters allows the letters to have form and allows them to be read. When you go outside and look around, your field of vision, or your field of sense perception, is articulated against a backdrop we call the horizon. As finite things present themselves to your senses, you can inquire after them and know them, but you never get to the end of the horizon, for it is constantly moving back to disclose even more to be known. The infinitude of reality becomes increasingly apparent. In all acts of understanding or knowing, Rahner contends that there is already present within those acts a preapprehension of Being, or what is ultimately real: God. But Rahner is careful not simply to equate being human with knowing God; after all, there needs to be room for what Christians call grace. Yet, for Rahner, there is a close connection between nature's capacity for grace and the actual experience of God's self-gift, or grace.

When discussing non-Christian religions, Rahner begins with humanity's capacity for and experience of God's self-communication. This anthropological starting point accounts for the salvation of those who do not know Christ explicitly. Though he maintains a **christocentric** theology—Christ is the lens through which everything is to be viewed—he does not negate other religions, for God willed these religions as a kind of preparation for the gospel. The salvific power of other religions, however, is to be understood and affirmed only through Christ. Therefore, other religions do not enjoy theological autonomy: their validity and salvific power are mediated by Christ. He grounds the logic of the anonymous Christian in the realization that the vast majority of human beings in history have not known Christ. He asks:

> Can the Christian believe even for a moment that the overwhelming mass of his brothers, not only those before the appearance of Christ right back to the most distant past (whose horizons are constantly extended by palaeontology) but also those of the present and of the future before us, are unquestionably and in principle excluded from the fulfillment of their lives and condemned to eternal meaninglessness? He must reject any suggestion, and his faith is itself in agreement with his doing so. For the scriptures tell him expressly that God wants everyone to be saved (1 Timothy 2:4).[6]

But precisely how does this love embrace all? For Rahner, true Christian faith is often *lived* by many who do not possess the *name* Christian. He writes elsewhere in the same essay:

> [Human beings], in experiencing [their] transcendence, [their] limitless openness—no matter how implicit and incomprehensible it always is—also already experience . . . the offer of grace—not necessarily *as* grace, as distinctively supernatural calling, but experience the reality of its content. (Rahner, "Anonymous Christian," 391)

Perhaps the classic example of what Rahner means in this last passage would be Gandhi. As a devout Hindu, Gandhi was committed to nonviolence, identified with the cause of the oppressed, and heroically brought freedom and a measure of justice to a subcontinent reeling from over a century of colonial exploitation and oppression. Gandhi is said to have remarked that it was a pity that Christians did not seem to listen to Jesus: "I like your Christ, but I do not like your Christians." For Rahner, and to some degree for all inclusivists, Gandhi was an example of a Christian in every sense of the word, only without the name Christian. Inclusivists could, therefore, affirm the salvation of Gandhi. He was saved because Christ was present in his life through the power of the Spirit even though he did not profess a Christian faith. This concept summarizes the idea embodied, to some extent, in the documents from Vatican II quoted above. It must be noted, however, that in the documents of Vatican II there is no affirmation of other religions as such, only of Christ being present in "elements" of the religious tradition.

Christian Perspectives on Religious Pluralism

Exclusivism	Inclusivism	Pluralism
This approach often focuses on the importance of the church and is termed ecclesiocentric (church-centered). It states that without explicit faith in Jesus Christ and incorporation into the Christian church, one is lost. The famous phrase from Cyprian of Carthage summarizes this position: "*extra ecclesiam nulla salus est*" ("outside the Church there is no salvation)." This position is still popular in many conservative Evangelical churches, less so in mainline Christian churches.	This approach emphasizes the unique priority of the Christian faith while acknowledging that elements of truth are found in other religions. The inclusivist position "identifies" those elements of truth as preparation for the gospel, and to the extent that adherents of these religions respond favorably to God's call, they can be saved. However, they are saved through the work of Christ. Karl Rahner coined the phrase "anonymous Christian" to describe those people who, without sharing in the public life of the Christian church, nonetheless share in the life of grace. Official Catholic teaching is inclusivist.	This approach to other religions has emphasized the relativity of claims regarding truth and privileged revelation. The pluralist position suggests that the result of historical criticism of the doctrines and practices of any religious tradition reveals a culturally bound system rather than the deposit of a pure, unadulterated revelation. The pluralist position advocates a sense of silence and awe in the face of the divine mystery to which all human experience of religion is related. The pluralist position can be theocentric (centered on God), pneumatocentric (centered on the experience of the Holy Spirit), or regnocentric (centered on the experience of God's kingdom).

Christology and Pluralism at the Turn of the Century

The inclusivist position has significant points of strength: it affirms the unique role of Christ as the mediator of God's saving work and provides for a way to understand the salvation of non-Christians, both within our own context and in the broader sweep of history. Yet many object to the idea of the anonymous Christian at the heart of the inclusivist approach. To those who object to the inclusivist position, the very idea of anonymous Christianity is patronizing and demeaning. It is like saying, "Though you think you are a devout Muslim you are really a good Christian. You just don't realize it." How would you feel as a devout Christian if a Hindu came up to you and said that you were a great devotee of Siva, it was just a pity that you did not realize it? Since the time of Vatican II, many scholars and laypeople have had a growing desire to move beyond the inclusivist paradigm to embrace a real pluralistic theology.

The **pluralist approach** rejects the inclusivist model for its uncompromising affirmation of Christianity over and against the other religious traditions. Pluralists also reject the inclusivist tendency to view other religions as incomplete realizations of Christianity and not as self-sufficient religious traditions in their own right. In the present context of religious plurality and dialogue, such inclusivism would seem untenable since it assumes that Christianity is the yardstick by which all other traditions must be evaluated. Interreligious dialogue is impossible without recognition of equality. A paradigm shift is therefore necessary.

Theocentric Pluralism

John Hick, a noted English philosopher of religion, has proposed just such a shift in Christian theology: a movement away from Jesus.[7] For Hick, a Jesus-centered (christocentric) approach to God and religious pluralism ought to be replaced with what he calls a "God-centered" (theocentric) approach. He argues that every religious faith is an historical-cultural realization of our experience of divine reality, but he does not mean by this that all religions are of equal value. Rather, Hick seeks to move the question of interreligious dialogue toward an assessment of religious traditions and their relative ability or inability to approach two objectives: (1) effectively mediate the divine reality, (2) promote a soteriology that seeks a "limitless better quality of human existence which comes about in the transition from self-centeredness to Reality-centeredness."[8] Jesus fits into all of this as a relative experience of God. For those who confess Jesus as Lord, Jesus may indeed save them insofar as their lives have been transformed according to the above principles. The language of the incarnation and the metaphysical concepts that governed the theoretical aspects of this doctrine must not be taken literally since they are, for Hick, merely historically conditioned (i.e., mythological) statements about God. This does not, however, mean that these statements and doctrines should not be taken seriously as "God-talk," but since we cannot have firm knowledge about God, all such talk must be circumscribed by humility and agnosticism.

Hick's proposal resonates with highly pluralistic religious culture like that found in India. Riamundo Panikkar, a Catholic priest born in Spain to Spanish and Indian parents, has lived in India for many years. He proposes an ecumenism, a unity among religions of the world, within diversity based on the acceptance of the "transcendental principle" that forms the basis for all religious experience.[9] Panikkar insists on the importance of religious diversity as a guard against any move to privilege one particular tradition, or against simplistic understandings of the divine reality. Within this diversity Panikkar develops the distinction between the "Universal Christ" and the "particular Jesus." For Panikkar, Christ is the universal symbol for salvation that cannot be objectified as a merely historical personage. However, what Panikkar calls "the **cosmotheandric fact** of Jesus" must be affirmed. That is, in Jesus we have the realization of God's connection to the world and specifically to human nature, but not to the exclusion of other concrete occurrences of this (such as Shakyamuni or Krishna). Panikkar thus adopts the Hindu concept of the avatar, or the incarnation of deity common among Vaishnavites in Hinduism. These devotees of Vishnu recognize that Vishnu has been incarnated at various points in history as the human beings Rama and Krishna, among others. Panikkar applies this concept of episodic incarnation to Christ and suggests that there is a functional equivalence between Christ and other saviors.

The Incarnation of God in Hinduism: The Avatars of Vishnu

Vishnu, along with Shiva and Brahman, is one of the chief deities within Hinduism. He is often called "the Preserver" and is characterized as loving, benevolent, and playful. Vishnu, of all the Hindu gods, is concerned with human beings and creation, so much so that he inserts himself into human events to bring about balance and harmony in the universe. Vishnu has several avatars, or historical manifestations, which have appeared nine different times with one still to come. The major avatars include Rama, Krishna, and for many Hindus, the Buddha.

Krishna is one of the most popular avatars of Vishnu. In the Hindu epic the Puranas, Krishna is depicted as a playful, often mischievous, cow herder who attracts the beautiful Radha with his flute playing. Krishna leaves Radha to go on a heroic mission and never returns. In the Hindu festival of Holi, women from Radha's village ceremonially beat the boys from Krishna's village. Additionally, Krishna appears in the Bhagavad-Gita as the charioteer of Arjuna on the eve of a great battle. Krishna instructs the young warrior on the importance of his duty as a warrior and exhorts him to shun all attachments.

Rama, the hero of the Ramayana, is another avatar of Vishnu. The Ramayana narrates the story. Rama has his wife, Sita, kidnapped by Ravana, the demon-king of Lanka. The Ramayana recounts how Rama, along with the help of his brother-in-law, Lakshman, and the army of monkeys led by Hanuman, defeats the demon and rescues Sita, whereupon the powerful goddess Durga gives him secret knowledge of how to kill Ravana.

Kalki is the tenth avatar of Vishnu. He is often pictured with a horse's head but also as a man riding a horse. He carries with him a sword with which he will judge the wicked and reward the virtuous at the end of the world. Additionally, the Buddha is often interpreted within Hinduism as one of the avatars of Vishnu.

The theocentric perspectives of Hick and Panikkar place God at the center of all the religious traditions of the world and stress that God has been manifested or revealed in various ways to different peoples in history. The diversity of religious traditions manifests the intersection between the divine mystery and the diversity of cultures and histories through which that mystery has been mediated. For example, all of the religious language used to describe Jesus in the New Testament has its origins in the Jewish and Greek world of the first century. Likewise, the classical christological doctrines of the fourth and fifth centuries were formulated within the particular contexts of philosophical and theological disputes characteristic of those particular places and times. The difficulty we have in understanding and appropriating those doctrines as modern people bears witness to their cultural remoteness. This is not true for just the Christian tradition, but for Buddhism, Islam, Hinduism, and all other religious traditions. In other words, all religions are in the same historically contingent boat. So is everything relative? Proponents of the theocentric position assert that the variety of religious traditions serve to complement each other in their differences. In this context dialogue is not only possible but essential. In that case, the dialogue envisioned by Vatican II is seen as real dialogue—Christians have nothing to gain or lose if they already possess the fullness of revelation.

Spirit Christology and Roger Haight

The contemporary problem of religious pluralism came to a head in the case of the prominent American Jesuit theologian Roger Haight. Haight issued his major work *Jesus, Symbol of God* in 1999 and has endured scrutiny and criticism ever since.[10] The book, which articulates a distinctive and challenging christological vision, set off a firestorm of controversy.

The book begins with the assertion that theology must be done in dialogue with the postmodern world. Through postmodern convictions about the intelligibility of ancient doctrines, Haight proceeds to narrate and assess classical Christology. He argues that the postmodern world is radically pluralistic in its outlook and thus challenges Christian claims of religious superiority and Christ as the absolute savior inherent in ancient Logos Christology. Differentiating between faith (trusting abandonment to the transcendent God) and belief (historically conditioned formulas that give concrete expression to our experience of faith), Haight argues for a fundamental change in Christian beliefs. Creeds are themselves the products of dialogue with particular cultures: Greek philosophical terms and ideas are at the heart of the debates at Nicaea and Chalcedon (e.g., *ousia and hypostasis*).

The language of the great christological councils was theoretical in some respects. For example, recall how *homoousios* was used as a technical, nonsymbolic term to overcome Arian interpretations of the creed. However, such language posited the primacy of symbol in Christian discourse. Moreover, the classical statement of Christology affirms that Christ is both human and divine—not one or the other—so a tension remains at the heart of Christian faith. Haight's characterization of Jesus as "symbol of God" is meant to capture this tension and make use of it constructively. For Haight, when Christians affirm that Jesus is the symbol or sacrament of God, they mean that in Christ they have had the experience of God. Haight contends that such an affirmation neither puts Jesus in competition with other religious traditions nor precludes the possibility that God would be revealed in other concrete historical mediations. Our encounter with God in Christ, like all encounters with the divine, can only be critically grasped and expressed through symbol and metaphor. To deny this is to introduce a theology that does not respect the reality of human encounters with the divine, encounters that are essentially analogical. Through such analogical perception, through the play of ideas and metaphors, through symbols, one is schooled in the things of God, in religious language, which is understood as the disclosure of God's real presence to us. For "without a sense of God's transcendent mystery, without a healthy agnostic sense of what we do not know of God, one will not expect to learn more of God from what has been communicated to us human beings through other revelations and religions."[11] Our language concerning Christ must respect this sense.

Haight believes that a **Spirit Christology** is the appropriate direction for contemporary Christology. In Spirit Christology the Spirit of God dwells within the human being Jesus from the first moments of his existence. Such an approach is in keeping, he argues, with the best insights of the Antiochene school of Christology, such as the orthodox theology of Theodore of Mopsuestia (see chapter 5). He argues that a Spirit Christology is faithful to the biblical testimony, as well as the decrees from Nicaea and Chalcedon, while at the same time providing the capacity to affirm the salvific presence of God in other religious traditions. For Haight, Jesus mediates a revelatory encounter with God. Yet, Haight also argues that God is immediately and immanently present to all creatures, and that this immanent encounter with God is always described as the presence of God's Spirit. The Spirit, universally present in the history of the world, is revealed in Christ, works for the salvation of all, and is not confined to one historical moment. Salvation is, therefore, not so much caused by Christ as it is revealed in Christ. Christ causes salvation for Christians insofar as he enacts God's saving presence among them, but this is not to the exclusion of other mediations, which can act independently of Christ. Haight sees this move as preserving Christian convictions regarding the saving work of Christ while at the same time affording recognition of God's saving presence, equally active and effective, in other religious traditions.

Jacques Dupuis and Participated Mediations

Jacques Dupuis (1923–2004), a Belgian Jesuit who for many years lived and worked in India before teaching at the Pontifical Gregorian Seminary in Rome, offers a major theological proposal in *Towards a Christian Theology of Religious Pluralism*. There he articulates a highly nuanced position that moves beyond the affirmations of Vatican II but does not go as far as the pluralist position. For Dupuis, a Christian theology of religious pluralism must always affirm that Jesus is at the center of God's plan of salvation for the world. But such an affirmation must also be nuanced and move beyond the inclusivism of the anonymous Christian. Dupuis affirms that Christ is the way of salvation and the universal mediator of God's universal offer of salvation. He believes that Christian theology loses itself when it wrestles with the false dilemma of theocentrism versus christocentrism. Rather, Dupuis affirms that authentic Christian faith eschews such a dichotomy: the Christian faith is theocentric precisely by being christocentric, and it is christocentric by being theocentric. Dupuis affirms, along with Vatican II's *Lumen gentium*, that Jesus Christ is the sacrament of God. Through Jesus, God acts in history to bring about our salvation and reaches people in a variety of ways, but how to best articulate this remains elusive. In an effort to construct a more christocentric and pluralist theology of religious pluralism, Dupuis surveys a variety of modifications to the theocentric approach discussed above.

One such modification emphasizes the reign of God as the appropriate paradigm. You will recall from an earlier chapter that the reign of God describes a relationship with God that is present now but will find its ultimate fulfillment in the *eschaton*. Through this approach, Christians can affirm the relationship with God found and promoted in other religious traditions, and that the fullness of that relationship is still to come. This approach has the merit of showing that the followers of other religious traditions are already members of the reign of God in history and that together with Christians they are destined to meet in God as pilgrims at the end of time. But such an approach, Dupuis concludes, neglects the fact that Christians affirm that the reign of God has broken through in history in Jesus, and that it is through the Christ and the work of the Spirit that all human beings might come to participate in God's reign. So, Dupuis concludes, the reign of God paradigm necessarily emphasizes the centrality of Christ.

Dupuis also considers the **pneumatocentric** (Spirit-centered) proposal. This modification to the theocentric approach involves the recognition, taken from the language of Vatican II, that the Holy Spirit is universally present and active in the religious traditions of the world. God's Spirit has always been active in the religious life of human beings outside the Christian community. The Spirit inspires, that is, breathes into people obedience to God and acceptance of God's grace. But such an emphasis, though true in every sense, does not really move us away from a christocentric approach, for the pneumatological perspective cannot be divorced from the Christian account of the universal role of the risen Christ. The work of the Holy Spirit is essentially bound to the universal action of the risen Christ. The Spirit's saving function consists in calling people to Christ. Thus Christ, not the Spirit, is at the center. Christocentric and pneumatocentric approaches cannot be alternatives; they are essentially bound together.

For Dupuis, various attempts to move away from a christocentric approach to the problem of religious pluralism are inadequate. When understood properly from a Christian perspective, all other paradigms lead back to a christocentric position. A Christian theology of religious pluralism, as a *Christian* theology, must be christocentric and bring out the full dimension of the mystery of God's self-disclosure in Christ. Such an approach must demonstrate that members of other religious traditions share in the reign established by God in history through Christ, and that the Spirit of Christ is active among them working for their salvation.

Any account of the saving work of Christ, Dupuis argues, cannot posit a personal distinction between the divine Son and the historical human being, Jesus of Nazareth. At the same time, however, one must always distinguish between the two natures of Christ. Without this distinction, the two operations of Christ become utterly confused. As a human being, Christ cannot operate as infinite or divine. This was precisely the point of the Third Council of Constantinople (Constantinople III, 680), which affirmed that Christ had two centers of operation and two wills. The "unconfused" natures, affirmed at Chalcedon, retained their proper operation and "energies." This point is important, for in the Incarnation, the divine nature of the Son is not lost or diminished, it does not lose its essential characteristics and functions. For Dupuis, the distinction between the two natures and their operations is significant since it allows for a discussion of the Son's saving activity in human history before as well as after the Incarnation. For the Son always remains present and active everywhere in the world working for the salvation of all. This universal activity of the Son is not diminished by the Incarnation and the historical life of Jesus. Dupuis insists that the eternal Son remains universally active while also being personally identical with Jesus of Nazareth. The distinction rests in the operations and not at the level of person. It is the divine Son who enacts God's plan of salvation, and this plan is unique. We are all called to participate in the life of God through the work of the Son and the Spirit.

Dupuis affirms the work of the Spirit in the life of the church and in the world bringing about salvation but also asserts that the outpouring of the Spirit, while connected to the Resurrection of Christ, is not confined to it. Dupuis notes that before the Incarnation the Spirit acted in a revelatory and salvific fashion. With the Resurrection and Pentecost, the Spirit, though working in total communion with the glorified Christ, does not lose its universal activity. Rather, if the Incarnation of the divine Son did not mean that the divine powers of the Son were lost or diminished, the same must be true of the Spirit: though poured out through the risen Son, the divine nature of the Spirit cannot be limited.

This activity of the Spirit reaches and enriches the members of various religions in and through their religious life and practice. How else could the Spirit reach them but through the elements of their traditions? Since these religions contain elements of truth and goodness, as Vatican II states, and the Spirit is mysteriously and powerfully present to them, it must be the case that members of these religious communities find salvation through their respective traditions. In other words, their religions are "ways of salvation" for them. In order to express this idea, Dupuis borrows an expression from John Paul II's encyclical letter *Redemptoris missio*: "Although participated forms of mediation of different kinds and degrees are not excluded, they acquire meaning and value only from Christ's own mediation, and they cannot be understood as parallel or complimentary to his" (no. 5). The notion of "**participated mediations of salvation**" is central for Dupuis as he constructs an inclusive pluralist approach to the theology of religions. Participated mediations maintains the integrity of other religious traditions as vehicles for the salvation of their adherents, while also remaining christocentric by emphasizing that Christ is the definitive source of salvation and is present within those traditions. Dupuis's inclusive pluralism thus relates the ways of salvation proposed by other religious traditions to the "event of Jesus Christ" (the Incarnation, life, death, and Resurrection). Additionally, these participated mediations are intended by God and various religious traditions to play a positive role for the salvation of their adherents. These religious traditions,

Person of Interest

Pope John Paul II

Pope John Paul II (1920–2005), or Karol Józef Wojtyła as he was called before becoming pope in 1978, was born in the Polish town of Wadowice. In his youth he was fortunate to be part of a community made up of both Jews and Christians. In fact, one of his best friends from childhood and throughout his life was a Jew named Jerzy Kluger. Karol Józef Wojtyła witnessed firsthand the impact of Christian anti-Semitism as many Poles turned on their neighbors and cooperated in Hitler's barbaric "final solution." When he became pope he tirelessly devoted himself to the issue of interreligious dialogue. He encouraged dialogue with the representatives of non-Christian religions, particularly in several prayer meetings at Assisi. His care and concern for the Jewish people and for Jewish-Christian relations drew particular attention. He was the first pope since the first century to visit a synagogue; he prayed for the Jewish people at the Wailing Wall in Jerusalem; and he approved the letter that recognized and expressed contrition for the role Christians played in the Holocaust. Perhaps most importantly, in 1982 he approved revolutionary guidelines for implementing *Nostra aetate*, Vatican II's declaration on non-Christian religions, which affirmed the continuing validity of Israel's call and covenant without neglecting the universal salvific mission of Christ.

as traditions, are necessarily secondary. The same is true for Christianity: there is a difference between the faith that saves and the religious tradition that conveys that faith. It is the work of the divine Word and the Spirit in history whereby God the Father seeks us out and saves us. In that one plan all things, all cultures, and all religions converge toward the eschatological reign of God.

The Return of a High-Descending Christology

Christology from Rome: *Dominus Iesus*

The Congregation for the Doctrine of the Faith (CDF), the chief doctrinal office of the Vatican, issued a document in 2000 titled *Dominus Iesus* that addressed the question of religious pluralism and Christology. The document begins with the evangelical mandate to "teach all nations," and then presents the entire text of the creed of Constantinople (the Nicene Creed) as the definitive statement of Christian faith. It goes on to identify the danger the church is confronting from "relativistic theories which seek to justify religious pluralism, not only *de facto* ["as a matter of fact," i.e., there are in fact many different religions] but also *de jure* ["in principle," i.e., the nature of God demands a plurality of religions]." The problem arises from certain philosophical and theological presuppositions that challenge the acknowledgment of "revealed truth." Some of these problems include the conviction that divine truth always remains inexpressible, the allure of relativism (the belief that all knowledge and values are relative to place and time and thus can have no universal claim), and the problem of making transcendent claims about the nature of God based on the historically contingent experience of Jesus of Nazareth. The document's account of revelation and the response of faith deserves note. In section 6 it states:

> The theory of the limited, incomplete, or imperfect character of the revelation of Jesus Christ, which would be complementary to that found in other religions, is contrary to the Church's faith. Such a position would claim to be based on the notion that the truth about God cannot be grasped and manifested in its globality and completeness by any historical religion, neither by Christianity nor by Jesus Christ.

Such a position is in radical contradiction with [the creed] according to which the full and complete revelation of the salvific mystery of God is given in Jesus Christ. Therefore, the words, deeds, and entire historical event of Jesus, though limited as human realities, have nevertheless the divine Person of the Incarnate Word, "true God and true man" (Council of Chalcedon, *Symbolum Chalcedonense*: DS 301; cf. St. Athanasius, *De Incarnatione*, 54, 3: SC 199, 458) as their subject. For this reason, they possess in themselves the definitiveness and completeness of the revelation of God's salvific ways, even if the depth of the divine mystery in itself remains transcendent and inexhaustible. The truth about God is not abolished or reduced because it is spoken in human language; rather, it is unique, full, and complete, because he who speaks and acts is the Incarnate Son of God. Thus, faith requires us to profess that the Word made flesh, in his entire mystery, who moves from incarnation to glorification, is the source, participated but real, as well as the fulfillment of every salvific revelation of God to humanity (Second Vatican Council, *Dei verbum*, 4). (*Dominus Iesus*, no. 6)

The document goes on in section 7 to make another crucial distinction between the theological virtue of Christian faith and the belief that is experienced and expressed in other religious traditions. For the CDF, religious belief—a common feature of the human condition—can be affirmed as a relatively vague though real experience of God's presence and our response to that presence, but it is primarily a search, or quest. Conversely, Christian faith is a supernatural gift whereby God offers nothing less than God's full self-communication. In Christian faith, we are not simply searching; rather, God has definitively reached out to us and given us the gift of God's very self.

For this reason, the distinction between *theological faith* and *belief* in the other religions, must be *firmly held*. If faith is the acceptance in grace of revealed truth, which "makes it possible to penetrate the mystery in a way that allows us to understand it coherently" (John Paul II, Encyclical Letter *Fides et ratio*, 13), then belief, in the other religions, is that sum of experience and thought that constitutes the human treasury of wisdom and religious aspiration, which man in his search for truth has conceived and acted upon in his relationship to God and the Absolute (*Fides et ratio*, 31–32). (*Dominus Iesus*, no. 7)

Dominus Iesus privileges the revelation of God in Christ as the definitive act of God's self-expression: Jesus of Nazareth is the Son and the Word, and the salvific mission of the Word is accomplished through Christ and no other. There can be no separation between an account of the Word and an account of Jesus of Nazareth, no account of the Word independent from the human being Jesus.[12] Additionally, although asserting that the fullness of God's revelation will be manifest in the future, *Dominus Iesus* does not imply that the revelation of God in Christ is to be regarded as temporary, limited, or provisional. Moreover, the revelation of God in Christ is not subject to modification or completion from other religious traditions, even though the particular practices of other religious traditions might be worthy of emulation (e.g., Buddhist nonviolence). *Dominus Iesus* also addresses the issue of the Holy Spirit and its activity in non-Christian religious traditions, asserting that the salvific action of the Holy Spirit does not extend beyond the one universal economy of salvation of the incarnate Word. While it is perfectly legitimate to affirm the presence of the Holy Spirit and the salvation of non-Christians through the "elements of truth and goodness" in their respective religious traditions, one cannot affirm the salvific character of those religious traditions as such.[13]

When *Dominus Iesus* was published, it was greeted with much rancor from a variety of quarters.[14] While many Protestant leaders rejoiced at the **christocentrism** of the document, they were also greatly offended by the documents attitude toward "ecclesial communities" of Protestant Christians; official Catholic teaching has refused to call these communities "churches" on the grounds that they do not preserve apostolic succession and do not validly celebrate the sacraments. Non-Christian leaders found the document offensive given its reaffirmation of the superiority of Christianity over other religious traditions. They felt it rolled back the progress that had been made in recent decades in official and quasi-official interreligious dialogue. Yet most theologians have recognized that the document was remarkable for the fact that it did not advance an opinion or an argument; rather, it simply reaffirmed the teaching of Vatican II and the teaching of John Paul II. The real question was whether cultural conditions had changed sufficiently to demand a new theological approach to ecumenism and interreligious dialogue. For many Christian theologians, the issue of religious pluralism threatens to demand that Christians marginalize their claims about Jesus. Many have sought to move away from a Christology from below, the Christology of Haight and others, to articulate a new direction for Christology. Such a shift finds energy in the work of the late Hans Urs von Balthasar.

The Drama of Salvation in von Balthasar

The shift to a low-ascending approach to Christology (one that begins with the human person, Jesus of Nazareth), along with the corresponding focus of the human being as the theological starting point of theology, led inexorably to the question of the uniqueness and universal mission of Christ. As we have seen above, *Dominus Iesus* responds to this development with an unambiguous affirmation of God's unique and universal self-communication in Christ. As such, the emphasis on revelation becomes normative for Christology in the Catholic Church. But are theologians obligated to embrace the extrinsicism and exclusivism that such a position seems to demand? Does one simply put one's head in the sand and dig out the old Christology textbooks from past centuries? The theology of the late Hans Urs von Balthasar emphatically answers, "No."

Von Balthasar was never interested in the christological controversies of the twentieth century that emphasized the human experience of openness to divine revelation (e.g., Rahner and Schillebeeckx). Instead, he seized on the importance of divine revelation for understanding Christ. Of particular interest for von Balthasar is the nature of beauty and the understanding of faith as an aesthetic act. For von Balthasar, God permeates all existence so that the sensible universe is teeming with the presence of God, and we can come to know God as creation announces the divine presence to us. Similarly, any understanding of Christ must place him at the heart of such aesthetic experience as the central actor in the drama, the unfolding narrative of salvation. One can see that for von Balthasar theology is less a philosophical science than a mystical art. Yet such an approach helps him articulate a Christology that resonates in many ways with concerns expressed in *Dominus Iesus*. His theology may

Person of Interest

Henri de Lubac

Henri de Lubac (1896–1991) exerted considerable influence on theology in the twentieth century. De Lubac joined the Jesuits as a youth in 1913, but still served in the French army during World War I, where he was seriously wounded. After the war he continued his education; he was ordained a priest in 1927 and given a position on the theology faculty at Lyons. Among his students were many of the most important theological minds of the twentieth century, including Hans Urs von Balthasar.

De Lubac became part of the *nouvelle theologie* (new theology) that sought to recover the spirit of the early Christian theologians and founded a series of books called Sources chrétiennes that offered new translations of important patristic texts. During the Second World War, he participated in the resistance and published widely against anti-Semitism. In the 1950s de Lubac's writings on grace and the supernatural—he had written a book titled *Surnaturel* (*The Supernatural*)—brought scrutiny from the Vatican, which eventually silenced him. His theology criticized the separation of nature and grace that had crept into Catholic theology in particular. He argued that it was precisely this kind of separation that had promoted a culture of secularism, which marginalized any talk of God and God's grace as utterly inaccessible and therefore irrelevant. His book *Surnaturel* helped to uncover this state of affairs and to right it by reintegrating theology and contemporary thought. His work was eventually vindicated in the text of several documents (especially *Gaudium et spes*) at Vatican II, where he was a theological advisor (*peritus*).

mark a way forward toward an authentically christocentric approach to religious pluralism.

Von Balthasar has written extensively on a variety of topics. His thoughts are organized into three multivolume works formed by his commitment to the transcendental properties of Being—beauty, goodness, truth—and their unity.[15] The scope and volume of von Balthasar's work can be daunting, but his theological vision possesses an elegant simplicity. He sees human existence as beset by a fundamental duality: the finite and the infinite, the particular and the universal. Von Balthasar affirms that human beings were created to seek the universal, that which is ultimately transcendent (God). But the human search for God can only find fulfillment if God has shared infinitude with human beings. For von Balthasar, the question is whether human beings will be able to receive God's infinite revelation. The God of the Bible (not simply the God of philosophy) is the God of creation, the one who has made the senses of human beings, the organs by which human beings come to wonder about God and their own finitude. God has created human beings with the capacity to know God, to find God through the experience of wonder, the experience of beauty that is at the heart of our existence.

A Divide within Contemporary Roman Catholic Theology: Rahner, von Balthasar, and Kant

Within contemporary Roman Catholic theology there are many divides. The rich texture of the tradition, the wide and divergent experiences of people in the church, intellectual influences, and a variety of other factors contribute to these divides in a way that both challenges and enriches the Church's tradition. One such divide in twentieth-century Roman Catholic theology has been articulated in the work of two of the greatest theologians of the past century: Karl Rahner and Hans Urs von Balthasar. Although they respected one another and engaged one another's work positively, they differed significantly in their respective responses to the great eighteenth-century philosopher Immanuel Kant.

It is difficult to overestimate the significance of Kant for Western philosophy, particularly his so-called three critiques and his book *The Critique of Pure Reason*. Suffice it to say that any presentation of Kant's position in such a small space will no doubt leave out much and run the danger of oversimplification. His approach to "pure reason" rightly helps to signal a major shift in Western thought. Kant challenged both Empiricists and Rationalists, who in the eighteenth century battled over the question of human knowledge of reality: was it accessible either through empirical observation or through the power of human reason to deduce truths (as in

mathematics)? Kant argued that the human mind contributes to our acts of knowing. In other words, although he offers a defense of natural sciences, he argues that such sciences do not reflect things as they are in themselves; rather these sciences reflect the role of the human mind in creating reality.

Rahner offered a positive appropriation of Kant's philosophy insofar as he saw Kant's emphasis on the human subject as decisive for an account of grace, revelation, and Christology. For Rahner, Kant had rightly pointed to the interior structure of human knowing as the place where the human being encounters self-transcendence, and this is therefore precisely the place to talk about the human experience of the Infinite, of Being, of God. Von Balthasar, on the other hand, rejected the human, or anthropological, starting point for Christian theology and argued that human beings first perceive the beauty of God in revelation, in the created order, in the life of Christ before any question about knowledge and structures of interiority. As such, von Balthasar set out to construct a refutation of Kant's critiques by constructing a systematic theology that began with a theological aesthetics (the glory of the Lord) rather than with the human person as did Rahner (Spirit in the world and hearers of the Word).

While the experience of beauty and wonder remain important in his theological and philosophical refection, the doctrines of the Incarnation and the Trinity are the real starting points for von Balthasar's theology. As such, he undoes the low-ascending approach that has been so character-istic of contemporary Christology. In the doctrine of the Trinity, Christians affirm that God is love, and love supposes the one, the other, and their unity. Such otherness within God—expressed in the idea of the Son as "other"—is echoed in the relationship between God and creation. Creation, like the Son, is an icon of God, though unlike the Son, creation is not God; it is "other" than God. The Son, as the eternal icon of the Father, can without contradiction unite himself with creation. In this union, von Balthasar understands Jesus as the **concrete universal**, the union of the finite and infinite. In the Incarnation, creation is made pure and brought into communion with the triune God. Such an event does not result in the dissolution of creation into God; rather, creation retains its identity as "other" than God. This involves the descent, self-emptying, or *kenōsis* of the Son. In this descent, the Son remains with the Father, and the Son continues to know "where" he is—he is with the Father—throughout his *kenōsis*, his Incarnation. Additionally, von Balthasar sees complete iden-tity between Christ's mission and his person: he is the one sent from the Father. This distinguishes him from other subjects who have thus been personalized by being given a mission, for example, the prophets. Jesus acts accordingly; he does not communicate a divine plan, but throughout his life he speaks as the personal Word of God. Christ is that plan.

The unity between Christ's mission and identity quite naturally link the Incarnation and the cross. For von Balthasar, the Incarnation cannot be separated from the cross since God assumed our sinful flesh in Christ to heal it and unite it to God. Von Balthasar's account of the Incarnation, therefore, is cruciform. Von Balthasar's theology of Holy Saturday provides readers with a provocative and vivid theological contribution. From the self-surrender on the cross, he moves to the abyss of sin and the abandon-ment that is death. It is this experience that Jesus embraces on the cross and in his descent into hell. Through such death, Christ embraces what von Balthasar calls "cadaver-obedience" (obedience in death), revealing and experiencing the full horror of sin. Jesus was thus truly dead, and only God could rescue him. In death Christ is in profound solidarity with each of us, and von Balthasar rejects any notion that the human being suffered apart from the divine Son because of the Chalcedonian formula, which affirmed not only a distinction between the natures in Christ but also their union in the person of Jesus. For von Balthasar the *kenōsis*, the self-emptying of the Son, is not simply a way of describing the journey of the Logos from his celestial abode, but is a description of what happens in the Trinity through the suffering and death of Jesus. The *kenōsis* of the Son is eternal.[16]

The Trinity, in von Balthasar's theology, is a unity with real difference. That difference is not oppositional but relational. Von Balthasar describes it as weakness, humility, and *kenōsis*. These features of the Trinity account for the dynamism within God's very nature. God is active, not passive or remote. God is relational and, above all, loving and gifting. This is reflected within human nature, particularly in the social dimension of human existence and its openness to the "other." Such openness is the condition for suffering. The more loving—and thus receptive—the relationship is, the more disposed one is to suffer. Yet this suffering is not a passivity or a defect in regard to the "other"; rather, it is an activity at the heart of human perfection: love. The Trinity, then, is a communion where there is room for active receptivity and where the suffering of Christ is contained. God is in solidarity with the universal experience of sin: suffering.

This solidarity produces a universalism in von Balthasar's soteriology. Building upon Origen's notion of **apokatastasis** (the restoration of all things), von Balthasar asserts that in Christ, God has destined all human beings for salvation. Deadly sin, the total rejection of God's love and mercy, remains a possibility. Von Balthasar rejects the idea that we can know such things. He rejects any speculation that would divorce our love from our hope, the union of which demands that we hope for the salvation of all.

Hans Urs von Balthasar's theology may strike many as a return to a pre-critical stage in theological reflection, yet his proposal does not embrace the mythological language and worldviews so predominant in pre-critical Christologies. Von Balthasar's Christology is mystical, yet rooted in the temporal and centered on the historic experience of God's self-disclosure in Christ. His emphasis on the aesthetic and dramatic nature of revelation and theology situate his thought within a post-modern context but in a different location than that of Roger Haight. The categories of beauty, drama, and logic provide fertile ground for re-appropriation of the Christian tradition in a post-Christian, postmodern world, but also provide common ground for understanding and dialoguing without encompassing other religious traditions.

Conclusion

If the history of Christology is the history of forgetting, the emergence of von Balthasar's Christology in recent years seems to recapitulate the history of Christology. The dangers inherent in a low-ascending approach to Christology are spelled out quite clearly in the thought of John Hick: Jesus is a remarkable cipher, an arrow pointing to God, but traditional Christological doctrines are ultimately dispensable. While Hick and pluralist approaches in general seem problematic, how can one affirm the definitive revelation of God in Christ while reverencing religious difference as difference? How does one overcome the violence some see as inherent in universalizing claims about Jesus? Such questions remain, but they nonetheless will be the questions that propel christological reflection into the future. It is the responsibility of all the faithful to wrestle with, argue over, and embrace new paradigms of christological orthodoxy, not despite the achievements of the past, but precisely because we revere those achievements and seek to be instructed by them. Although the Magesterium (the official teaching office of the Church) has laid out guidelines and limits for contemporary Christology, these must be viewed as conversation starters, invitations to the next generations of the faithful to reflect on the power of Christ for the salvation of the world.

Questions for Understanding

1. Why is religious pluralism such a pronounced issue for Christians today?

2. Define the exclusivist position. Is this position still held by Christians in our day?

3. Why do many theologians find the concept of the anonymous Christian problematic?

4. What are the main characteristics of *Dominus Iesus*? How do these characteristics make the document problematic in the eyes of some?

5. Identify two important differences in the christological approaches of Haight and Dupuis.

6. Explain the place of beauty and wonder in the theology of von Balthasar.

Questions for Reflection

1. Can Christians remain faithful to the gospel and adopt a pluralist position? Explain. How should Christians respond to Christ's command to go and teach all nations?

2. Research the CDF's procedure for dealing with problematic theologians. Are these norms fair in your opinion? Explain. Why do many people, both religious and secular, find these procedures problematic?

3. Construct a chart listing each of the proposed paradigms for dealing with the issue of religious pluralism discussed in this chapter. In a separate column, list the arguments in favor and against each of these positions. Finally, which paradigm offers the best option for the Christian church in dealing with religious pluralism? Explain.

Endnotes

1 See William Loewe, "Lonergan and the Law of the Cross: A Universalist View of Salvation," *Anglican Theological Review* 59 (1977): 162–74.

2 Letter 73 *(To Iubaianus)*, 21. I have cited the more famous phrasing cited often in church history, but the actual text of Cyprian reads, "*salus extra ecclesiam non est.*"

3 There is some debate among Evangelical Christians regarding the place of the sinner's prayer in the experience of salvation. The prayer simply indicates the acknowledgements necessary to receive Jesus as Savior within the Evangelical tradition. Billy Graham helped to make the sinner's prayer a staple of twentieth-century American Evangelicalism.

4 Nicholas of Cusa, *The Peace of Faith (De pace fidei)*, various editions.

5 Translations are from A. Flannery, *Vatican II: Conciliar and Post-Conciliar Documents* (Boston: Daughters of St. Paul, 1988).

6 Karl Rahner, "Anonymous Christian," in *Theological Investigations* (New York: Seabury, 1974), 6:391.

7 For most of what follows, see John Hick, *God and the Universe* (New York: St. Martin's, 1973) and his essay "Jesus and the World Religions," in *The Myth of God Incarnate*, ed. John Hick (London: SCM, 1977), 167–85.

8 John Hick, "On Grading Religions," *Religious Studies* 17 (1981): 451–67; at 463, 467.

9 For what follows, see Raimundo Panikkar, *The Unknown Christ of Hinduism*, revised edition (Maryknoll, NY: Orbis, 1981).

10 Roger Haight, SJ, *Jesus, Symbol of God* (Maryknoll, NY: Orbis, 1999).

11 Ibid., 417.

12 *Dominus Iesus*, 10.

13 Ibid., 8, 11.

14 For a compendium of reactions and opinions on *Dominus Iesus,* see *Sic et Non: Encountering* "Dominus Iesus," ed. Stephen J. Pope and Charles Hefling (Maryknoll: Orbis, 2002).

15 For an overview of von Balthasar's work, see Hans Urs von Balthasar, *My Work in Retrospect* (San Francisco: Ignatius, 1993).

16 John O'Donnell, *Hans Urs von Balthasar*, Outstanding Christian Thinkers (New York: Continuum, 1991), 46.

Glossary

A

Adoptionists – This heretical Christian group believed that Jesus was God's son through adoption and not essentially. In other words, at some point in the life of Jesus, God chose to grace Jesus with a unique relationship. The Jewish-Christian sect known as the Ebionites were essentially Adoptionists, as was Paul of Samosata.

Alexandrian school – The Egyptian city of Alexandria was a center of learning long before the Christian era began. It eventually became the most important center of Christian life and thought in the third century. Alexandrian theologians developed a highly allegorical method for the interpretation of Scripture and emphasized a form of philosophy centered on Plato. The Alexandrian approach to Christology is often described as Logos-sarx because it emphasized the importance of the divine Logos and tended to diminish the humanity of Christ, making it merely functional and reducing it to flesh (*sarx* is Greek for "flesh"). The chief representatives of this school were Origen, Arius, Athanasius, Apollinaris, Cyril, Eutyches, Dioscorus, and Leontius of Byzantium.

Allegory – This word literally means "to read again." It is a literary genre as well as a method of interpretation that sees within a given story (narrative) another story. More precisely, an allegory is a story in which every element or character in the story has a corresponding element outside that story and within another plot. Many early Christians, particularly those in Alexandria, emphasized an allegorical approach to the interpretation of the Bible, an approach which they inherited from Greek writers and Hellenistic Judaism.

Analogia entis – This Latin expression is usually translated as "the analogy of being." For Thomas Aquinas, the created order reflects something of God's being. As such, human beings can make analogical statements about God, but all statements about God must first be negated *(via negativa)*. To say that God is "Father" means first of all that God is not a Father. God does not contribute genetic material to create a new life; God does not, strictly speaking, have a spouse. Rather, our experience of fathers provides the basis for saying that God is like a father: faithful, strong, dependable, and loving *(via positiva)*. But every positive statement of this sort must be rounded off by the conviction that whatever qualities even the most idealized fathers might possess, God's love, faithfulness, and other qualities are infinitely beyond our experience *(via eminentiae)*. This principle was officially endorsed by the Catholic Church in the Fourth Lateran Council (1215), and is particularly important in contemporary feminist theology.

Anonymous Christian – This phrase was used by Karl Rahner to describe those non-Christians who have responded to God's grace and who live God's call faithfully; such people are saved through Christ, although they do not formally recognize it. Many have faulted this notion on the grounds that it patronizes and devalues other religious traditions.

Antiochene School – The Syrian city of Antioch was one of the oldest Christian communities (Acts 11:19–26) and became an important center for Christian thought. The Antiochenes preferred a comparatively historical or literal approach to Scripture, as opposed to allegory. They also preferred the philosophy of Aristotle to that of Plato. Their approach to Christology is often called Logos-anthropos because it emphasizes the full humanity of Jesus (*anthropos* is Greek for "human being"). The Antiochenes approached the christological question by beginning with the human being Jesus and then asking how the divine Logos is connected to or united with him. Some chief representatives of this school include: Paul of Samosata, Diodore of Tarsus, Nestorius, John of Antioch, St. John Chrysostom, and Theodore of Mopsuestia.

Anti-Semitism – This is the denigration or hatred of all things Jewish, especially the Jewish people. The word *Semite* refers to the descendants of Noah's son Shem in Genesis 10:21–31. He became the father of the "race" of the peoples of Mesopotamia, including both the Arabs and the Hebrews, or Jews. Throughout the Christian era many interpretations of Jesus' teachings have portrayed Judaism negatively and have thus provided a foundation for modern anti-Semitism. The experience of the Holocaust has given impetus to Christian self-criticism for theological positions and attitudes that have condoned anti-Semitism. Additionally, the work of numerous scholars has painted a more accurate picture of first-century Judaism by drawing attention to Christian prejudices and setting Jesus and his followers firmly within a Jewish context.

Apatheia – Greek for "without suffering," apatheia refers to the Greek philosophical concept that God is remote, unconnected to the plight of the world, and unable to suffer. Moltmann challenges this doctrine and its appropriateness for understanding the God of Israel and Jesus.

Apocalyptic eschatology – This theology, which emerged within Judaism in the centuries around the time of Jesus, is characterized by an anticipation of God's decisive act in human history to bring about the destruction of evil and the vindication of the righteous. Apocalyptic eschatology comforted those who suffer persecution. It envisioned a final cosmic battle with the forces of evil and the resurrection of the dead—the righteous to eternal reward and the wicked to eternal punishment.

Apokatastasis – This Greek word, meaning "restoration," was used by Origen to describe the hope that at the end of time all things would be restored to God, including Satan and the damned. Others who held this position include Gregory of Nyssa and Clement of Alexandria.

Apology – The Greek word *apologia* means "defense." An apologist offered a defense of something. Since Christianity was largely unknown to most people (and highly suspect), Christian apologists emerged in the early church to offer arguments in defense of Christianity. Justin Martyr was an important early apologist.

Authenticity – Bernard Lonergan used this term to express what human beings are created to be. It represents the full potential of human existence.

B

Babylonian Exile – Following the Babylonian capture and destruction of Jerusalem in 587 BCE, the Babylonian king Nebuchadrezzar (Nebuchadnezzar) led a significant portion of the city's inhabitants into forced exile hundreds of miles away in Babylon (modern Iraq). During that time, exiles from Judah longed to return to Jerusalem and restore their kingdom. The exile came to an end in 539 BCE when Cyrus the Great conquered Babylon and allowed the Jews to return home.

C

Canon, canonization – From a Greek word meaning "measuring rod" (*kanōn*), these terms have come to refer, respectively, to that which is normative and the process of making something normative. A canon is usually the collection of texts a group regards as sacred: the Bible, for Christians.

Catechism of the Catholic Church *(CCC)* – This is a compendium of the Roman Catholic Church's teachings presented thematically and used to help educators and those preparing educational material. It contains both highly authoritative material as well as basic material for teaching the truths of the Catholic faith. It is a helpful resource for exploring many teachings that are basic to Catholic Christianity as well as to other Christian traditions.

Chalcedon, Council of – Convened by the emperor Marcian in 451 near the imperial capital, the council affirmed the full humanity of Christ and the union of that humanity with the divinity of Christ. The union of the two natures, divine and human, was affirmed over and against the Alexandrian position articulated by Eutyches and Dioscorus.

Christ – The Greek word *christos* translates the Hebrew word *messiah* (anointed one). The title evoked the hope in Israel that God would raise up a descendant of David, and perhaps even a new high priest, to restore the nation and usher in the final age. The title was applied to Jesus early in the Christian tradition.

Christocentrism – In the discussion of religious pluralism, the christocentric position emphasizes the place of Christ in the discussion and how other savior figures might relate to Christ as the Incarnation of God.

Christological moment – This term refers to a scene in the Gospel stories that the evangelists used to express and crystallize their understanding of Jesus—an understanding that was the product of the Resurrection. The scene is a vehicle for the expression of a post-resurrectional Christology rather than a recollection of an event from Jesus' life.

Concrete universal – This expression comes from Hans Urs von Balthasar and refers to the conjunction between the finite and the infinite at the heart of the human experience of God. For von Balthasar, Jesus is the concrete universal.

Constantinople – The imperial city Constantine built to unite the eastern and western parts of the fractious Roman Empire. It became a place of great political and ecclesiastical intrigue when Antioch and Alexandria began to vie for influence in the imperial court.

Constantinople, Councils of – *The First Council of Constantinople* was held in 381 to deal with, among other things, the doctrine of the Holy Spirit and various heresies, especially the Christology of Apollinaris. This council issued an expansion of the creed formulated at Nicaea that is often misleadingly called the Nicene Creed. *The Second Council of Constantinople* was held in 553 in an effort to reconcile the Cyrilian-monophysite churches, but succeeded only in condemning the great Antiochene theologians (Theodore of Mopsuestia, Ibas of Edessa, and Theodoret of Cyrus). *The Third Council of Constantinople* met in 680 to affirm that since in Christ there is a union of the divine and human natures, there must be two wills and two "operations." Interestingly, Pope Honorius (†638) was posthumously anathematized, or condemned, for supporting the doctrine of "one will" in Christ.

Convenientia – This Latin word, often translated "appropriateness," refers to a contingent matter of fact, not a matter of necessity, in God's plan of salvation.

Cosmotheandric fact – This expression was used by the Spanish-Indian Jesuit Raimundo Panikkar to describe the inherent connection between God *(theos)* and the world *(cosmos)* in human beings *(andres)*, particularly in the man Jesus.

Counter Reformation – Following the success of Martin Luther and other leaders of the Protestant Reformation, the pope convened a council in 1548 at Trent to address the concerns and challenges of the reformers. The council of Trent met periodically over two decades (1548–1563) and instituted many positive reforms in the life and theology of the church. The general tenor of the council, however, as well as its implementation over the subsequent century was often defensive and aggressive. The Roman Catholic Church did not adopt a more positive posture toward Protestantism until the Second Vatican Council (1962–1965).

Creed – From the Latin word *credo* (I believe), the term has come to designate any formal statement of faith.

Cultural imperialism – The practice of intentionally imposing cultural norms and practices on other cultures as a matter of policy. Alexander the Great was an important proponent of cultural imperialism.

D

Day of Atonement – The solemn Jewish feast that celebrates the removal of Israel's sins is called Yom Kippur in Hebrew. The biblical ceremony includes a sacrifice of purification and the transfer of sins to the "scapegoat," which is then expelled from the community.

Demythologizing – This is the term used by Bultmann and his disciples to describe the process of "peeling back" the elements of a first-century Jewish (apocalyptic) worldview that are no longer applicable or meaningful for contemporary people. The process of demythologizing yields a contemporary existential interpretation of the gospel.

Deuteronomist, Deuteronomistic history – The Deuteronomistic tradition is one of the four or more traditions that make up the Pentateuch, or first five books of the Bible (Genesis–Deuteronomy). This tradition emerged in the northern king-dom of Israel in the eighth century BCE and was carried to the southern kingdom of Judah following the collapse of Samaria in 722 BCE. It became the basis for Josiah's reforms before the destruction of Jerusalem in 587 BCE. The Deuteron-omistic history is the account of Israel's history that runs through Joshua, Judges, 1 and 2 Samuel, and 1 and 2 Kings. The basic tenet of this theology was that YHWH would grant long life and prosperity to those who were righteous and faithful, while the wicked would be destroyed. The Deuteronomistic theology suffered greatly as righteous Jews began to experience more and more suffer-ing. In some ways, apocalyptic eschatology compensates for the inadequacies of the Deuteronomistic tradition by making the afterlife, or the resurrection, the primary place where God's justice and mercy are vindicated.

E

Ecclesiocentric position – This term, meaning "church-centered," refers to the approach to religious pluralism that is centered on membership and participa-tion in a particular church for the attainment of salvation. Cyprian of Carthage famously expressed the most extreme ecclesiocentrism, saying, "Outside the church there is no salvation."

Enoch, First Book of – This nonbiblical book is an example of apocalyptic escha-tology. Although written in the second century BCE, it is attributed to the bibli-cal figure Enoch, who was said to have been assumed into heaven (see Genesis 5:24). The book was widely read in early Christian circles, and is particularly important for understanding the origins and meaning of the Son of Man figure.

Ephesus, Council of (431) – Nestorius, the bishop of Constantinople, argued against calling Mary *Theotokos* (Mother of God), saying that she was only *Chris-totokos* (Mother of Christ). Cyril of Alexandria arranged for a council at Ephesus to condemn his teaching. The council met before the supporters of Nestorius arrived, condemned Nestorius, and reaffirmed the unity of Christ against Nesto-rius, who had argued against a union between the divine and human natures in Christ.

Essenes – This group, one of the "sects" within first-century Judaism, is com-monly thought to have produced the Dead Sea Scrolls found in a series of caves near Qumran. These scrolls contain a number of biblical books, commentaries on biblical books, and sectarian documents that reflect the distinctive worldview and theology of the Essenes. They believed that God was about to visit his judg-ment upon the corrupt temple in Jerusalem and the priests who operated it. The Essenes retreated to the desert to prepare themselves for this event.

Ethical monotheism – This scholarly term refers to the prophets' demands that the Israelites sustain their status as YHWH's people by behavior that mirrored YHWH's behavior toward Israel. Thus they must protect the widow and orphan, treat neighbors and aliens with justice, and worship YHWH alone. The exclusive worship of YHWH, however, is meaningless without the corresponding ethical behavior (Isaiah 1:11–17).

Exclusivism – This position on religious pluralism contends that one cannot be saved from destruction without explicit faith in Christ.

F

Formula of Reunion (433) – This document ended the schism between Cyril of Alexandria and John of Antioch (and the Alexandrian and Antiochene churches) following the Council of Ephesus in 431. The Formula, a synthesis of Alexandrian and Antiochene Christology, brought balance to the question of the natures in Christ and became a major source for the Formula of Chalcedon.

G

Gnostics, Gnosticism – A complex religious movement that emerged in the second century CE, some forms of Gnosticism blended well with elements of orthodox Christianity. Gnostics denied the goodness of the material world, from which "prison" human beings can be liberated through special knowledge. Gnosticism was particularly insidious because it used aspects of Christian thought and Gnostics' works often claimed to have been authored by prominent early Christians (for example, *Gospel of Mary* or *Gospel of Thomas*).

H

Han – The unresolved resentment and indignation, the sense of helplessness and total abandonment in the face of injustice accumulated over years and even centuries of oppression suffered by the *minjung*.

Heresy – From a Greek word meaning "sect," it has come to mean any false teaching or a teaching that contradicts a central doctrine.

Hermeneutics of retrieval – In liberation theologies (feminist, Latin American, black, womanist, and *mujerista*), it is the principle of interpretation that gives a central place to forgotten or suppressed elements of the Christian tradition (such as texts, symbols, traditions, and practices) that promote the well-being and freedom of oppressed groups.

Hermeneutics of suspicion – In liberation theologies (feminist, Latin American, black, womanist, and *mujerista*), it is the principle of interpretation whereby one looks for stories, symbols, traditions, and practices, in the Christian tradition that have been used to support or legitimate the oppression or marginalization of certain groups of people.

Hilasterion – This Greek word translates the Hebrew word *kapporeth*, which refers to the golden cover on the ark in the "holy of holies" of the Jerusalem temple. This cover was the place where YHWH was thought to have sat and received the blood of the atoning sacrifices on Yom Kippur (the Day of Atonement).

Homoousios – This Greek term, meaning "same being," was suggested to the bishops at Nicaea under imperial pressure as a way to describe the relationship between the Father and the Son. In this context it means that whatever makes the Father God makes the Son God.

Horizon – The horizon is the place where the earth appears to meet the sky. It is the limit of our field of vision—we cannot see beyond the horizon. Bernard Lonergan uses the term analogously for that which defines our field of moral vision and our understanding of reality. When confronted by the world, our horizon of meaning and value determines our understanding of the world and presents us with possible courses of action. When our horizon is infected by bias, it becomes extremely limited, like a cataract. For Karl Rahner a horizon represents the infinite presence of Being as the source and goal of all human knowing. It is where the finite and the infinite meet.

Hypostasis – This Greek term is roughly equivalent to the Latin word *substantia*, meaning underlying reality or subsistence. The term was problematic in the christological debates between the Alexandrians and Antiochenes because there was no general agreement about its meaning or its precise relationship to *physis* (nature) and *prosōpon* (mask or person). Clarifications were made at Chalcedon between the concepts *physis*, *hypostasis*, and *prosōpon*, making it possible to speak of a hypostatic union of the divine and human natures in Christ. Whereas *physis* ("nature") has to do with "What?" questions, *hypostasis* and *prosōpon* deal with "Who?" questions.

Hypostatic union – This phrase is often used to denote the union of the two natures (human and divine) in Christ. The concept is probably best attributed to Leontius of Byzantium's notion that the human nature of Christ had its hypostasis in the divine nature.

I

Inclusivism – This position on religious pluralism, which forms the heart of contemporary Catholic Church teaching, asserts that non-Christians can be saved from destruction if they respond to God's offer of grace through Christ. This grace is offered to women and men of goodwill who seek to do God's will but who, through no fault of their own, do not know Christ. Those who do so are, to use Rahner's term, anonymous Christians.

Indulgences – This practice had a complex theology, but the essence of it was the offering of some act as a form of penance so that time in Purgatory (the place of penance in the afterlife) could be reduced. In indulgences, the benefits of an act of penance were transferable: one could do an act of penance for the sake of another, perhaps a friend or deceased relative. At many times, particularly in the sixteenth century, indulgences were given to persons who made monetary contributions to the Church; this "selling" of indulgences incensed Luther and many of his contemporaries.

Infancy narratives – This genre of literature is common in the ancient world; the story of an important figure in history was often prefaced by a tale of remarkable birth. This literary tradition can be traced as far back as Sargon the Great of Assyria in the third millennium BCE. Two of the Gospels (Matthew and Luke) contain infancy narratives combining material of historical significance with other material that primarily reflects post-Resurrection Christology.

J

Jubilees – This nonbiblical book of the second century BCE is a commentary and expansion upon material found in Genesis and Exodus. It also offers an account of the afterlife as disembodied spirits.

K

Kapporet –This Hebrew word refers to the covering on the ark of the covenant on which God (YHWH) was enthroned, otherwise known as the mercy seat (*hilasterion* in Greek). It was the focal point of God's presence with Israel and the place where blood was sprinkled on the Day of Atonement (Yom Kippur).

Kērygma – This term, Greek for "proclamation," refers to the faith proclamation of the earliest disciples of Jesus (stage two). This proclamation of faith also served to call others to faith.

L

Liberal theology – This theological movement emerged in the nineteenth century and sought to accommodate the Christian tradition to modern Western sensibilities. The result of this blending was a form of Christianity with little capacity to critique modern culture and only a diminished sense of the supernatural and the holy or transcendent.

Liturgy, liturgical – The Greek work *leiturgia* means "public work" and refers to acts of public worship as opposed to private prayer. Public worship is formal, regular, and symbolic.

Logos – This Greek term means "word," "reason," or "speech." In late Second-Temple Judaism (around 100 BCE), the Logos emerged as an important aspect of God and became personified as Wisdom. The Fourth Gospel begins with a hymn to the Logos and the Incarnation of the Logos in Jesus.

Logos Christology – This approach to Christology emphasized the idea that God's self-expression, God's Word, became incarnate in Christ. It has its origins in Greek (Stoic) philosophy and in the Hebrew Bible (Old Testament), particularly associated with the creation story in Genesis.

Logos spermatikos – This phrase, Greek for "seminal word," expressed an important concept in Stoic philosophy. It refers to the notion that the divine Logos permeates the created order—in particular, human beings. It is the duty of every human being to cultivate logos, or reason, and thereby cultivate a connection with the divine. Justin Martyr appropriated this expression in his apologetic works and identified Christ with the Logos and the cultivation of reason in Greco-Roman culture.

Lord – At the close of the Old Testament period, the divine name, YHWH, was never pronounced (except by the high priest on Yom Kippur, the Day of Atonement). Instead the word *adonai* (Hebrew for "Lord") was pronounced. For Paul, the Greek equivalent, *kurios*, refers to (1) the glorified risen Christ; (2) the fact that this figure merits the same worship and honor as YHWH; (3) Christ at his return in glory (Parousia), and eventually to Christ before his return; (4) the fact that Jesus is something more than human; and (5) Jesus' dominion over people.

M

Maccabees, Maccabean – This is the name of a Jewish family who, in the second century BCE, led a revolt against the Greek kingdom (the Seleucids) that controlled Jerusalem and had outlawed Jewish religious practice. During this period many Jews suffered torture and death because they would not violate the commandments of YHWH (2 Maccabees 6:18–7:42). Their deaths were seen as sacrifices for the sins of Israel from current and past generations (4 Maccabees 6:27–29). The Maccabees defeated the Seleucids, but eventually compromised their religious and nationalistic idealism. The successors of the Maccabees, usually called the Hasmoneans, were regarded unfavorably by pious Jews in Jesus' time since they had compromised their original zeal and corrupted the priesthood.

Messiah – Hebrew for "anointed one," the equivalent word in the New Testament is *christos* (Christ).

Messianic secret – This is a feature of Mark's Gospel first identified by William Wrede. In Mark, Jesus admonishes many people not to disclose his identity as Messiah to anyone. Wrede asserted that such secrecy was an apologetic device used by early Christians to explain the fact that no one claimed that Jesus was the Christ during his lifetime, but only after his Resurrection. For Wrede, the messianic secret explains this problem by claiming that everyone knew that Jesus was the Christ; their silence on this point was due to Jesus' instructions not to reveal it until later.

Metanoia – This Greek word, often translated "conversion," designates the appropriate response to Jesus' proclamation of the nearness of the *basileia* (kingdom of God). William Loewe and Bernard Lonergan have argued that this religious conversion, a radical transformation of one's horizon of meaning and value, is made possible through the recognition of God's love flooding one's being, of "being in love in an unrestricted fashion." Thus metanoia becomes the centerpiece of any responsible account of salvation.

Middle Judaism – This expression has come to designate a step in the process of the transformation of Judaism following the destruction of the temple in 70 CE. Middle Judaism thus signals that time when various battles to reorient Judaism without a temple led to the end of the diversity of the late Second-Temple Period and the formation of normative Judaism, a form of Rabbinic Judaism.

Midrash – This is a distinctively Jewish style of writing popularized among the Pharisees. It is a homiletic or sermon-like exposition of a biblical text, which usually attempts to address questions not directly answered in the biblical text. For example, *Jubilees* is a *midrash* on Genesis and Exodus.

Miracle – This word is derived from the Latin *miraculum*, meaning "something to be wondered at." The New Testament (written in Greek) uses words like *dunamis* (power), *ergon* (work), or *sēmeion* (sign) rather than miracle. A miracle has often been understood as an observable event with religious meaning that can only be attributed to God since it is outside the natural order of things. Jesus' miracles can, however, be understood apart from this definition, as symbolic acts whereby Jesus proclaimed the kingdom of God. They are dramatic parables in action where Jesus confirmed the faith of the recipient and challenged onlookers to be converted and accept the advent of the *basileia* (kingdom).

Minjung – This Korean word, meaning "the popular mass," has become a popular term for describing the status and suffering of the vast majority of Asians.

Modalists – This heresy denied any real distinction between the Father and the Son. The Father and Son were mere energies, or modes, of encountering God. Sabellius and Praxeus were two prominent Modalists.

Monarchia – This Latin term means "power," or "authority." In the early church many theologians attempted to explain the relationship between the Father and the Son with reference to how they shared the divine power, or *monarchia*. Two different solutions emerged in the third century: Dynamic Monarchians or Adoptionists believed that the Son's share of the divine power was granted to him because of his virtue, while Modalists denied any real distinction between Father and Son (see above).

Monophysitism – This word (literally "one nature-ism") is the label given to the heresy of Eutyches, who insisted that any mention of two natures in Christ necessarily implies that there were two persons *(prosōpoi)* in Christ. Eutyches's insistence that Christ had but one nature—the divine nature—was condemned at Chalcedon in 451.

Myth – The Greek word *mythos* has a wide range of meanings. In the context of the work of Strauss and Bultmann, it becomes a technical term that refers to the symbolic narrative found in Scripture. Myth, in this context, has to do with the attempt to communicate truth, not deception.

N

New quest – Ernst Käsemann launched a "new quest" for the historical Jesus in the 1950s. This quest, conducted mostly by former students of Bultmann, focused on retrieving the historical Jesus for theological reasons. It was precisely the theological motivations as well as their devotion to Bultmann's thought that distinguished this quest from both the "old quest" and the "third quest."

Nicaea, Councils of – The *First Council of Nicaea* (325) resulted in the condemnation of Arius and the articulation of the orthodox faith in the form of a creed. The *Second Council of Nicaea* (787) addressed the issue of breaking images, or "iconoclasm."

Normative – A norm acts as a control, a limit, but also a source. Scripture and church doctrine are both norms of Christian faith. One major question is, to what extent should historical Jesus research be normative for Christian faith?

O

Old quest – The quest for the historical Jesus in the nineteenth century focused on attacking traditional Christianity and vindicating one or another contemporary philosophy. It was brought to an end with the work of Albert Schweitzer in the early twentieth century.

Orthodox – This Greek word refers to correct belief. While the term is normally used positively, it has also been used pejoratively to describe a firm, fixed, and unnuanced position that is blind to other ideas.

P

Parable – The Greek word *parabole*, meaning "comparison," refers to a provocative story or image that teases or plays with the hearers' imagination and expectations. In so doing, the parable forces the hearers to reconsider their position or worldview. As such, Jesus' parables were an important tool in his proclamation of the *basileia*.

Parousia – This Greek word means "presence," or "visitation." Theologically, it refers to the second coming of Christ, at which time the dead will be raised and judged, and evil will be defeated. The Parousia oriented one of the earliest patterns of New Testament Christology: Jesus would become Messiah in the fullest sense only upon his return.

Participated mediations – Jacques Dupuis uses this phrase from John Paul II's encyclical *Redemptoris missio* (no. 5) to lay out his theology of religious pluralism, in which other religious traditions are the means of salvation for their adherents. As such, they participate in the saving work of Christ to bring about the salvation of all.

Penal substitution – In this approach to soteriology, espoused by the reformers, sin incurs punishment from God, and this punishment was inflicted upon Christ instead of humanity. So Christ's suffering takes on cosmic dimensions: it is not simply the suffering of a human being, but the suffering that is the punishment due for all the sins of the world throughout time.

Pharisees – This is another of the sects or groups within first-century Palestinian Judaism. The word *pharisee* means "separate one." This group emerged during the second-century BCE as opponents of those who wanted to find some accommodation with Greek and Roman cultural forces that had emerged in Palestine in the Maccabean period. The Pharisees were the great "democratizers" of Judaism: they sought to make purity a goal not just for the priests who served in the temple, but for all the people of Israel. The Pharisees were generally popular in the first century, though they often argued with one another over the appropriate interpretation of the Mosaic law. Jesus seems to fit in with this group in some ways. Both Jesus and the Pharisees were laymen, and both were addressed as "teacher," or "rabbi." Both Jesus and the Pharisees sought to instill in the people of Israel a concern for righteousness and complete dedication to God.

Physis – This Greek word, often translated "nature," is perhaps best understood as dealing with "What?" questions. The response to such a question tends to involve identifying the nature of something. (See also *hypostasis*.)

Platonic – This word refers to the philosophical school of thought begun by Plato. A characteristic is the distinction between the concrete world and the ideal world of "forms" (see, e.g., Plato's *Republic*, Book 7).

Pluralist approach – This approach to religious difference sees religious diversity as a natural outcome of human contact with the divine. Pluralists resist any talk of the superiority of one religious tradition over another; rather, they affirm the relative worth of religious traditions. Christian pluralists insist that Christ is the Savior of Christians, but they also insist that there are other saviors who operate independently of Christ or the Christian church.

Pneumatocentric – This phrase, meaning "spirit centered," refers to the approach to religious pluralism that emphasizes the universal saving work of the Holy Spirit—rather than the role of Christ or the church—in mediating salvation.

Post-Christian – This expression has come to describe much of the Western world. The history of the West was dominated by Christian faith and its institutions, but such dominance is a thing of the past. Culturally, the West can no longer be regarded as Christian.

Postcolonial Christology – This theological movement addresses the violence and structural marginalization of indigenous or native peoples connected with the promotion of the gospel throughout history. Such an approach to Christology has rendered pictures of Christ that are a far cry from those generally dominant in the West.

Praxis – The significance of this Greek word is derived from Aristotle. It refers to action upon which there has been critical reflection. Praxis also signals an ongoing engagement, rather than an isolated act, that is informed by ongoing critical reflection.

Prosōpon – This term is often translated as "person," though it did not always seem to have that meaning. It was used interchangeably with *hypostasis* and conveyed the idea of concrete existence. (See also *hypostasis*.)

Ptolemaic Kingdom – This was one of the kingdoms or empires established by Alexander the Great's generals following his death. This empire was centered in Egypt and controlled Jerusalem for a century until the Seleucids took control of Palestine in the second century BCE.

Purgatory – In Roman Catholic doctrine, Purgatory is the name given to that "place" or time when, after death, one is purified and made holy to enjoy full union with God. This purification entails suffering and penance, which can be assisted by those on earth and those in heaven through the communion or fellowship of believers (saints).

R

Rabbi, rabbinic (See **Pharisees**)

Ransom – The Greek *apōlutrosis*, usually translated as "ransom" or "redemption," is a commercial term reflecting the buying of a slave's freedom. It is used frequently by Paul and throughout the New Testament to describe the saving work of Christ's death.

Rationalists – In the eighteenth century, many had come to accept the autonomy of reason over and against religious faith. Rationalism argued that the only things that are real, true, and good are things that can be affirmed through scientific reason. A corollary to this was that faith had nothing to contribute to an account of the world or of God.

Reformation – Martin Luther inaugurated an attempt at church reform in 1517. The condemnation of Luther by the pope and other church officials precipitated a fracture within Western Christianity. Luther was followed by other reformers like Ulrich Zwingli and John Calvin, all of whom shared Luther's emphasis on Scripture as theological norm (as opposed to tradition), and faith (as opposed to works) as the criterion of salvation, conceived as God's gift (grace). On other points, however, the various reformers held different ideas, leading to further splits within the church. The Reformation is a complex religious, social, and political event (see also Counter Reformation).

Religious pluralism – This expression simply describes the contemporary situation, which is characterized by pluralism of religious belief and practice. For example, the identification of North America or Europe as Christian belies that these cultures have become more open to and permeated by people professing other religious faiths or none at all.

Re-symbolization – In feminist theology, re-symbolization refers to the construction of a theology, stories, liturgy, and symbols that can become the vehicle for transformation from an androcentric (male-centered) church to an inclusive church.

Robber Council (449) – Also known as *latrocinium* (the Latin expression Pope Leo I used to describe it,) this council was engineered by Bishop Dioscorus of Alexandria and the emperor Theodosius II to vindicate Eutyches and Alexandrian theology over and against its opponents, especially the Antiochenes. The council condemned Flavian, the bishop of Constantinople, and even forced the pope's legates (his representatives) to flee for their lives. The results of this council were rejected by Leo and many others. When the emperor, Theodosius II, died unexpectedly, his successors convened the Council of Chalcedon in 451 and deposed Dioscorus and his supporters.

S

Sadducees – This is another sect or group within first-century Palestinian Judaism. The term derives from the name of King David's great high priest Zadok (2 Samuel 8:17). From the late second century BCE this group, largely comprised of priests, held control of the temple and Sanhedrin, and were the primary link with the Roman government in the region. While not as popular as the Pharisees, the Sadducees were highly influential and pragmatic.

Sanhedrin – In the Roman Period the Sanhedrin was that body of Jewish leaders, under the leadership of the high priest, who administered the temple and oversaw the application of Jewish law and observance in and around Jerusalem.

Satori – The Japanese term C. S. Song borrows from Zen Buddhism to describe insight or enlightenment; it is the function of theologians to provide or provoke insight or enlightenment primarily through the art of narrative.

Scapegoat – In the Yom Kippur ritual (Leviticus 16), the high priest transfers the sins of the nation to a goat, which is then driven out into the desert to be destroyed by the demon Azazel.

Seleucid Kingdom – This was one of the kingdoms or empires that arose following the death of Alexander the Great. The center of this empire was in Persia and Syria, and its main cities were Antioch and Ecbatana. The Seleucids took control of Jerusalem in the second century BCE. When Antiochus IV Epiphanes came to the throne, he outlawed the Jewish religion and precipitated a major crisis.

Sheol – This is the Hebrew word for the abode of the dead. Sometimes it seems to be equivalent to "the pit," or "the grave." At other times it appears to be a place much like Hades in Greek mythology—a place not of torture or despair, but of silence, forgetting, and sleep.

Shema – This traditional Jewish prayer found in Deuteronomy 6:4–9 has been recited daily by Jews for centuries. Its monotheistic emphasis presented the earliest Christians with a challenge: how does one affirm God's presence in Christ and God's oneness at the same time?

Son of God – This is both a christological role and title. As a role, it refers to angels and any individual or group characterized by a special intimacy with God. As a title, it was an important way for early Christians to express their faith in Christ and his intimacy with God. The Fourth Gospel (John) and other early Christians go further by describing Jesus as "the only begotten Son of the Father," thus stressing the uniqueness of Jesus' relationship to the Father.

Sophia Christology (See **Wisdom Christology**)

Soteriology – The theological discipline that seeks to articulate an understanding of how Christ's life, death, and Resurrection bring about salvation.

Spirit Christology – This modern approach to Christology has been espoused by many figures, including Roger Haight and Piet Schoonenberg. Rather than emphasizing the incarnation of the Logos, this approach emphasizes the Incarnation of the Spirit in Christ. To its proponents, Spirit Christology is attractive, because it does not limit God's saving work to the historical life of Christ but can include other saviors.

Spiritualization – The term refers to the metaphorical interpretation of sacrificial ritual so that its meaning applies to the intimacy between God and the believer.

Subordinationism – The tendency within Christology, particularly with Tertullian and Origen, to understand the Son as something less than God the Father.

Suffering Servant – This is modern biblical scholarship's name for an enigmatic figure in Isaiah (Isaiah 42:1–7, 49:1–7, 50:4–9, 52:13—53:12). The Servant is often thought to be a collective figure, that is, he represents a group of people, usually interpreted as Israel or the righteous in Israel. Through the suffering of the Servant, the covenant with YHWH will be renewed. The Suffering Servant thus became an important image in Jesus' ministry and in the early Christian community for understanding the meaning of Jesus' suffering.

Symbol – In Bernard Lonergan's thought, a symbol is an image evoked by or evoking feeling. Symbols are important as vehicles for the expression and apprehension of value.

T

Theory – the Greek word *theoreō* means "to see." Theory, then, is abstract language that reflects formal clarity—it helps one to see things more accurately. Theory is contrasted with metaphor and symbol, both of which are essential, but both metaphor and symbol are examples of "thick" language (language with a wide variety of meanings). Theory is just the opposite.

Theōsis – This Greek word, often translated as "divinization," reflects the soteriology operative in the work of theologians like Athanasius, who argued that in Christ, human beings participate in the life of God: "God became human so that humans might become divine."

Theotokos – This Greek term, meaning "God bearer," was a title given to the Virgin Mary. It was especially popular among the Alexandrians. Nestorius caused a major controversy when he insisted that Mary could only be called *Christotokos* (Christ bearer) since she had given birth to Christ (the *prosōpon* of the conjunction between the divine and human natures) and not God. The title and the controversy it provoked, like all doctrines concerning Mary, are not primarily about Mary but about Christ.

Third quest – This phrase, coined by N. T. Wright, designates a distinct movement in historical Jesus research. Among some of the elements that distinguish the third from the second or "new quest" for the historical Jesus are the consistent use of standard criteria, emphasis on the Jewishness of Jesus, and the ecumenical and interreligious nature of the research.

Toledot – This Hebrew term, meaning "begettings," refers to a literary device, common to many parts of the Old Testament, in which narratives are connected to one another through lists of "begettings," which record and connect the descendants of various protagonists in the narrative.

Typology – This approach to biblical interpretation maintains that texts, personalities, and events of the Old Testament prefigure or point to events in the life of Christ and the early church.

W

Wisdom Christology – This approach to Christology borrowed heavily from the wisdom tradition of Israel, in which God's wisdom is personified. Wisdom personified is regularly female (the word for wisdom in both Hebrew and Greek is grammatically feminine). Many contemporary feminist theologians have emphasized a wisdom approach to Christology.

Wisdom tradition – This is one of the movements or literary traditions within Judaism that contributed greatly to the development of Christology. The wisdom tradition is embodied in Proverbs, Job, and some Psalms. The wisdom tradition emphasized, among other things, the nearness of God in the practical, everyday world. In Second-Temple Judaism, the wisdom tradition began to emphasize the personification of God's wisdom. The communication of personified Wisdom is God's Word, the Logos.

Y

YHWH – This is the name of God given to Moses in Exodus 3:14, often translated "I am." It is usually written without any vowels out of reverence (pious Jews traditionally do not pronounce the divine name), and contemporary translations of the Bible often render it as LORD. In scholarly circles it is often used to differentiate the God of Israel from other conceptions of God. Most scholars believe it would have been pronounced "YA-way."

Index